A Useable Past

~~~

Volume 2: A New Life
The Religion of Socialism
in Britain 1883–1896:
Alternatives to State Socialism

A Useable Past

A History of Association, Co-operation, and un-Statist
Socialism in 19th and early 20th century Britain.
In 3 volumes.

Volume 2: A New Life
The Religion of Socialism in Britain 1883–1896:
Alternatives to State Socialism

Stephen Yeo

*Historian, University of Sussex,1966–1989;
Principal of Ruskin College, Oxford, 1989–1997;
Chair of the Co-operative College and then the
Co-operative Heritage Trust, 1999–2015*

EER
EER Edward Everett Root, Publishers, Brighton, 2025

EER
Edward Everett Root, Publishers, Co. Ltd.
3rd Floor, 15 West Street, Brighton, Sussex, BN1 2RE, England

www.eerpublishing.com
edwardeverettroot@yahoo.co.uk

First published in Great Britain in 2018

© Stephen Yeo, 2018

This edition © Edward Everett Root Publishers 2025

ISBN 9781915115713 paperback
ISBN 9781911204572 hardback
ISBN 9871911204824 eBook

Stephen Yeo has asserted his right to be identified as the author of this Work in accordance with the Copyright, Designs and Patents Act 1988 as the owner of this Work.

All rights reserved. No part of this publication may be reproduced, stored in a retrieval system or transmitted in any form or by any means, electronic, mechanical, photocopying, recording or otherwise, without the prior permission of the copyright owner.

Design and typesetting by Pageset Ltd, High Wycombe, Buckinghamshire

The three volumes in this set are

Volume 1. *Victorian Agitator, George Jacob Holyoake (1817–1906): Co-operation as 'This New Order of Life'*

Volume 2. *A New Life, The Religion of Socialism in Britain 1883–1896: Alternatives to State Socialism*

Volume 3. *Class Conflict and Co-operation in 19th and 20th Century Britain. Education for Association: re-membering for a new moral world*

For Robin Murray (1940–2017), without whom...

Contents

Preface and Acknowledgements   1

Part I THREE SOCIALISMS: STATISM, COLLECTIVISM, ASSOCIATIONISM

1. *My Own Conflicts?* A personal preface	14
In the plural	14
Differentiation, to enable choice	17
Position and positions, autobiographical and social	19
Hornsey Labour Party	22
Childhood	24
Sussex again	26
2. The three socialisms	30
2.1 Statism	30
William Hazell and 'a Socialism which is no longer social'	31
'A workers' socialism or a state socialism'	32
'Caesar for the time being'	35
The ship of state	37
Our Societies: 'Our Union, constituting the society for whom we work'	39
Free association, civil society, and The Party	43
Production	46
Associations	48
2.2 Collectivism	51
The 'quintessential Fabian' on 'bygone socialisms'	51
Collectivisms	52
Fabians	54

Whose knowledge, for and about what?	57
Architects or bees?	62
'The new class'	64
'A collectivist spirit': 'the secular and the religious are one'	66
2.3 Associationism: 'mostly guessed at'	70
'A field of iterance and echo'	71
Twenty-six workers	74
'Pluralism'? 'Community'? Delivered to, or made by, us?	76
'We shall have …'	79
The scandal of associationism	81
Through association, 'it is being done'	85
Associations and the liberal-democratic state	88
Self-management – 'the general end of every known workmen's organisation' – and its enemies	90
Describing ellipses: 'a new age does not begin all of a sudden'	92
Back to where I began	96
An emergent, new social economy?	98

Part II A NEW LIFE: THE RELIGION OF SOCIALISM IN BRITAIN 1883–1896

1. *'We have a glorious and inspiring work in hand'* **(Tom Mann, 1894)**	111
'Lo! I was one of the band … I was born once long ago; I am born again tonight' (William Morris, from 'Pilgrims of Hope', 1886)	118

'The separation of politics and religion has ceased to be ... politics are henceforth merged in morals' (Belfort Bax, 1884) 123
'As the early Christians founded Brotherhoods and Sisterhoods, so in a sense must we if we are to convert the people' (Katherine St John Conway, 1893) 127
'Religion' usurped? 131

2. A single social group? *'I belonged to all these bodies, neither caring much for the dissensions'* **(Ben Turner)** 142

Unities: 'making it whole' 162

3. Failure or defeat? 169

Part III SOCIALISM, THE STATE, AND SOME OPPOSITIONAL ENGLISHNESS

Preface 187
Keep smiling through 189
Flesh and blood, in the cupboard 191
Before the idea of 'Englishness', England and its State 194
Cut to 1984 and The Modern Leviathan 202
Yeast was in that dough 214
News from Somewhere 244
Thomas Kirkup (1844–1912) 244
William Morris (1834–1896) 249
So, what went wrong? 260

NOTES AND REFERENCES 277

INDEX 323

Illustrations

Cover image: Kuzma Petrov-Vodkin, *Fantasy* (detail) 1925.

James Ensor, *The Artist Surrounded by Evil Spirits* (detail) 1898, copyright DACS 2018. 12

Walter Crane, *Cartoons for the Cause*, London, 1896 106

A Co-operative Wholesale Society invitation, from *The Producer* (April, 1927) 186

Preface and Acknowledgements

In Volume 1 of *A Useable* Past, a study of the life and ideas of George Jacob Holyoake (1817–1906), I described how *association* and its *-ism* were articulated in the Co-operative Movement. I use 'articulate' in both senses: to utter and to join. Active co-operators associate in ways which would now be called 'political' and even 'socialist' by their competitors and by some of their protagonists. Only a few – just as committed – people in the movement would have described their work in those terms until the 1920s, and most members of the Co-op still do not.

In *Victorian Agitator, George Jacob Holyoake (1817–1906)*, I celebrated Holyoake's work in the Co-operative and Secularist movements: how he constructed, in his words, co-operation as 'This New Order of Life'. Holyoake lived during the radically ambitious phase of the Co-op's presence in Britain. This lasted from the mid-nineteenth to the mid-twentieth century. He was a remarkably eloquent educator, agitator, and organiser, and the most stylish prophet of 'associative intelligence' that the British co-operative movement has produced so far. He was also well known internationally.

'Association' is a neglected nineteenth- and twentieth-century 'keyword' in Raymond Williams' sense of that term. It was once used to describe a variant of 'socialism' not all of whose advocates or activists saw themselves as socialist. Words in the same cluster of meanings are currently enjoying a revival in Europe as well as in Britain, among proponents of a commons-based, equitable, sustainable, co-operative and mutual, solidaristic, commun-istic *social* economy, polity, culture, and society. Along with the awkward terms 'associational' and 'associationism', 'association' is now returning to the vocabulary of radically practical politics, in productive settings which are designed for the *making* of socialism from below. Networks are multiplying in which the Here and Now is preferred to the There and Then, in linked projects for material 'world-making'. World-making was the term which Holyoake – a latter-day Owenite – preferred to 'utopian'.

Until recently, in everyday and academic conversations about civil society and voluntary organisation, 'voluntary' as applied to this or that has tended towards generality. Like 'civil' – and 'community' for that matter – 'voluntary' and 'voluntarism' have been used to refer to all kinds of getting together by anyone for any purpose or set of relations. As Holyoake argued in the case of the word 'co-operation', such generality has served as a sort of vaccine against co-operative and mutual enterprises and movements when their members and associates propose them as 'a new order of life'. Co-operation and mutuality can be made safe for the powers that be when they are corralled into – or self-defined as – a 'sector' in a 'mixed economy' with Capital in command. If humans everywhere and always co-operate because by their very nature they (we) get together and associate, what is so special about co-operative societies or voluntary associations? Like 'social' or 'society' – keywords with a better-traced social history than 'association' – associations are always there as part of human life. So what? What have they got to do with socialism? Something quite important, I argue in this second Volume of *A Useable Past*. This book is intended as a contribution towards making more fully *social* relations, which Holyoake playfully described as a 'social' – as opposed to an anti-social – society.

*

As a social historian working at Sussex University in the 1970s, I was lucky to work with Robin Murray (1940–2017) and with a group of (mostly) social economists and Marxists which he brought together.

Robin's capacity to blend the practice of theory with the theory of practice in associational socialist settings was unique. Since his premature death in 2017, his work on *Co-operation in the Age of Google*; on really fair trade; on popular and regional planning; on the equal exchange of goods and ideas; on the nature of money; on Zero Waste (his term); on accumulation for located Labour in and against global Capital; and on the river of a *social* economy fed by innumerable tributaries ... his work on all these things (relations) is now being collected and used in inspirational ways. Robin urgently wanted to understand what a materially available and fully social economy could mean. He argued that we – living cells of people with the capacity to divide and multiply – are already in a position to associate in order to produce (make) labour's (all peoples') new order of life, and that we could become even more able to do so.

The group of which I was an apprentice member all that time ago was known as the Brighton Labour Process Group. It was affiliated to the Conference of Socialist Economists (CSE). Reading Volumes 1 and 3 of Marx's *Capital* while in that group helped me, an historian among political economists, to see my work on the Co-operative Movement in Britain and on wider (mostly working-class) association differently.

So I took a (mostly historical) paper to the Labour Process

Group which came directly from my reading of *Capital*. From there I took it to a conference of the British Sociological Association. I called it 'Some Problems in Realizing a General Working-class Strategy in Britain'. Not surprisingly, it was quickly forgotten. This was at a time when history, sociology, and social movements of old, old, pre- or un-socialist labour were not valued highly by value-theory economists or, for that matter, by many Marxist labour historians. Robin Murray's mind, however, was quintessentially positive and open, on the lookout for value in its widest sense from everyone he met. He welcomed the paper, helping me to build on it towards the revival of an 'associational' socialism. It was when his essay on 'The Three Socialisms' was published in the *Bulletin of the Conference of Socialist Economists* that I felt able to develop earlier papers which have now grown into Part 1 of this book as 'The Three Socialisms: Statism, Collectivism, and Associationism'. That is why I dedicate this volume of *A Useable Past* to Robin.

*

I explain my intentions for this book's three Parts at the start of each of them and, in the case of Part III, in another prefatory note. I also make my main acknowledgements within or at the beginning of each essay. My debt to Ursula Howard – a constant and skilled reader and companion in difficult as well as in easy times – is immense. And thanks to Alan Allport for introducing me to Catherine Robinson, the kind of professional editor I wish I had always had. And to Pat Connaty, Henry Tam, Hilary Wainwright, Cilla Ross, and Mike Hales for wanting me to go on when half of me wanted to stop. At a meeting of the Labour History Society in Leeds to honour the life and work of Asa Briggs, I was happy when

Eileen Yeo encouraged me to persist with the three socialisms.

The extended References and Notes at the end of the book will show how wide and deep is my indebtedness to other writers and activists. As with the Holyoake book, I also hope that the discursiveness of some of the Notes will enable readers to follow my winding path wherever they wish to walk. I owe thanks to John Spiers, with his new EER imprint, for giving me the freedom to lay such long trails at a time when other publishers would not.

It is for the same reason that I have chosen to use long and frequent quotations in this book, to make room for voices more vivid than my own. All three of the essays which follow as Parts I, II, and III have been developed from earlier texts which were originally published in pre-digital days, between 1977 and 1987. The utter transformation from those times to today's world – more changed, more disappointingly, for socialists and would-be socialists than for anyone else – made it essential to intervene in the original texts in 2017–2018, for better or worse as I prepared them for publication. The web and digitalisation at least made the task easier. Without attempting anything like a comprehensive overview of masses of material published on my themes during the last forty years, I have added and subtracted material and ideas. As I did so, I was often overwhelmed by a sense of growing insignificance, as a same old, same old socialist in catastrophic, seemingly Endist, twenty-first-century neo-liberal times. Delete, undo, delete, undo …

Asa Briggs, my supervisor at the University of Sussex, used to remind his students that, whether we acknowledge it or not, historians write from time- and place-based 'vantage points'. Allowing more than one such vantage point into the same text – in this case the 1970s–80s and the transformed late-teens of the twenty-first century – may be a challenge for today's readers. I apologise if it makes some among them squint too painfully. All the more so, perhaps, because the 1970s and 1980s are now much reviled from the Right, Left, and 'New' centre-ground of politics in Britain. There is at least some continuity: my own commitment to socialism of a particular kind has not changed. And, it must be admitted, neither has the slim (receding?) chance of its general – as distinct from its local – achievement

As in Volume 1 of *A Useable Past*, I have not been afraid of the first-person singular, declaring my own commitments and beliefs, my disappointments as well as hopes. In spite of the darknesses of the latter years of the first decade of the twenty-first century from the point of view of the political Left, I also continue to use the first-person plural, whistling up a *We* which I know to be there, while also wishing that it – and I – were more robust.

I also recognise that there will be readers irritated by repetitions that I have deliberately retained in the texts, particularly in the overlap between Parts I and III. That the underlying arguments are similar is to be expected. But I have allowed instances and quotations to appear more than once, because I know that some readers will want to follow their own specialist interests, rather than reading through from page one to the end.

The order in which Parts I, II, and III were written is not the same as the order in which they appear in the book. The sequence here is deliberate. Part I is the least conventionally historical. While based, as historians like to say, in 'my period', which in my case means the late nineteenth and early twentieth centuries, Part I darts between places and times, designed, as it is, to put socialism in the plural and to set up a quarrel in readers' minds among and between socialisms. It is designed to provide a lens through which the particulars of Parts II and III may be read.

Part II is the most conventionally historical part of the book. It is designed to give a presence to – and in part to celebrate – a 'moment' between the mid-1880s and the late 1890s when something like a 'religion of socialism' was at its height. 'New Life Socialism' can certainly be found before 1883 and after 1896. These were the too-tight brackets between which I originally confined it. My interest in such a socialism during the hopeful 1970s has survived into the sometimes despairing second decade of the twenty-first century. It also explains why I still find George Jacob Holyoake so compelling. Shortly before he died in Brighton in 1906, Holyoake was still watching 'the growth and trend', through his chosen movement, of nothing less than 'a new Order of Labour'. In my own old age now, had I the energy (and the doctoral students) to follow this through, I would urge myself and the students to get inside, for example, the largest working-class movement of the late nineteenth and early twentieth centuries: the Friendly Society movement. This movement had four million members in 1900. I would be asking how many of these mostly working-class members, in giant Orders and Unities like the Ancient Order of Foresters and the Manchester Unity of Oddfellows – Liberal and Conservative as many of them must have been even after the Labour Party was formed – asking how many of them thought, with Holyoake, that 'with or without "signs and portents" heralding this new order of life, it is appearing'. And how many of them thought that a new order of self-governing life – deliberately decentralised while efficiently federated at their apex or centres – was prefigured in their own intricate associations?

In Parts II and III my aim is at least as much to celebrate as to explain, and certainly not to explain away. I want to give a presence to a socialism which had an attractive power and an absolute value for those who lived and died in it, living and dying before the next 'phase' of socialism began to dominate. Defeat should never be moralised into 'failure'. I believe 'New Life' (Part II) socialism and the 'peculiarities of the English' (Part III) can still be seen as opportunity and resource, rather than as departures from a known timetable. They constitute more than a recessive gene in the evolution of labour's self-realisation; more than a stage in an assumed advance of secularisation; and more than an immature, 'pre-political', or 'post-religious' phenomenon in the history of (British) socialisms. In any case, New Life socialism and the opportunities for a socialism which grows from an old, politically protestant, self-organising culture like our own will continue to speak for themselves, and in voices less full of hesitation and foot-and-note disease than my own. While I hope that the book as a whole will pass muster among professional historians, I also hope that it will speak to socialists and would-be socialists, making our past more useable, serving, in Raymond Williams's fine phrase, as one among many 'resources for a journey of hope'.

May 2018

PART I. THREE SOCIALISMS: STATISM, COLLECTIVISM, ASSOCIATIONISM

Digging historically to sow politically, looking forwards to NOW, from late-nineteenth and early-twentieth century Britain

James Ensor, The Artist Surrounded by Evil Spirits *(detail) 1898, copyright DACS 2018.*

I thought it would be presumptuous to reason from myself to the Party. In reality, it was still more presumptuous to imagine that I was exceptional, and that other people, and the political organisations which act only through them, were immune from my own conflicts.
Alick West, *One Man in His Time* (London: Allen and Unwin, 1969)

There is a socialism which is not afraid to say what it is for and begin to put the values of free association into effect in the process of resistance.
Sheila Rowbotham, 'Welfare rebels', in *New Society*, 18–25 December 1980, p. 573

Anything is possible
that we are not dead yet
A door opens
And I prefer
new errors
to every certainty
in my mouth
a taste of earlier times
Can you help me?
....
late news
and radio talks
on neo-capitalism and the avant-garde

The opening lines of Hans Magnus Enzensberger's 'Summer Poem' (1964), to which poem he added an explanatory 'Note':

Its formal principle is that of openness. One can regard poems either as closed and sealed, as impermeable structures, or as net-like constructions with which new experiences can be caught again and again – even when the writing of the text is finished.

1. *MY OWN CONFLICTS?* A PERSONAL PREFACE

In the plural

The following thoughts on conflicting socialisms began during the early 1970s, in my office opposite Tom Bottomore's, on a corridor that we shared in the School of Social Science at the University of Sussex. They started as feelings, experience-based, and have been developing as thoughts – based as much in practice as in books – ever since that time.

Tom Bottomore (1920–1992) was an expert on class, socialism, and the Austrian school of Marxism – and Professor of Sociology at Sussex from 1968 to 1985. In what follows I will mix the unashamedly personal with particulars mostly from late-nineteenth- and early-twentieth-century British social history, which in historical terms is the period and place that I know best. I will also mix material from two essays that I published in the late 1980s with insights taken from more recent historians of socialism. The original two essays were inspired by working with a group convened by Robin Murray during the 1970s: the Brighton Labour Process Group. It was there that I learned that socialisms, like other ideas and practices, are *made* against, within, and in anticipation of *differing* sets of social, anti-social (class) relations. Like other cultural products and producers of cultures, socialists and -isms are as material as boots, coal, and beans, differing from one another not only intellectually but also in terms of the old class relations in and against which they are produced, and the new, fully social relations which they anticipate and, at best, prefigure. In the Brighton Labour Process Group, inspired by Robin, the question became: how to design and construct cells of a fully social – productive, political, economic, cultural, sustainable, local, universal – democracy? Cells, that is to say, which are capable of multiplying – accumulating their own (fully social) capital – in the face of powerful oppositional forces which depend on destroying them: how to associate, in other words, in such a way as to make for an *associational* rather than a *statist* or *collectivist* socialism?

In this essay 'the run of the argument' (as Robin liked to call it) does not constitute a settled history written from a single point in time. And nor is it a set of sociological ideal types, in the manner of Max Weber. Stretching readers' patience, my (somewhat extended) argument also contains long quotations in the main text as well as epigraphs. This is because I wanted to overhear voices other than my own. As in the 'Note' which Enzensberger published with his twenty-page *Summer Poem* in 1971, quoted above, my 'formal principle is that of openness' in the hope that 'new experiences can be caught again and again – even when the writing of the text is finished'.[1]

In the case of socialism, I began to reach for the plural – socialisms – in a seminar which became a *festschrift* published in 1987 to mark Tom Bottomore's retirement.* I wanted to characterise three socialisms: the socialism that focuses on capturing state power, whether by election or revolution; the socialism that is about rule by those with the knowhow; and the socialism that is about association or associations: getting together. I hoped to enable choices to be made between them among my students, but I also had more general aspirations. I decided to bend the stick in the direction of the differences between the three socialisms, rather than the overlaps between them. I called them *statism, collectivism,* and *associationism.* The overlaps between them are more extensive than I will admit here, particularly in the case of statisms and collectivisms. These -isms have long been in conflict with each other, as *-isms* tend to be. And all three of them extend well beyond positions which can in any way be described as socialist. From time to time, and not only as socialisms, they have been in explicit struggle. But there is still truth in Richard Sennett's observation in 1977: 'class antagonism within the ranks of revolutionary cadres remains the great unwritten history of nineteenth-century radical politics'.[2]

Gathering pace since the late 1980s, good work has been done on the intellectual history and, to a lesser extent, the social history of socialism. I cannot take proper account of this work here, but John Dunn, Gregory Claeys, and Mark Bevir, among others, have placed socialism in and against intellectual traditions in Britain stretching back at least to the sixteenth century.[3] These traditions include 'republicanism' and its radical variants, beginning in the Roman republic; liberalism, democracy, and their 'social' variants; and post-Enlightenment sciences of society and their Positivist, Marxist, and modernist or 'policy' variants. They also include revolutionary and counter-revolutionary 'positions', with their multiple 'revisionist' offshoots, and Protestantism and its fecund theological and organisational (or, as I would call them, 'associational') descendants.[4] The relative autonomy of *language* – as in the language of Chartism and other -isms – has been a matter of dispute in much of this work, as has a related preoccupation of the 1970s and 1980s: the place of 'theory' in history.[5]

In *The Making of British Socialism* (2011), Bevir occasionally writes 'socialisms' in the plural. He seeks to liberate a singular, essentialist, or 'must be' idea of socialism from what he calls 'the old historiography'. This historiography tied socialism to assumed – but now halted – inevitabilities such as 'the forward march of labour', 'the progress of the working classes', and the Hegelian apotheosis of The State, or to one of the many other anticipated 'Ends' of History. Trying to loosen its ties with Marxism, 'socialism', Bevir suggests,'arose contingently, and also variously … had no correct or developed form that was bound to come to the fore and triumph over more primitive rebellions'.[6]

Bevir's preferred 'new historiography' unravels three strands of socialism in Britain, focusing on the 1880s and 1890s as I did in the 'New Life' essay republished in this book. Bevir's three strands – themselves internally differentiated – are 'the Marxists', 'the Fabians', and 'the Ethical Socialists'.[7] Arguing for the 'contingency' of socialism, Bevir suggests that, as idea and as preliminary practice, socialism has been made and unmade by individual heads and hands, working together at particular times and in particular places to transform the social and political traditions that they inherited. As a set of shifting concepts and relations rather than a singular essence, socialism is therefore re-makeable in differing forms, fortified, Bevir hopes, by historical explanations of its past. He sees his new historiography as a necessary preliminary to the making of new socialisms: 'a new historiography should recover the diversity, contingency and contestability of socialist ideas and the movements they inspired'.[8]

Differentiation, to enable choice

My characterisation of statism, collectivism, and associationism is similarly committed to a useable past. But it is designed to assist construction in the present, not mainly by using the professional historians' approach which places socialisms among their antecedents in order to explain them. Instead, I will assemble types and examples, to enable today's would-be socialists (whether calling themselves that or not) to recognise, and so be able to choose between, very different projects on what is still sometimes seen as a singular (whether 'far' or 'moderate') Left.⁹ Alternatives to state socialism as well as to government by expert social-ists – a usage favoured by Tony Blair in the run-up to the Labour election victory of 1997 – are now being opened up. G.D.H. Cole's most original work, *The World of Labour* (1913), is being revisited, as are Guild Socialism, Distributivism, and pluralism more generally. The past and the present of trade unions, co-operatives, dissenting chapels, women's groups, and community organisations are being untied from orthodox Labour and other Party forms as those forms begin to atrophy. Something of an oppositional 'tradition' is being reassembled. Associational life is being actively rebundled for 'civil society after state-socialism' and for a 'Left after Social Democracy'.¹⁰ And voluntary action is acquiring a more cutting edge than 'voluntary organisation' customarily has.

For some people on the Left side of the old Left–Right divide, it continues to be important to act in a united and disciplined way, pretending that there are 'no enemies to the Left'. Following the twentieth century – E.J. Hobsbawm's 'age of extremes' – however, it is clear that socialisms, where they still exist in people's heads or on the ground, remain wildly, not to say tragically, different. Some of them have been corralled into 'One Country'; others have been appropriated as 'National'; still others belong to dogs who eat dogs and for whom LOVE – the word that Edward Thompson once shouted out in an effort to shock a sectarian socialist meeting – is something of a sideshow. This does not mean that socialism is dead, or that, where it lives on, it would be better put out of its misery. Trying to kill *any* kind of socialism once and for all has been the project of free-market fundamentalists for forty years now – for half of this socialist's life. But it remains a good word for what I, and a persistent number of people who share ideas and practices, believe in, along with people of all ages who I see living wonderfully socialistic lives *sans le mot*. So my aim in this Note is not to explain – an over-used word among historians – but to encourage would-be socialists to change things in the present, by cleaning rear-view mirrors, and acknowledging well-differentiated contemporary models. I do not seek to dismiss *any* 'old historiography'. Human agency can be made more or less accessible by historians, ancient and modern. It is made more available and useable in the best of the old historiography of socialism, as it is in the best of the new. Boris Kolonitsky described the presence of October 1917 in modern Russia as 'a very unpredictable past'. Socialism in general may have exactly such a past in and against contemporary global capitalism. It may have to wait for its present until it becomes necessary and unavoidable, rather than merely desirable.

Position and positions, autobiographical and social

Before I moved to Ruskin College in Oxford as Principal in 1989, I taught history at Sussex University for twenty-five years, including a course in Comparative History called Labour Movements. Soon after 1968 I started to teach (with Tom Bottomore) a student-initiated course called 'Social Movements and Political Action'.[11] It was on our corridor in Sussex's School of Social Science that I began to feel the oppressiveness of some socialism, among faculty members rather than among the 1968 generation of students.

I wanted (needed) a socialist practice that did more than fetishise ownership (statism) or control (collectivism). If class may be defined as 'the grouping and re-grouping of practices in the course of people's struggles to direct their own futures',[12]

I aspired to a socialism that was about majority self-direction, or most people's own futures. And 'class' seemed like a set of (productive) relations to be *made* rather than a concept to be refined. Within the university I began to experience what socialism (mostly 'Marxism' at that time) was like, in hands other than those of working-class people – as an ideology, in fact, for academic heads. At that time I was also teaching a Special Subject in History called 'Poverty and Society in Britain, 1880–1914'. In their Special Subjects students were encouraged to use primary sources. In that topic and period, there was no shortage of documentation of socialism in its many competing guises – and even more evidence of large-scale associations of working people dedicated to collective Self-Help. However, it was not generally felt that there was much connection between the two, whether between 1880 and 1914 or among radical Sussex students in the late 1960s and early 1970s. I found this puzzling.

The clash of interests between social groups – classes? – in the same social movement was, of course, fully recognised then as it is now. During the late 1960s and 1970s students were particularly interested in who their antagonists, but also their allies, might be: *operai e studenti, as the 1968 poster had it, uniti si vince!* (Workers and students, united you win!). As the course 'Social Movements and Political Action' (SMPA) developed with students over the following fifteen years, we assembled worksheets for teaching and learning. Talks by activists were recorded and kept in the university library.

We assembled chains of examples of the relations between class and socialism, past and present. One example was Hugh Gaitskell, Leader of the Labour Party in Britain from 1955 to 1963, who grew anxious about his coterie, including his young friends Roy Jenkins and Tony Crosland. Beatrice Webb had been similarly worried about Gaitskell, as contemporaries had been about Sidney and Beatrice – and for similar reasons. Richard Crossman's *Diaries* report a remark of Gaitskell:

> 'I am sometimes anxious about Roy and young Tony. We, as middle-class socialists, have got to have a profound humility. Though it is a funny way of putting it, we've got to know that we lead them because they can't do it without us, with our abilities, and yet we must feel humble to working people. Now that's alright for us upper middle class, but Tony and Roy are not upper, and I sometimes feel they don't have proper humility to working people.'[13]

After a visit from Gaitskell and Eileen Power in 1940, Beatrice Webb bracketed the two of them with Gaitskell's friend Evan Durbin:

> What is wrong about this group of clever and well-meaning intellectuals is the comfort and freedom of their own lives, they have everything to gain and nothing to lose by the peaceful continuance of capitalist civilisation.[14]

To complete this particular chain, Belfort Bax, a British Marxist and member of the Social Democratic Federation (SDF), had been clear about the likes of Sidney and Beatrice Webb as early as 1901. 'Fabianism', he wrote, 'is the special movement of the government official, just as militarism is the special movement of the soldier and clericalism of the priest'.[15] In his novel *The New Machiavelli* (1911), H.G. Wells raised his eyebrows in a similar way, parodying the Webbs and putting them, lightly disguised, among a scientific, professional, and managerial *nouvelle couche sociale*.

Hornsey Labour Party

I arrived at Sussex for my first academic job after activity as a parliamentary Labour candidate in Hornsey, North London, in the 1964 and 1966 general elections. I was a left-winger in a lively constituency party which was divided on class and geographical lines as well as on left–right, ideological ones. Gender divisions were also fundamental, but less theorised than they soon became. The then working-class wards (Harringay [sic] and Finsbury Park) in Hornsey were to the 'Right' of the professional–managerial wards (Highgate and Muswell Hill). In the latter, the activists were (as I recall particular people) architects, lawyers, doctors' wives, Ford Motor Company managers, teachers, advertising copy-writers, and high-tech small-business owners. In the early 1980s some of them left for the Social Democratic Party (the predecessor of the Liberal Democrats), finding the Labour Party 'stuffy', 'old', insufficiently 'radical'. These people were the activists in the more affluent wards of the Hornsey constituency as it was then constituted: Highgate, Muswell Hill, and Crouch End. It was those wards that were drawing an increasing proportion of the Labour vote.

But they were not active in the same sense that working-class members in the working-class wards were. These people – London Transport workers, local-government workers, office workers, London artisans such as drapers and upholsterers, apprentices, unemployed people – literally kept the party going, as a social entity or club. It was more than marginal to their social lives, which did not, at that time, include much non-work contact with the growing number of Cypriots and people of Caribbean origin who lived locally. They were mostly white, including wartime and pre-war refugees from European fascism. They ran the outings, the tote schemes, the celebrations after election results, and the women's sections.

The party was their social home. Without them it would have died, dependent on subscriptions paid by Bankers' Orders rather than subscriptions collected personally by the Road Stewards who still visited members door to door in many wards in Hornsey. In many areas in Britain since the 1960s, professionals and managers have come to dominate the Party.

I identified with the working-class wards, North and South Harringay, and Finsbury Park, finding myself increasingly at odds with the others. As a recent Oxford history graduate, I was a cadet member of the professional–managerial class, but I did not feel like it. I lived in South Harringay, in an 1890s 'ladder' of roads to the west of Green Lanes which were named after Disraeli's novels, including *Sybil, or The Two Nations*. I kept wondering why the professional-managerial class (PMC) felt that the Labour Party was their ideological home, even as I put on my Gannex coat to welcome Harold Wilson to the constituency. The happiness in North and South Harringay wards when Wilson succeeded Gaitskell as Leader of the Labour Party in 1963 was palpable.

As an active parliamentary candidate, I was involved in what would now be called local campaigning, or community politics. I enjoyed this more than the doctoral research in History for which I had a state grant. We ran good campaigns designed to dissolve the divide between Party and Place, on such matters as the closure of railway lines, leasehold reform, rent control, overcrowded public transport, race relations, and the loss of public spaces in the borough to private commercial development.

In the then-developing rifts within London Labour, I was surprised to find that my support came more from the working-class wards than from elsewhere. On the way to being elected to the Executive of the London Labour Party, I learned the importance of membership of the wider movement. In my case this consisted of membership of the 1/420 Branch of the Transport and General Workers' Union, Clerical and Supervisory Staff Section, and membership of the Co-operative movement and Party. The Webbs' distinction between people organised as producers in trade unions, as consumers in co-ops, and as citizens in local government and the (Labour) Party made some analytical sense but not much experiential sense to me at that time.

My version of socialist activity did not appeal to the professional and managerial class (PMC) or, for that matter, to the revolutionary entrists in the Party from International Socialism (IS, the predecessor of the Socialist Workers Party). The Communist Party had a strong presence in the 'North London' wards of the Hornsey constituency – Highgate and Muswell Hill – but the Labour Party seemed to be more of an enemy in their eyes than the Conservatives. A slogan painted on a railway bridge near where I lived stays in my mind: *Vote Communist and Cut the Rates*. The Regional Office of the Labour Party forbade me to debate nuclear disarmament on the same platform as the local Communist candidate. After a talk that I gave on 'Lenin or Bevan?' to the Young Socialist branch, I remember being inspected (on a CND march) for possible recruitment to IS. I was too 'voluntarist', and – as the naive alternative in the title of my talk demonstrated – too weak on theory. At regional training sessions for Parliamentary candidates, I learned what the Party as 'a broad church' meant: Bob Maxwell, later Sir Robert, of Pergamon Press (and subsequently of the *Mirror* Group) was being trained, alongside John Palmer of IS and the *Guardian*.

Childhood

I went up to Oxford to do a degree in History from a second-generation middle-class, professional home. I was born in

1939 and grew up in a class-divided commuter village near London, where there were 'village boys' (Them) and Us: the ones who went away to school. We had bigger houses, often with a 'daily woman' and 'someone in to do the garden' two mornings a week. A full-time gardener would have been too expensive. Nevertheless I saw that our household's entries to the village flower and vegetable show were presented in the 'gardeners' class rather than the 'cottagers' class. During the war there was also a fair amount of free labour in our household, provided by what were otherwise known as evacuees. My mother's helpers, with their children, came from South and East London.

An earnest child, I worried a lot about class. In the context of honouring Tom Bottomore, perhaps I should express my anxiety as a concern with Max Weber's theodicy problem: in other words, how to respond to the unequal distribution of life chances. This has fuelled my politics – as Weber argued that it fuelled most religions – ever since. I identified with the village and against the commuters and RAF officers who ruled it, thanks also to a repulsive prep. school and to strong mothering by and affection for our 'daily', Mrs Martin. Her husband, a permanent-way worker on British Railways, also taught me much about class, particularly when he told me that whereas his group had to meet to arrange their interests, the gentry did not. They met anyway, as already-*made* classes do. Having also been a servant – and a skilled poacher – on an estate, he was an acute analyst of class.

As a child, I was particularly attracted by any associational life in the village that crossed class lines: something which I could see that the Anglican church was not really doing. There were two Churchwardens in the parish church, a Vicar's Warden (my father) and a People's Warden (Mr Tilley, the local carpenter). Through my father, I saw that the Cricket

Club was one example of a mixed association; through my mother, the Women's Institute offered another. I enjoyed attending meetings of both.

Sussex again

When I arrived at Sussex as a doctoral student in 1966 and then as an Assistant Lecturer, I began to study the history of voluntary associational life in nineteenth- and twentieth-century Britain in a town (Reading) near my home village. I included everything from Friendly Societies to Pleasant Sunday Afternoon (Brief, Bright and Brotherly) meetings, from Congregational chapels to branches of the Social Democratic Federation, from football clubs to branches of the Workers' Educational Association. As I was working with Asa Briggs, I adopted a 'local studies' approach to my book, *Religion and Voluntary Organisations in Crisis* (1976).

At Sussex, I joined the School of Social Studies. In one of the earliest of subsequent Sussex University bids to assimilate external dominant styles, the School soon substituted 'Science' for Studies. This was part of the same shift that led to the Mantell building *not* being named after Tom Paine. Paine had strong associations with Lewes, where many university faculty members lived: but his name was not felt to be good for marketing purposes. With the changing academic population on our corridor during the 1970s, I began to worry about socialism. I observed the growing number of militantly professional scientists, including political ones. They were called behaviouralists. I sometimes wondered why they were there, since they seemed to be opposed to most of what Sussex's radical, interdisciplinary 'New Map of Learning' stood for.[16] That was not the problem. What became a problem for me was watching some of them change. In the spirit of the times they became socialists – no: Marxists, some of them 'leading' ones. I was puzzled, because their practices, as far as political class relations were concerned, did not seem to change. They seemed not to share Walter Benjamin's view that 'the mind which believes only in its own magic strength will disappear. For the revolutionary struggle is not fought between Capitalism and mind. It is fought between Capitalism and the proletariat.' [17]

Social-scientific Marxism in the 1970s, often much harder to follow than Marx, appeared to be about 'positions'. But a position seemed to connote something in the head, as in 'What's your position on ...?' ('unproductive labour', ' the law of value', 'Europe', etc.), rather than any actual relationship on the ground. Feminism was soon to alter that. 'Correct' became a terribly important, tight, little word. I heard it more and more from militant students in my course on Labour Movements, as well as from Militant Tendency 'entrists' in the Labour Party. I was seldom 'correct'. I found the category oppressive. I still remember the tone of voice in which I heard it said – by a colleague who had discovered Gramsci – that 'common sense' is despicable. Similar persons, I noticed, were inclined to describe first-person narratives – even oral history as a whole – as 'mere' anecdotes, meaning intrinsically unreliable evidence. 'Ethnography' was not highly rated among (socialist) scientists of society, who began to talk of 'humanism' with disdain and to do tough things like 'interrogate' texts.

And then there was the all-or-nothing revolutionary position which, however deep its understanding of the world, seemed to make changing the world by common, available, popular action so much more difficult. In the world as it is transformed by the immense power of capital – so it was said – institutions constitute a closely interlocking *system*. Whole lives were devoted to interpreting this, often in language as opaque as the system itself. There is no hope, or so it was said, for partial successes, only for global ones – however paralysing (but also self-pardoning) this might be. The crucial criterion for the assessment of partial measures was whether they were capable of functioning as 'Archimedean points': i.e. as strategic levers for a radical restructuring of the global system of *social control*. This was Revolution as One Big Heave. This is why, his latest interpreters alleged, Marx spoke of the vital necessity of changing, 'from top to bottom', the conditions of existence in their entirety, short of which every effort towards the emancipation of mankind is doomed to failure.[18]

I felt the doom myself, in a world which seemed to have nothing, but nothing, in common with Hornsey Labour Party outings to Folkestone five years before. I wondered what all this Marxism had to do with working people's interests in East Brighton or South Harringay. In the face of a lot of scientists who knew what 'the class's' trajectory was, and who were experts in capital's logic, I turned away to work in what I now see to be a very far from simple place – 'the community'.[19] I ducked the difficult task of reaching a labour-process understanding of intellectual (in my case historical) production. Or, rather, I ducked it in the university, and worked with the Federation of Worker Writers and Community Publishers. I started to work with QueenSpark, an East Brighton community action group based in Brighton's Hanover ward which produced a community newspaper and books of working-class autobiography and poetics. That is another story: not entirely a success story, but not one which the word 'failure' adequately captures either.[20]

Not long afterwards, like many socialists at that time, I began to re-read *Capital*, Volume I. As mentioned, I joined a faction of the Conference of Socialist Economists called the Brighton Labour Process Group. Through their instruction, my way into Marxism was the one recommended by Engels, namely the history of changing patterns in the division of labour. I learned what 'the labour process' meant, and what distinguished large-scale industry – 'machinofacture' and 'the real subordination of labour' – from earlier relations of production. It was this group that first theorised the 'three socialisms' in a way which I then began to historicise.[21]

In most quarters on the Left during those years, there was a growing sense that socialism had lost its guarantees. In *Modern Tragedy* (1966), Raymond Williams described this starkly as a 'loss of the future'. Socialism, many began to feel, has to be made or produced, rather than rising like the sun; and made – if at all – now, not 'after the revolution'. Unless socialism exists already, in some sort, it is unlikely that 'it' will ever come into being. 'The project of Socialism', wrote E.P. Thompson in *The Poverty of Theory* (1978) 'is guaranteed *BY NOTHING* – certainly not by "Science", or by Marxism-Leninism – but can find its own guarantees only by *reason* and through an open *choice of values*. And it is here that the silence of Marx, and of most Marx*isms*, is so loud as to be deafening.' It was through that silence that Thompson listened so hard and with such intricate, urgent, field-working skill to the pre-Industrial Revolution world of popular, 'class struggle without class', moral economy of *Customs in Common*.[22] 'Now', as Sheila Rowbotham wrote in 1979, 'it seems to have become inescapably important to bring the real differences about how to make socialism which exist on the Left and in the Labour Movement out into the open, in order to develop new understandings.'[23]

2. THE THREE SOCIALISMS

2.1 Statism

Our central grievance is that we ourselves are not the Cabinet. With the rise of Labour to power, many of the parliamentary difficulties would tend to adjust themselves.
Labour Leader, 31 May 1912

We are no longer petitioning for a place in the counsels of the state, we are the state.
W. H. Harrison at the 1946 Annual Conference of Trades Councils

Then they called the general strike for December 17. Undoubtedly, this would have meant the confrontation ... the bloodshed, the civil war. At this moment, the only alternative to martial law was to raise our arms and let ourselves, the state itself, be destroyed.
M. F. Rakowski, interviewed about Solidarity, February 1982

When, therefore, I identify myself with my office or title, I behave as though I myself were the whole complex of social factors of which that office consists ... I have made an extraordinary extension of myself and have usurped qualities which are not in me but outside me. 'L'état c'est moi' is the motto for such people.
C. G. Jung, *Two Essays on Analytical Psychology* (1953)

Socialism is concerned with many other matters beside the exercise of state power, but it is politically puerile to ignore the centrality to socialist politics of the struggle to acquire, and to exercise state power for what are hoped to be good ends. In political theory socialism must be defined in the first instance in terms of the exercise of state

power and the organization of the economy; it cannot simply be dissolved into the name for an assemblage of miscellaneous cultural enthusiasms which happen to be current at a particular time.
John Dunn, *The Politics of Socialism: An Essay in Political Theory* (Cambridge: Cambridge University Press, 1984), p.xvi

William Hazell and 'a Socialism which is no longer social'

In an article in the *Co-operative Review* in April 1953, directed at delegates to the Llandudno Co-operative Congress that year, William Hazell (1890–1964) called for 'A Congress Creed: Democracy for Man – Not Man for Democracy'.

Hazell was a remarkable Co-operator from the South Wales coalfields. A lifelong critic of state socialism from a democratic, non-Communist, Co-operative position, he embodied Gramsci's idea of an organic intellectual. Hazell celebrated the immanence of the Co-operative Commonwealth by practising the presence of his own and other Co-operative Societies in Wales and England, federated in a Co-operative Union based in Manchester and supplied by a singular Co-operative Wholesale Society with depots all over Britain. Hazell liked to contrast the State's capacity to 'card-index, note, record, number and administer' with the social movement to which his consciousness and his being belonged. He celebrated 'discovery, believing, journeying, questing and searching by the chart of a slender hope, an awful longing, and the keeping alight of the dying smoking flax of a pure idealism: this is not for bureaucracy, but for joyous, co-operative, hopeful travelling'.

'The people', he warned in 1953, 'are in danger of perishing upon a cross of ideologies and spurious-State worship, an erection which is democracy degraded into anti-democracy and a Socialism which is no longer social but retains only the "ism".'[24]

Three years earlier, in December 1950, Hazell anticipated the demise of the 1945-51 Labour Government. There had been major achievements. A state dramatically enlarged for warfare had not been cut down to size, but extended for the purposes of national health and people's welfare, and in order to plan for a crisis-ridden peacetime economy. But that state had not been trans*formed* in such a way as to make for an economic as well as a political, materially *social* democracy. So Hazell published an article in *Co-operative News* with the title 'LOST: A Co-operative Commonwealth'. A friend had asked him 'what had become of the Co-operative Commonwealth – that "State within a State!" which had Co-operation for all purposes of life?'. His friend lamented the Labour Government's missed opportunity. Labour politicians had, for decades, 'picked our brains and substituted for our beloved Commonwealth a Socialist State run by Fabians and Ruskin College students, plus retired trade union officials'. Statist politicians had, he continued, favoured 'nationalisation' over the Rochdale Pioneers' purpose: to 'arrange our powers of production, distribution, education and government' by means of a giant federation of Co-operative Societies.[25]

'A workers' socialism or a state socialism'

Supported by hopes and fears as explicit as those of William Hazell and his friend, the first of my three socialisms is the easiest to characterise. The common usage of 'statism' is near enough to mine to prevent too much confusion. This will not be the case with 'collectivism'; and 'associationism' – an awkward word – has, as yet, very little modern currency.

Durkheim was clear in his 1896 book on *Socialism*:

> There are two movements under whose influence the doctrine of socialism is formed: one which comes from below and directs itself towards the higher regions of society, and the other which comes from the latter and follows the reverse direction ... according to the place occupied by the theoretician, according to whether he is in closer contact with workers, or more attentive to the general interest of society, it will be one rather than the other ... The result is two different kinds of socialism: a workers' socialism or a state socialism.[26]

Until Margaret Thatcher's challenge, our problem – even as socialists – was to see the state as phenomenon, let alone as problem. Every move to extend its reach seemed like progress. Having been reared in 'the most state-planned and state-managed economy ever introduced outside a frankly socialist country',[27] my generation – I was twelve when the Labour Government was defeated in 1951 – literally has (welfare) statism in its bones. Many of my generation secured public-sector employment during the 1960s, more than ten years before the boom came down in the mid-1970s. Some of us later settled for state-sponsored early retirement, in careers of exceptional public comfort.

There are many things which are still obscure about statism, such as precisely whose movement it is. It may be no-one's. Or maybe the notion of 'the political class' is more than the much-used phrase that it has become during the last twenty years? What does statism do, and for which 'class', when class is seen – to use Mike Hales again – as 'the grouping and re-grouping of practices in the course of people's struggles to direct their own futures'? After all, 'the state', or some 'it' or 'thing' standing in for it as a screen for conscious or unconscious human projection, long precedes 'class', whether as classification or as liberation struggle. Thanks to Margaret

Thatcher and believers in the religion of 'the market', sceptics on the Left have become sufficiently conscious of 'the state' by now to recognise that it does not, as yet, appear to belong to producers (workers) by hand; nor, for that matter – however many of them are in one way or another employed by it – does it appear to belong to producers by brain. As far as the latter are concerned, apparatchiks, as Brecht observed, fear conception and prefer execution. They find production – even of new social relations – too likely to get out of control.[28]

As a concept, 'statism' is as helpful for understanding Social Democratic regimes as it is for understanding Communist regimes. As socialist project and as 'actually-existing' (Rudolf Bahro's phrase, in *The Alternative in Eastern Europe,* 1978) 'socialist' regimes, statism starts with the state: the state as a thing rather than a set of relations, and certainly not as a relation of production.[29] Statists (a seventeenth-century word for politicians in general) commonly personalise the state: 'We are the state'. Personality packages with the capacity to grow into cults sometimes follow.

In Britain, there has been a common slide from state to *government* in general, or even to 'the present' government and thence to normality or parliamentary-democracy-as-we-know-it. As early as 1883 Seeley complained that 'the temptation of our historians is always to write the history rather of Parliament than of State'.[30] In 1985, during the trial of Clive Ponting (accused – but ultimately acquitted – of breaching the Official Secrets Act by leaking official documents about the sinking of the *General Belgrano* during the Falklands War), the way in which the interests of the government of the day hid behind the interests of the state or 'national' interests in Britain became notorious. One way to understand this historically is to look at the way in which Ministers in Britain inherit monarchical styles of personal rule. It was a

German king, George II, who grasped the realities here. He once murmured to Lord Chancellor Hardwicke: 'Ministers are Kings in this country'. 'That', wrote Nevil Johnson in his book *In Search of the Constitution* (1977), 'is the core of it all'.

'Caesar for the time being'

In late-nineteenth-century Britain, statist – even Caesarist – 'structures of *feeling*' (to use a concept invented by Raymond Williams) informed socialist bodies such as the Independent Labour Party (ILP). Sentiments that look ugly in the light of twentieth-century National Socialist history were commonly expressed.[31] Painful though it is to rehearse them, in the present state of world politics it may be salutary to do so. For example, T.D. Benson, the ILP Treasurer, wrote an article on socialism and syndicalism in the *Labour Leader* (the main ILP newspaper) for 7 June 1914. In a socialist state, Benson thought, 'there will be a governing or organising class, corresponding to the brain, but an organising class whose only motive for existence is service to the community – a class which, also, may be hereditary under Socialism, perhaps must be so'. In the same newspaper on 14 February 1897, George A.H. Samuel, who had a regular column in the *Leader* under the by-line 'Marxian', awaited the arrival of 'a man strong in the pride of birth or in the conquest of fortune, a man destined to play the great card in the grand style; and the people will follow him to Social Democracy as they have never followed one of their own class'.

For 'Marxian', in the same paper on 1 October 1898, 'socialism was essentially an aristocratic creed ... just imagine or study the clod-pated bundles of nerves and appetites that constitute the human produce of the Capitalist system: and then picture the sort of "Democrat" who seeks definite and helpful guidance from such a mob'.[32]

And Henry Hyndman, who led the Marxist Social Democratic Federation, the ILP's main rival, wrote an article in February 1901 on 'Democracy'. It was published in the Federation's newspaper, *The Social Democrat*:

> If enfranchisement of a mass of deteriorated, uneducated voters would tend to throw back ... essential education, then I am not in favour of such enfranchisement, of such 'democracy', however convinced I may be of the truth that the whole adult population will take an active and intelligent part in the administration of socialism when Social Democracy itself is constituted. If however anyone could thoroughly convince me (seeing education must inevitably come, in the first instance, from above, that is to say from those who are already themselves educated) that we should make more progress in educating the people under a capable Caesar than we should with a fully enfranchised democracy – then I am for a Caesar for the time being, always provided the capable Caesar presents himself.

Whenever 'the state' is made into the active subject of a sentence, as it was in Ramsay MacDonald's early books of socialist theory, warning lights should flash:

> *The State regards* [my emphasis] the man as a carrier of human life between the Past and the Future, and assigns to him the work of realising the Future from the Past. It shows him the path ... A right is the opportunity of fulfilling a duty, and it should be recognised only in so far as it is necessary to the performance of duty ... Nor should the state grant 'the right' to the franchise unless by doing so it is promoting its own ends.[33]

There are passages in MacDonald's *Socialism and Society* (ILP Publications, 1905) which anticipate Lenin after 1917. Substitute 'the Soviet State' for MacDonald's reference to 'the democratic state' and 'the proletariat' for his reference to 'the people' in the following passage: 'the democratic state is an organisation of the people, democratic government is self-government, democratic law is an expression of the will of the people who have to obey the law.' In the same work MacDonald called biology into play:

> The Socialist refused to regard the State as a mere collection of individuals, the majority of whom coerce the minority; he regards it as the means of expressing a will which belongs to the minority as well as the majority, because the minority is organically connected with the community for which the State is acting ... (and) because the communal life is as real to him as the life of an organism built up of many living cells.[34]

The ship of state

Statism ends as well as begins with the state. Unable to replace or transform it, statists seek 'reforms'. In order to achieve them on a consistent basis, however, they have an underlying problem: how to reproduce themselves as a ruling class, when they have no direct power in production.[35] Their characteristic route to political power or 'office' is to recruit a boarding party, capture the bridge, and take the helm. Official channels, whatever they are at the time, are sufficient and self-justifying, however much they become powerless in the face of international money (funds) and global market (players) The 'ship of state' was a metaphor much favoured by Ramsay MacDonald. Once 'in power', Social Democratic statist regimes are then frequently (always?) 'blown off course', to use Harold Wilson's phrase. Foreign interference or invasion;

defeat at the polls; economic destabilisation; being rendered 'uncompetitive', or hoist by their own petard of nationalisation – as in National Governments: these are all common ways of sinking statist vessels.

Left statist regimes are frequently followed by much uglier ones, National Socialist as well as 'Stalinist'. The trouble that statist-socialist regimes get into often comes from their own side: the labour movement. Allende and the truck drivers in Chile are a notorious example. Salvador Allende (1908–1973) was the first Marxist president of a Latin American country to come to power by means of open elections. A truck drivers' strike was instrumental in destabilising his rule, and that of the Chilean Socialist Party in 1973. One function of statist socialism has been to shift the blame for capitalist crisis from 'system' to labour movement, and thus to clear the decks for open authoritarianism. The Callaghan Labour government did exactly this during the years preceding Thatcher's election to power in 1979 in Britain. The 'Winter of Discontent' led to an aggressive period of anti-Union legislation.

Would-be-socialist statists bidding for power patrol the border between 'industrial' and 'political' action as actively as any of their non-socialist party-political competitors. The use of 'industrial action' for political ends is as threatening to social democratic statists as it is inconceivable, in theory, to holders of power in Communist states. While such divisions of labour between politics and the rest of life are characteristic of modern capitalism, statists work entirely within them, 'freezing the imagination within the official compartments'. Alternative visions are simply excluded, so that crude alternatives between, for instance, 'governmental direction' and 'the market' remain firmly in place.[36]

Our Societies: 'Our Union, constituting the society for whom we work'

In their early days, movements-for-labour, like movements-for-Capital, start within 'civil society' and then move out beyond it. They do not begin as anything Official such as, for instance, Her Majesty's Opposition. The term 'civil society' is now used somewhat loosely, to refer to social (or 'voluntary') organisations away from the state and away from 'business'. In its original, eighteenth-century usage, it referred, more precisely, to economic or business formations as the future carriers of the wealth of nations.[37] So as long as it stays as a fully *social* movement, labour's movement, which is not the same as its Party, shares none of the 'civil', 'official'/ 'unofficial', 'industrial'/ 'political', 'indirect'/ 'direct', 'representative'/ 'delegatory' divisions of labour that are embodied in the 'British way of doing things'. In the early nineteenth century, the tone of the incipient labour or social movement was distinctly uncivil and explicitly anti-state. 'To us brethren', wrote an Owenite in 1834 in a series of Letters on Associated Labour,

> it matters little who or what may be the men that direct the crazy machine called *the State*. We have little to do with them ... while we adhere to *Our Union*, we have nothing to apprehend either from them or their precious legislature ...You have worked in pain and want, for society; you have resolved to constitute the society for whom you work.[38]

The labour of constituting the society for which associated labourers worked became an active, creative, cultural struggle until, by the 1890s, the Webbs acknowledged that 'the trade unions offer the century-long experience of a thousand self-governing working class communities'.[39] Visiting Lancashire in 1883 before she became an expert in social science, Beatrice Webb asked herself, in her diary, 'how had this class, without administrative training or literary culture, managed to initiate and maintain the network of nonconformist chapels, the far-flung friendly societies, the much-abused trade unions, and that queer type of shop, the co-operative store?' Beatrice went on to ask herself:

> ... were the manual workers what I was accustomed to call civilised? What were their aspirations, what was their degree of education, what their capacity for self-government? ... I can't help thinking ... that one of the best preventives against the socialistic tendency of the coming democracy would lie in local government ... A strong local government, with considerable power to check individual action ... for the active regulation of their own and their neighbours' lives will be far less dangerous than theorising and talking about things of which they have no knowledge.[40]

It was the possibility that people 'who do not know *at all* what they are talking about' might control affairs of state that deterred J.M. Keynes from joining the Labour Party. 'I do not believe that the intellectual elements in the Party will ever exercise adequate control.' [41]

The Webbs had more confidence than Keynes that their class fraction could act as Labour's social scientists. They were the most powerful 'intellectual elements in the Party', putting in formidable work on behalf of local as well as central aspects of government and administration. Between 1906 and 1929 they traced the evolution of local government, which was controlled, as they projected it would be, by a central Party and State. They produced no fewer than ten volumes on the *History of English Local Government*. They patiently mapped the growth of 'social institutions' through which what *should* happen was being carried by what *had* happened and would pattern and permeate a progressive state of affairs in England. For the controls that they wished to keep in expert hands, the Webbs relied on specialist organisations and institutions whose laws of motion could be traced in positive(ist) ways. They were wonderfully open and honest about themselves and their class, particularly when writing privately. In a diary entry for August 1940, Beatrice Webb speculated whether Beveridge could or should work with the more socialistically inclined G.D.H. Cole. Was Beveridge any kind of a socialist? 'If the socialist state means that he (Beveridge) and his chosen colleagues are to enquire into the facts with a view of ordering them – Beveridge is a socialist ...What he despises is the working man who acts by instinct.'[42]

Large-scale self-government by working people, as Beatrice and Sidney projected, could not but involve the law and thus the state. Thomas Burt, the President of the 1891 TUC and leader of the Northumberland miners, warned Congress that 'the great dividing line among us is as to the proper functions of the State'.[43] As soon as private associations of labour manifested any ambition towards universality, their enclosure became a problem for associations of private capital. The contest or class struggle between unions for private labour and their equivalents for private capital constituted, and was in turn constituted by, 'the state'.[44]

Prolonged struggle between associational forms may indeed be what class struggle – as opposed to class conflict – mostly consists of: the conscious struggle (conscious at least from Capital's point of view) between opposed, materially possible directions for a whole society to take.

But this is not how statists see things. Statist parties and experts produce their own decontextualised, unsystematic (in the sense of ignoring capitalism *qua* system) diagnoses of the consequences of their own activity, which they then naturalise as normal human behaviour, even as human nature. These diagnoses have been sociological and psychological, organisational and personal. The 'iron law of oligarchy' is one example; the inevitability of 'apathy' among 'the masses' is another.[45] Paradoxically, 'the freedom of the market', seen as the opposite of the inherently oppressive state and as the *only* modern form of freedom, can become yet another way of blocking the deconstruction and reconstruction of (plural) states.[46]

Perhaps because they do not clearly represent any coherent class, statists are weak on class as conflict and as struggle, preferring 'class' as classification and as social-scientific sociology. Or they wish it away altogether. Statists may gain a genuine proletarian following – 'following' being the right word in this setting. Here again, Mike Hales's already-quoted definition of class as 'the grouping and regrouping of practices in the course of people's struggles to direct their own futures' would be foreign to statists, even as rhetoric. The statist project is more about what its beneficiaries can do for 'the people', rather than what the people can do for themselves. As D.H. Lawrence wrote in his poem *When wilt thou teach the people?*:

> ... Lenin says: You are saved, but you are saved wholesale.
> You are items in the soviet state,
> and each item will get its ration,
> but it is the soviet state alone which counts
> the items are of small importance,
> the state having saved them all.
>
> And so it goes on, with the saving of the people.
> God of justice, when wilt thou teach them to save themselves?

The much-used phrase 'our people', used by Labour statists during elections in Britain, conveys a sense of ownership. It explains the jilted-lover behaviour in constituency Labour parties when 'our vote' fails to materialise, for instance in 'the North', on former council housing estates, and on the so-called Celtic 'fringe' – 'after all we've done for them too'. It also explains a phrase that Keir Hardie fell into at the 1907 Labour Party Conference, when he threatened to resign from the Parliamentary Party because of its hesitation over women's suffrage. After all, 'with great respect and feeling, the party is largely my own child'. [47]

Free association, civil society, and The Party

Statists are ambivalent about civil society. Social democratic and communist statists have dealt with this concept either by neglecting it or by confining it to its original meaning in the Scottish Enlightenment, namely as private, economic activity. A more recent way of neutralising 'civil society' has been to confine it to the 'voluntary' sector, by which is meant the 'economically inactive' or 'unproductive' sphere. Statists generally choose not to follow Mao Zedong's revolutionary route through the Chinese countryside to the cities. They proceed directly to the metropolis by means of general elections, supplemented by (rather than constituted by) local elections. In metropolitan capitalisms and in post-1917 state socialist regimes, there are short-term gains from such a choice of route. Leaving the private to remain as private, the personal as personal, and keeping people quiet, happy in their social (= domestic, producing, and consuming) lives, can bring popular, even populist, gains. 'I get impatient', Hugh Gaitskell wrote in 1955, 'with those who think that everybody must continually be taking an active part in politics or community affairs. The vast majority find their happiness in the family or personal relations, and why on earth shouldn't they? There will always be a minority who are genuinely interested in social activity and social work. They can get on with the job.'[48]

There will always be a minority ... so why shouldn't 'we', seeking power, constitute that minority? Why don't 'the masses' leave *The Future of Socialism* (Anthony Crosland, 1956) in our capable heads and hands? 'Most people', after all, 'don't have the head for it'. With such a deliberate, commercial-populist division of labour between a providing Us and a grateful Them – 'the vast majority' – the power of the people 'in power' is either exercised in authoritarian ways or turns out to be as intermittent as that of Labour in modern Britain.

There has been plenty of evidence that the Labour Party when in power or 'office' has had as much trouble with its own party and trade union affiliates as it has had from any other group. It is striking how much political capital – and force – has been used by statist leaderships – social democratic as well as communist – 'managing' their own movement, rather than facing up to their enemies outside. Labour has never much cared for independent ('free') association among working people.[49] Unions and Co-operatives are partners, preceding and helping the Party to recruit and survive. They have their place. But they are not *in themselves* the cells of a new social order. They do not prefigure an entirely different way of 'doing business', producing and consuming. They are seen as less than the whole – or even as less than *a* whole. As interest-groups they necessarily lack the 'overview' or capacity to supervise which belongs exclusively to statespersons. The rest of us, in our (voluntary) associations may be economically active but, from a fully social point of view, we can only ever be partially sighted.[50] Hence the necessity of 'the market', alongside the Party, to deliver the goods, take care of 'the economy'. Until the women's movement of the 1970s challenged them in Britain, social democrats held their hands over the private, letting capitalism divide it, license it, provide for it, with disastrous long-term political and psychological consequences even for themselves.

In their most extreme, Communist, states of mind, statists end up by seeking to obliterate civil society altogether. A critique of Lenin's Bolshevism put it sharply:

> A concept of politics as identical with the issue of the possession of state power must of course abolish politics as activity and replace it with politics as apparatus ... the politics of the people were rendered redundant. Politically the people were abolished.[51]

An anthropological study of the USSR during the 1980s exposed unresolved issues in the minds of collective farmers in 'Karl Marx Collective':

> If we are to understand the rationality of collective farmers we must address the question of whether the state is actually seen as in principle distinct from its economic institutional creations, or whether it acts within and by means of them. Are collective farmers taught to see themselves as the object of state planning, or as the instrument by which state planning is executed? Marx's theory assigns the state under capitalism to the superstructure, but the question arises for socialism whether it remains in this status, or whether, in view of its creative and participant role in the socialist economy as 'subject' in Soviet terminology, in the infrastructure. What is perhaps remarkable is that it appears that this central problem has not been resolved.[52]

Production

Statism is primarily about distribution or circulation, not about production. British Railways did not manufacture railway engines, and the National Coal Board was actively prevented from branching out into ancillary industries. Statists have no particular place in industry or, rather, no particular place in large-scale industry as defined and contrasted with 'manufacture' in *Capital*, Volume I. Statism in its pre-socialist forms is parasitic upon productive activity. In its developed socialist forms, when 'in power' it may well constitute a brake upon production. This is how Trotsky characterised it in *The Revolution Betrayed* in 1937. The New Right in Britain from the 1980s onwards would agree. And now they can crow – *I told you so* – about Venezuela and China, and laugh as well as cry about North Korea. Statists are thus in an awkward position. In so far as they are associated with regimes in which the state is the largest single employer, as in Britain during the 1980s, feelings against them and their 'socialism' can be mobilised from the Left as well as from the Right in populist ways (against 'bureaucracy', 'inefficiency', failure to meet 'targets', etc.), all in the name of private labour's 'freedom to choose'.

In so far as it remains socialist in ambition (and has any power in the face of the world market), the project of statism is to weaken the political and economic power of private capital while selling policies designed for, rather than by, 'ordinary' people. The project therefore gets near to realisation only to the extent that private capital is weak and subject to national control, not having assumed its large-scale, 'liberalised', global forms. This has been the context in which the more successful twentieth-century socialist governments have operated.

Against private capital, statists (left and right) occupy 'the state', from whose heights they hope to command the economy. In the name of the movement that they seek to represent, they attempt, at their strongest, to establish power – with a plan or even a monopoly – over circulation. They attempt to determine the division of labour *between* units of production and thereby to control the allocation of use-values and labour, surplus product, and investment. 'Free markets' within national economies, or between national economies and their competitors, are inimical to this project. Hence the 'insoluble equations' faced by Labour economic policy-makers in modern Britain. After five years of the Callaghan Labour government, and Labour having lost the election of May 1979 to Margaret Thatcher, a key Labour economic policy-maker, Peter Shore, used 'Insoluble Equations' as the title of an article in *The Observer*:

> There are ... major lessons to be learned from ... economic management in 1974/9: and the most important by far is the weakness of the contemporary State. The British people overwhelmingly will the ends of economic revival, industrial growth, full employment, and more stable prices. Yet the Government they elect is palpably unable to exercise sufficient persuasion or control over the institutions concerned to make these ends achievable. And the State power is increasingly hobbled and fettered by external authorities ... Until these trends can be changed, the economy will continue to weaken and so too will confidence in political democracy itself.[53]

If the economic foundation of statism at its most ambitious is national planning, it needs protection from the World Market.[54] It was William Morris who gave this market – emergent rather than dominant in his times (1834-1896) – its definite article and capital letters, knowing that its version of everywhere and *Nowhere* would never be the same as his. Because would-be controllers of a central state base their power on economic synthesis (rather than direct production), they try to reproduce that power by centralised control of political synthesis. This is why they need to prevent the independent political organisation of the classes whose base is in (economic) production.[55]

There are of course weak, would-be, or ex-, statisms which get nowhere near such controlling ambition. Raymond Williams characterised the politics of the post-1966 Labour Party (or the Labour leadership) as 'post social democratic'.[56] One way of not being blown off course is to decide never to leave harbour, though such caution does not necessarily lead to any greater electoral success. Even at their strongest, statists are in difficulty rather than in power. From their base in the political, they reach out to control the economic. But they cannot bring it to heel. Bits of planning, national ownership, sticks and carrots, do not work. The fact that they do not work is seen by statists as contingent rather than necessary. So more and more of them need to be piled on, in a situation in which control has to be either absolute or ineffective. Formality of control from above is not the same as real control from within, or universal, *social* control from below.

Associations

Statism neglects the details of the forms, and in particular the *relations*, of production. Statists tend not to see the potential *sociality* of these forms and relations, that is to say their politics and economics united in the most inclusive sense of *social* – or that which Raymond Williams theorised as *cultural* – production. Statists, as I am characterising their socialism here, are not cultural materialists in Williams' inclusive sense of *culture*, a keyword whose uses he traced in *Culture and Society 1780 to 1950* (1958), alongside 'industry', 'democracy', 'art', and 'class'.[57] Statists tend not to acknowledge the possibility of fully social production, that is to say the making of society by means of Societies or Associations: 'constituting the society for whom (we) work' by means of a multiplicity of mutuals, co-operatives, unions, guilds, companies, partnerships, clubs, campaigns, licensed commons, foundations, charities, etc. federated as actual rather than abstract 'society'. Statists are prone to emphasise the forces of production (as in 'technology') as if they were separate from the relations of production and can be altered by 'policy' rather than through practice. The details of the labour processes at work in factories, fields, workshops – or in political parties and in the culture more generally – are either neglected or held constant. To reform or reinvent them might be regarded within a statist mindset as 'political interference'.

When social democratic movements or parties become large enough, they appear to activists, but not always to their Parliamentary leaders, to provide a basis for industry or society more generally. Social Democratic movements have sometimes grown very large, for example the pre-1914 German Social Democratic Party (SPD). For millions of its members and their associates, the SPD provided a whole way of life or culture which was alternative to and relatively autonomous from the wider culture. Such party forms can then become their own cause or nation, with a revolutionary ideology (in the case of the German SPD, Kautsky's Marxism) which legitimises their day-to-day, 'reformist' practice.[58] They grow large enough to reflect, mimic, or even anticipate large-scale modes of organisation more familiar in an industrial or economic setting – modes that are championed, as we shall see, by collectivists. This was the problem that Lenin identified and which led to the Lenin-ism of *What Is To Be Done?* (1902). Such forms of political association can now be seen as achieving the 'real subordination' or 'de-skilling' of the voter/citizen in the same way as adequately capitalist forms of material economic production did for workers in the workplace. This was made plain in chapter XXII of Schumpeter's *Capitalism, Socialism and Democracy* (1942). As befitted a one-time Minister of Finance in a Social Democratic government, the divisions of labour between the producers and consumers of politics were celebrated – seen as being as technically determined as an iron law – rather than contested from a majority, working-class, associationist point of view.[59]

In sum, the change for which statists work is expected to come through the narrow (capital P) Political conduit within which they seek to come to power by means of Party Politics, rather than through wider associational life. So they suffer a permanent crisis of agency as far as socialism is concerned. Statist socialism at its worst takes from Labour ('the masses', 'ordinary' people) all 'available forms' of social-political-cultural production. From their (big P) Political, National (nationalising) point of view, there is something illegitimate about 'politics' entering into football, the family, the classroom, the bed, the Co-op store, even into the labour processes of newspaper and television production. Such aspects of productive life are either contained within the movement, echoing the rest of the culture sometimes on a large scale, or they are neglected as not being the movement's or the Party's business. The idea of associational forms that are neither simply alternative nor narrowly oppositional, but which attempt to be both, gets lost. The result is predictable and unpredicted. Such aspects of life get left, in the long run (which is where we are in modern Britain), to be socialised, but on private capital's terms, not on private labour's. The common sense of the entire culture shifts, through changes which are wrought a long way away from politics (and often, now, in confidential or secret places) against even statist socialist priorities. To the extent that these have become dominant within 'socialism' itself, the common sense also shifts, tragically, against socialism *tout court*.

2.2. Collectivism

...He came shouting by
as if the art of thinking were a pommel
to pound the world into conformity...
From Alice Oswald's poem 'The Three Wise Men of Gotham Who Set Out to Catch the Moon in a Net' (1996)

Many think that a government of the wise would be a good thing, but such government has this disadvantage – it prevents anyone else being wise.
G.J. Holyoake, *The Jubilee History of the Leeds Industrial Co-operative Society from 1847 to 1897 Traced Year by Year*
Leeds: Central Co-operative Offices, 1897, p.217

The 'quintessential Fabian' on 'bygone socialisms'

'We must rid ourselves resolutely of all those schemes and projects of bygone socialisms which have now passed out of date', wrote Sidney Webb in 1899, in an apotheosis of 'collectivism', as I will characterise it here. 'If our aim is the transformation of England into a Social Democracy, we must frankly accept the changes brought about by the Industrial Revolution, the factory system, the massing of population into great cities, the elaborate differentiation and complication of modern civilisation, the subordination of the worker to the citizen and of the individual to the community.'[60]

So what were some of the characteristics of late nineteenth-century 'collectivism' as I will set it up here? To use Sidney

Webb's 1899 statement, to which he gave the title 'Socialism True and False', they included an excited modernity, with a corresponding sense of the 'out of date'; a fondness for 'system'; a fondness for evacuations or purges, as in 'we must rid ourselves resolutely' (of x, y or z); a sense of social change as something wrought abstractly and objectively, as in 'the transformation of England into ...'; a welcome for 'subordination' (by 1916 Webb was advocating Universal Submission); and an acceptance of key capitalist divisions of labour, like the 'elaborate differentiations' between city and country, heads and hands, conception and execution, which make simple co-operation and 'primitive democracy' inadequate. And all this was articulated at a time when Ebenezer Howard's practical work towards creating the first Garden City at Letchworth and William Morris's practical work (in wood and other materials) on work-pleasure as art and art as work-pleasure were well under way. No wonder William Morris is reported as saying to Sidney in 1895, 'The world is going your way at present, Webb, but it is not the right way in the end'.[61]

Collectivisms

Confusions can easily arise because there have been almost as many different uses of the word 'collectivism' as there have been of 'socialism'. It is very difficult, not to say impossible, to differentiate some carriers of statists, as I have characterised them, from some collectivists. And the earliest citation of 'collectivism' in the *Oxford English Dictionary* is from 1880, and it is very similar to the meaning that I will assign to 'associationism'.[62] J.T.W. Mitchell, chair of the giant Co-operative Wholesale Society between 1878 and 1895, often described his work in 'associational' terms, as did George Jacob Holyoake, with whom he seldom agreed on the best way forward for Co-operatives. In 1894, Mitchell described himself as 'a collectivist, but not by Act of Parliament'. And the use of 'collectivism' by the early New Right in Britain, for example in Max Beloff's *The Tide of Collectivism – Can It be Turned?* (1978), is not very different from statism as outlined above.[63]

In the face of such overlaps I will continue to press differences heuristically here, in the hope that a quarrel between my three ideal types or models of socialism will lead to easier recognition of the differences between them, followed by sharper questions from activists about the real, inevitably mixed historical and modern instances that people on the Left encounter every day. Individuals are often, perhaps even usually, at least two things, espousing at least two -ists or -isms at the same time: associationists, after all, want and need a (trans-formed, by them) state rather than no state at all.

Collectivism's heyday as a disputed label was between 1885 and 1910, much used during those years against, as well as among, socialists. This is a period of intellectual history which has been brilliantly characterised by Stefan Collini.[64] During that time, 'collectivism' was one pole in a field-of-force of ideas, the other pole of which was often labelled 'individualism'. Each of these -isms shared characteristics, criss-crossing liberalism and socialism, in a discourse which sometimes had negative consequences for working-class identification with *any* socialism. To quote the Co-operative Wholesale Society journal, *The Wheatsheaf*, in 1898:

> Amongst all these contending -isms clamouring for support, the ordinary working man may well be perplexed, wondering which of them is the most likely to fulfil the promise of its advocates, and in many cases he may refuse to discuss or adopt any of the systems offered him … Co-operation is not an -ism.[65]

When Asa Briggs, a founder of the Society for the Study of Labour History, was selecting writings and designs by William Morris for a collection published by Penguin in 1962, he reminded readers that 'many working men who joined a wide variety of labour organisations cared little about the varieties of socialism they expressed'.[66]

The welcome for collectivist socialism by many middle-class figures in this period was explicitly intended to prevent what Durkheim called 'workers' socialism'. And self-identified Collectivists were by no means all on the Left. They included many who simply thought that 'society was something more than an aggregate of so many individual units'.

Fabians

'We must rid ourselves resolutely of all those schemes and projects of bygone socialisms'; 'our aim is...' But who were the first persons plural, the 'we' and the 'our' in Sidney Webb's *Socialism True and False*?

'Nothing in England is done without the consent of a small intellectual yet political class in London, not 2,000 in number. We alone could get at that class', wrote Sidney in a letter to a fellow Fabian, Edward Pease, in 1886.[67] 'We' in that instance meant the Fabians – a group who, as Webb explained in the same 1886 letter, were deliberately trying to form a political association which was unlike an orthodox political party. Fabians could be as self-conscious as Lenin about the political party as a form to be adapted for the purpose of obtaining power for the ideas and the people they were interested in. Lenin, for his part, was very interested in the work of the Webbs: he 'attached the highest importance' to *Industrial Democracy* (1897), translating it while in exile. Its influence on *What Is To Be Done?* (1902) is not hard to detect.[68]

Fabians used machine language about 'public opinion'.

Beatrice Webb thought there was no such thing as 'spontaneous' *public* opinion. It 'has to be manufactured from a centre'.[69] They used similar language about 'government', 'outside organisations', and how 'the policy of a political association is deterermined'. In Thomas Kirkup's *History of Socialism*, first published in 1892 and revised for publication in 1913 by the first historian of the Fabian Society, Edward Pease explained how:

> to the ordinary citizen, and especially to the workman, the Government is a thing apart, a great machine of which he knows little and over which he has no control, except as an elector, and then only, so to speak, by force. The Fabians were many of them in government service as first division clerks. The Society itself, at this period, had its only headquarters at a table in a Downing Street Office. To Government clerks at Whitehall, even the juniors, Government is a delicate machine whose working they have to control. They draft the despatches which ultimately determine policy in remote dependencies or in post offices and custom houses throughout the country. They prepare the information for ministerial speeches, and make the first outlines of new legislation. To men in such service many ways of influencing political action are apparent which the outsider cannot realise: The country is not so much governed by the votes of the electors, as by the ideas put into the heads of official persons whether parliamentary chiefs or permanent civil servants. What is true of government is equally true of outside organisations. The policy of a political association is determined – within limits – by the man who drafts its resolutions and reports. Know more than other people, know what you want, and you can make other people carry out your ideas. It is easier to get control over existing machinery than to make machinery for yourself.[70]

Such men knew with scientific certainty what 'the people' were unable to do, and so would be best advised never to try. According to Bernard Shaw,

> The people want a policy (at least 1% of them do), but they can't make one, they must go to the thinker and tactician for it ... In offering them the Fabian make of shoe I don't question their capacity or loyalty, I only assume what everybody knows as plain matter of fact, namely that they can't make the shoe themselves.[71]

And Fabians knew, with some relish, what they, the Fabians, *could* do, which was – like all potential ruling classes – to fold their own tools and interests (in their case, knowledge) into what *must be*. My ideal-type Collectivists – who can surely still be recognised in the Westminster village and its love-hate media – stated their interests as sociological laws, turning social movements into 'objective' tendencies.[72] Their confidence is itself significant. As experts they are less deferential than statists. They would not be as surprised as Harold Wilson was when he got to Downing Street in 1964 and found that 'everything worked'. They had the hubris of an emergent ruling class, and the theoretical reach to go with it. To others, on the populist Right as well as on the Left, their project often appeared unattractive. H. G. Wells, L.T. Hobhouse, and John Burns, for example, expressed some disgust at the time. But to Fabians the project had 'poetry' in it. In 1890 Sidney wrote excitedly to Beatrice: 'to play on these millions of minds, to watch them slowly respond to an unseen stimulus, to grade their aspirations without their knowledge – all this, whether in high capacities or in humble is a big endless game of chess of ever extraordinary excitement'.[73] Others on the Left at the time knew what kind of a class movement this was, perhaps more clearly than most socialists since. 'Fabianism', wrote Belfort Bax in 1901, 'is the special movement of the government official, just as militarism is the special movement of the soldier and clericalism of the priest'.[74]

Whose knowledge, for and about what?

It would be a mistake to lean too heavily on the Fabians in this setting.[75] 'Collectivism' as a type of socialism – but also as the ideology of a type of person in typical modern, professional-managerial 'positions' – can also help to situate the academic Marxisms to which I was party in the School of Social Science at Sussex University in the 1970s. It may also apply to the socialisms of the Soviet Union and its satellites in Eastern Europe before 1989.[76]

I will return to the University of Sussex later, ending this essay where it began. In a less local setting, however, it is the growing presence of a self-conscious knowledge-producing estate or class which the modern Left has had to try to come to terms with, complacently or otherwise. It goes without saying, perhaps, that its presence extends way beyond 'socialism', and way beyond universities.[77] However, a professional and managerial class *has* been central to the production, as well as the distribution and exchange, of pervasive – even dominant – notions of 'socialism' in our time. That class also tends to keep 'knowledge' in the singular rather the plural, afraid not only of the 'relativism' which might result from the admission of 'knowledges', but also, perhaps, of the loss of their own position in dominant arrangements for the production of knowledge and, increasingly, of 'representative' democracy itself. The politics of knowledge are the politics of its production, as well as its distribution and exchange.[78]

In 1977 Barbara and John Ehrenreich posited the Professional and Managerial Class (PMC) as a 'new' class, distinct from the working class, and from the old middle class of small- and medium-sized business owners, and from a wealthy class of owners. At that time, they welcomed the PMC as progressive porters for socialism.[79] In recent work, notably in an article published by the Rosa Luxemburg Stiftung's New York office in 2013, they modified their expectations.[80] In introducing this new work, the Co-Directors of the Stiftung related it to socialism in general and to 'class analysis for the twenty-first century':

> Historically, members of the PMC have designed and managed capital's systems of social control, oftentimes treating working-class people with a mixture of paternalism and hostility. As advocates for rational management of the workplace and society, however, the PMC has sometimes also acted as a buffer against the profit motive as the sole meaningful force in society. Today, members if the PMC face a choice. Will they cling to an elitist conception of their own superiority and attempt to defend their own increasingly tenuous privileges, or will they act in solidarity with other working people and help craft a politics capable of creating a better world for all?'[81]

As self-critical intellectuals who chose to see themselves as cultural producers, both Rudolf Bahro in the German Democratic Republic and Raymond Williams as a 'Welsh European' were acutely aware of the same questions.[82] During the 1970s and 1980s, they each moved critically within and against modernist, professional and managerial, versions of 'class, politics and socialism'. Expressing their own, subjective conflicts concerning roles and positions, they described the objective obstacles and opportunities facing 'ordinary' working people. They produced positive proposals for cultural, participatory, and democratic 'New Left' versions of socialism on which socialists have been working ever since.[83]

Building on such work from the late 1970s, starting with his *Living Thinkwork: Where Do Labour Processes Come From?* (1980), Mike Hales has been an unusually insightful, self-conscious as well as class-conscious, socialist thinker and activist. Born into a working-class family in Halifax in 1947, and employed in professional-managerial or 'technical' situations for most of his working life, he is painfully aware of the objective, systematic difficulties, as well as the subjective choices involved in moving through 'collectivism' as I am using the word here.

With a First Class degree in chemical engineering, Mike Hales worked as an apprentice engineer at ICI, Britain's leading chemical manufacturing company, lectured on the history of science and technology, and worked in the Greater London Council's Economic Planning Unit with Robin Murray as a researcher/developer of regionally-based work ('employment' would be a more PMC word). He designed and led a six-country research project on national systems of innovation, and worked as a consultant on the design of IT systems. He remains someone who is, in his own words, 'deeply committed to the production and development of "theory", centering on discovering how freedom-and-necessity works in the sphere of technologies and the hands-on organisation of paid work'.

In his work in progress during 2018, provisionally called *Activists and the Long March Home – Class Geography, Conviviality, Melancholy Territory. A Prospectus for Libertarian Socialist Activism*, Hales continues to evoke and analyse his 'journey in cultural materialist, labour-process oriented, professional-managerial occupational territory'.[84] He is preoccupied with a '*radical professional* politics: of redesign of wage-work workplaces, and design of design', 'adopting radical professionalism as an organic intellectual politics'. He offers the most sensitive contemporary register that I have found of all the difficulties involved. Using 'class' as the best reality from which and with which to describe 'the grouping and regrouping of practices in the course of people's struggles to direct their own futures',[85] and believing that 'anyone who chooses, in any place in the class landscape can find socialist activities', he finds that 'being a professional-managerial gives us a place to stand and dig'.[86] But, but ... within actually existing capitalisms there are real, material obstacles: if the socialist project is that of 'subjective socialisation' for the many rather than for the few – in other words, in more than my 'collectivist' sense – how is this to be accomplished within current conditions? In Hales's words:

> One thing which is clear is that capitalist production achieves, through time, a massive socialisation of work. Or, to be more precise, what is clear about capitalist socialisation of production is that it is objective socialisation. Labour processes in different parts of the world depend on one another for their raw materials and tools, in a complex and geographically far-reaching division of labour quite different in kind from that of pre-capitalist economies. But alongside this objective socialisation of labour there is no corresponding subjective socialisation of labour at the immediate level of the labour processes making commodities. Not only are different workers employed in subsequent stages of production, but also, the necessity of direct communication between these distinct work groups is systematically extruded, as labour becomes increasingly objectively ordered – notably by specialised instruments of labour, machines. This is a major fact of political life, in the context of activism and organising

in a world of productivity-hungry multinational and multi-site capitalist enterprises. What the term fragmentation refers to, but does not describe, is the subjective isolation of workers. The political project which it implies, but does not point clearly to, is the subjective socialisation of labour, which as a historical process must proceed in opposition to capital's merely objective socialisation.

The task is daunting, he continues:

> To socialise labour power means to make it possible for all to know what any can do, and what would be necessary for them actually to do it; not necessarily so that all *can* do it, but so that they can grasp the meaning and the objective conditions of others' actions....
>
> .... It is the ability to raise a structure in imagination before erecting it in reality that marks off human activity from other kinds. Yet even when this major thought was first put in these terms – by Marx in the nineteenth century – the separation of 'architects' and 'labourers' was deeply entrenched in social practice. Today – in our chemical plant design process – there is one obvious and terrible fact: labourers and architects are not the same people. The process worker is not the design engineer. Nor do they work together. The pre-conceptualising power of the collective architect is vastly greater now than in Marx's day, the forces of conceptual production (state planning bureaucracies, NASA, the R and D establishment) have developed quantitatively and qualitatively. And the collective labourer is relatively more powerless, more *ignorant*, because of the existence of this knowledge producing estate. To put it mildly, for socialists this is a big problem.[87]

For the working class the Professional Managerial Class holds a threat; the systematic undermining of conditions of autonomous working-class cultures, even identity. But equally, how socialism can be won in industrialised countries without the PMC and working class working at it together is hard to see.[88]

Architects or bees?

As a project as well as a finished achievement, I am using 'collectivism' as a word to describe modern forms of near-monopoly or 'new class' control over a particular kind of productive knowledge in an era when such knowledge(s) and its resulting systems are crucial. At a time when fragmentation becomes a very common human disadvantage point – the frog's view of the sky from the bottom of a well – a social group who can literally 'get it together' becomes important. This may be to put the causal relationship the wrong way round. It is *because* of the PMC's stock-in-trade, which is, precisely, a supervisory or bird's-eye view – supervising 'knowledge' itself – that there are so many frogs so deeply stuck in a hole, without a horizon. What is to be done? Their (our) frogs-in-winter situation cannot be dealt with effectively either by simple workerism or by complex scientificity, however tempting each might be. It is too late for either. At the risk of being sent to the back of the class as 'relativists', we may need to put 'knowledges' in the plural, alongside socialisms. There is no such *thing* as abstract, a-historical, class-neutral, capital-K Knowledge. But there is certainly a modern *relation*(ship) (of production) which encourages, no, *produces* the idea of such a *thing* (or corpus). As many of the quotations that I am using here surely indicate, that set of modern relations of production has produced a particular usage (and practice) of 'socialism', characterised by particular ways of acting towards other (plain, ordinary, mass, *working*-class etc. etc.) people. Collectivism is deeply rooted not only in large-scale 'private' capitalist industry but also in state-capitalist industry. The connections here are well known, not only through Lenin's enthusiasm for Taylorism – that is to say the active de-skilling of the working-class 'line' in modern machinofacture – but also in symbolic details such as the fact that a foundation-subscriber to the *New Statesman* in Britain, L.F. Urwick, produced a three-volume eulogy of Taylor and Taylorism.[89]

Self-conscious knowledge or 'theory', elevated to the status of a science and 'applied' in offices and lecture rooms as well as fields and factories, distinguishes collectivists from statists: that is to say 'scientific' knowledge of bureaucracy, technology, labour processes, 'democracy', and then of 'society' itself. The PMC are 'in power' in the work-place (the bank, the agribusiness, the corporation, the 'plant') already. They understand modern labour processes and how to connect them as *their* 'system': *the* labour process, as Marxist economists began to theorise it in the 1970s. The notion of an a-historical 'objective' 'economics' and 'organisation theory' is theirs. It does not matter whether they actually own the fields and factories: they possess the knowledge that is the principal ingredient of emergent forms and relations of production. They have the know-how. They can bring 'it' all together. Theirs is a 'knowledge' which is separated self-consciously and materially from the practices it is *about*. They work *on* things, on 'them' or 'it' as object rather than as (equal) agent or subject. Theirs is a way of knowing which is also a mode of production: a knowledge which is both organised by and organises how things (relations, including 'public opinion') are made in a society in which labour is really subordinate to capital.

Professional, managerial, and technical supervision becomes important in modern, large-scale, production, when the 'social' relations characteristic of such production are extended to entire, global, corporate, financial, cultural, economic, social (or anti-social) systems. As in the syntax characteristic of the Webbs, already quoted, ' the transformation into ...', abstract nouns become dominant as -*isations* without a clear subject to the sentences that they impose, but with many objects in their viewfinders. In global relations of production, synthesis within and between different units of production is achieved, or its absence palliated, by means of newly defined 'social' sciences – soci-ology, social-ism, and social-work. Such synthesis is attempted within politics as well as within economics, within public administration as well as within private production. 'Social science(s)' are devised – as they were being devised along the corridor in the University of Sussex where this essay began – to link politics and economics, but from above rather than from below.

'The new class'
'Whether a theory and set of practices that goes beyond, but also on occasion includes, 'socialism' can be linked directly with the PMC is the question behind the controversy among historians (and participants such as Milovan Djilas of *The New Class* published in 1958) concerning the 'New Class' in the post-1917 Soviet world. But it is also a more general question, going back to Saint-Simon's conception of 'the organizer' and, before him, to Goethe's Faust, 'the developer', who can 'bring material, technical and spiritual resources together, and transform them into new structures of social life'.[90]

In his *Philanthropy and the State, or Social Politics* (1908), Kirkman Gray, a 'sociologist and besides, a socialist of the progressive type', described how 'the modern sociological agitator regards every abuse in its relation to the whole range of social life, that is to say he adopts the method of science'.[91]

In the hands of ambitious collectivists like Gray, 'the method of science' was used to characterise the state, or the 'social' division of labour (who does what and where?) not from a working-class disadvantage-point but from the vantage point of a class which has actual or potential control of an entire mode of production: as architects rather than bees.

Statists are at some disadvantage here, compared with collectivists. Statists have to reach out from their public positions in politics (or parliamentary-democracy-as-we know-it) to try to control economics (or 'business'), using 'systems of representation' and indirect tools like 'nationalisation', 'accountability', 'planning'. Collectivists, on the other hand, have a place *within* the 'private' or economic sphere and – using similar languages to understand them both – they can reach out from that place towards 'public' politics and 'the state'. Compared with statists, they can wait. The Fabian word 'permeation' describes their project well. They do not have the same urgent need to 'capture state power'. Whereas statists are advised that 'they must acquire political power and the sovereignty of the State to be enabled to put an end to the reign of the robbers',[92] collectivists are, in an important sense, in power already. Whether or not they are 'in office' or 'form an administration', they constitute an emergent and material force (a set of social relations) within capitalisms as well as within actually existing socialisms. Because the PMC has a real site in production (as contrasted with statists' site in, or attempts to control, circulation), 'the state', on behalf of the PMC, is likely to defend or protect the changes made or projected in 'the economy'. Political and economic unity (synthesis, system making, social control) can be achieved not only through state planning, but also through limited competition and the market. Hence the 'reforms' attempted in Czechoslovakia up to 1968 and in Hungary in the 1980s.

Whatever formation is in play or in power, conflicts are endemic and likely to turn into overt struggles for more power, both economic and political. Emergent collectivism within modern capitalism presents problems of control for would-be 'private' capital. Emergent collectivism within modern statist regimes also presents problems of control for the would-be 'public' ruling party, or state. The issue becomes not merely the old capitalist problem of separating labour from the means of production (as in the emergence of large-scale industry from manufacture), but of separating technical labourers from each other. This is a struggle in which technical labour, in so far as it tries to realise its own external-to-capital project, tries to re-compose itself as a class against capitalist efforts at class decomposition, familiar in their more common, historical, proletarian settings. These struggles in a capitalist setting have been well described by Mike Hales as a 'politics of knowledge', and in a statist setting by George Konrád and Ivan Szelényi in *The Intellectuals on the Road to Class Power* (1979).[93]

'A collectivist spirit': 'the secular and the religious are one'
At its strongest, the collectivist project can be radically puritanical, to the point of selflessness. During the 1880s Sidney Webb wrote of the necessity for programming the individual person to 'self-deadness'. This was in the interests of a Roman-republican type of citizenship or public service, releasing formidable external energy.[94] Full of internal feeling, albeit repressed, collectivism despises 'sentimental' socialism in favour of the 'scientific'. It is radical about the family, property, democracy, religion, morality – all the sacred cows that Bernard Shaw and Oscar Wilde had such fun attacking.

The *Letters and Recollections* of a rank-and-file Fabian, Frederic

'Ben' Keeling (1886–1916), provide vivid documentation. Keeling became manager of the Leeds Labour Exchange in 1910:

> I have noticed several times that my entire disregard of any individual feelings when I am aiming at what I conceive to be a social end strikes many people as simply horrible ... I care more for the State than I care for or have ever cared for myself, or for any other human being ... I have lost all my dogmas except a passionate faith in the development of a collectivist spirit in relation to property and breeding.
>
> We have got to be better capitalists than the capitalists are. When we – that is the administrative classes – have more will, more relentlessness, more austerity, more organising ability, more class consciousness than they have, we shall crumple them in our hands.[95]

It was not only 'the capitalists' who were to be crumpled. Characteristic working-class modes and aspirations were to be superseded as well, in an ambitious, systematic, collectivist vision of a new industrial civilisation. 'Primitive' democracy, autonomous collective bargaining, producer co-operation, face-to-face mutual insurance, building societies in which the borrowers and lenders were the same people ... were all interesting but, in the end, baggage. 'Local government' had its place, but, as we have seen when characterising statism, subordinate to central government. The local was, perhaps, as the Webbs saw it, a bit 'primitive', but viewed systematically and historically it could function as 'one of the best preventives' 'against the socialistic tendency of the coming democracy'. 'The Webbs', Carl Levy has suggested, 'were evolving a model of social organisation where the salaried brain-workers were gradually becoming the fulcrum of all political activity'.

'Industrial democracy' on the Webb model has never

happened yet, anywhere – least of all in Britain. But during the 1930s a 'new civilisation' in Stalin's Russia became available as a screen on to which the Webbs and others could project their dreams. In the first (1934) edition of the Webbs' *Soviet Communism: A New Civilisation?* the title included a question mark. The second edition took account of changes achieved between 1934 and 1937. The question mark was dropped. The new civilisation was the apotheosis of *system*. 'It is based on an intellectual unity throughout all its activities.' 'The utilitarian calculus' had replaced 'the economic calculus' of capitalism. 'The ancient axiom of "Love your neighbour as yourself" is embodied, not in the economic but in the utilitarian calculus, namely, the valuation of what conduces to the permanent well-being of the human race. The citizen acts in his factory or farm according to the same scale of values as he does in his family, in his sports or in his voting at elections. The secular and the religious are one. The only good life at which he aims is a life that is good for all his fellow men, irrespective of age or sex, religion or race.'

The texture and tone (including their dominant masculinity) are distinctive, alongside the 'theory'. From time to time, perhaps, all socialists should meditate on the Webbs' *Soviet Communism*:

> It is clear that everyone starting adult life is in debt to the community in which he has been born and bred, cared for, fed and clothed, educated and entertained. Anyone who, to the extent of his ability, does less than his share of work, and takes a full share of the wealth produced in the community, is a thief, and should be dealt with as such. That is to say he should be compulsorily reformed in body and mind so that he may become a useful and happy citizen. On the other hand, those who do more than their share of the work that is useful

to the community, who invent or explore, who excel in the arts or crafts, who are able and devoted leaders in production or administration, are not only provided with every pecuniary or other facility for pursuing their chosen careers, but are also honoured as heroes and publicly proclaimed as patterns and benefactors.[96]

In the USSR in 1919 'collectivism' was seen by the 'Suprematist' group in Vitebsk as 'one of the paths marked out on the road map which leads to the "world men"... in it each ego preserves its individual force, but if we want to attain perfection, the self must be annihilated – just as religious fanatics annihilate themselves in the face of the divine, so the modern saint must annihilate himself in the face of the "collective", in the face of that "image" which perfects itself in the name of unity, in the name of coming-together.'[97]

Perhaps G.W. Balfour MP, a well-connected Conservative, had a point in his 'critical lecture on Socialism' to Co-operators in the People's Hall, Albion Street, Leeds in April 1894. He fused statism and collectivism – perhaps always joined in practice – when he warned working people that, under socialism:

> the first duty of the State would be to enforce discipline. It would be impossible for a workman to withdraw from his employment because he was dissatisfied, unless he was to cease to be a citizen. The State having monopolised the whole employment of the country, there would be no other employment for him. On the other hand, it would be impossible for the State to dismiss a citizen; it would be bound to see that all had employment. The Collectivist State of the future would have to be organised on the military model. That was really what it came to.[98]

2.3 Associationism: 'mostly guessed-at'

Are these our days of heaven, in the end?
These days when the world is mostly
guessed-at, all conjecture, orphic ventures in a field
of iterance and echo, creatures

bidden from the grass to take new forms,
the absences that make us what we are
unravelled from a maze of being
heard and called for, answering and answered?

John Burnside, from *Still Life with Feeding Snake* (London: Jonathan Cape, 2017), p. 26

Many associationalists did not see associative democracy as a supplement to existing social relations but as a 'new society'... Many associationalists did seek to replace entirely representative democracy with a new functional democracy, and also to replace the market-based economy with a socialist system of a non-collectivist type.
Paul Hirst, *Associative Democracy: New Forms of Economic and Social Governance* (Cambridge: Polity Press, 1994), p.19

'*You can hardly imagine it, the amount of talent there is locked up within the working class is enormous. If we had socialism, you'd see all that talent come out, it would be a most wonderful awakening. You don't see it under capitalism. You can hardly imagine it. The Labour Party has always talked about what it will do for you; never what you can do for yourself, and that's where it has made its mistake.*' [99]
A South Wales miner (b.1919) interviewed by Jeremy Seabrook in *What Went Wrong?Working People and the Ideals of the Labour Movement* (London: Gollancz,1978)

'A field of iterance and echo'

The verb *to voice* (an opinion etc.) is a close cousin of the verb *to vote*. I hope I have given statists and collectivists enough voice for would-be socialists to recognise them and either choose (elect or anoint) them, or get together (associate) to *make* an altogether different kind of socialism.

To achieve similar recognition for associationists, they too need to be heard in their various voices. So I will continue to listen, unafraid of lengthy quotation. Associational – there is no way of making *assoc-* words attractive, but *commun-* words have their own problems too – associational voices can be as confident as those of collectivists and statists. But they are also, by contrast, often discordant, incomplete, and seemingly un- or anti-'political', sometimes un- or anti-'socialist'. They come from all over the place ideologically, as if stemming from some kind of *ur-*, or natural human impulse. Even the word 'individual' was sometimes used to mean 'undividable from' as recently as the eighteenth century.

A confident example of a deep associational impulse comes from an unexpected quarter: William Beveridge (1879–1963). Although for much of his life a Liberal in party political terms, and widely known as the architect of the 'welfare state' following the Second World War, earlier in his life he had been a thorough-going collectivist.[100] The Labour Government of 1945–51 did not actually consult Beveridge on the details of the engineering of the welfare state following his iconic Reports on *Social Insurance and Allied Services* in 1942 and *Full Employment in a Free Society* in 1944. He had already written a series of social policy reports for twentieth-century governments, starting with *Unemployment: A Problem of Industry* in 1909.[101] The final report that he published, in 1948–9, is the least well known. Its first volume was published as *Voluntary Action: a Report on Methods of Social Advance* (London: George Allen and Unwin, 1948-9). A second volume on *The Evidence for Voluntary Action* followed in 1949. This consisted entirely of testimonies, as is characteristic of effective encouragements of associational life as a method of social advance.[102]

Voluntary Action was funded by the National Deposit Friendly Society, not by the state. Late in his life Beveridge became a member of the Hearts of Oak Friendly Society. This may explain the confident vision of 'human society as a friendly society, an Affiliated Order of branches' with which he concluded his Report:

> None of the Victorian pioneers dreamed of a world with dangers such as ours. None of them doubted that man could and would be master of his fate. To restore the conditions in which these pioneers did their work will not be the work of any one man. But restoration may come through one spirit breathing again through many (people) ... So at last human society may become a friendly society – an Affiliated Order of branches, some large and many small, each with its own life in freedom, each linked to all the rest by common purpose and by bonds to serve that purpose. So the night's insane dream of power over other men, without limit and without mercy, shall fade. So mankind in brotherhood shall bring back the day.[103]

It is not surprising that William Hazell, the South Wales Co-operator whom I have already quoted, was enthusiastic about Beveridge's chosen *Method of Social Advance*. Beveridge, Hazell thought, had recognised that

> fields still lie open, outside the realm of compulsory State acts, for associations of voluntary, non-conscripted, Rochdale-minded men and women ... The greatest mistake any State can make is to ignore or neglect the possibilities and potentialities

of Consumers and Producers Co-operation ...The live dynamic of voluntary mutual aid will outlast and outshine many schemes of state coercion by State or commune.[104]

'All conjecture' is the poet John Burnside's way of putting it. Voices from the world of free association can also be poetic, *poesis* being the ancient Greek word for *making*. Unlike collectivists, associationists do not, as yet, have a definitive programme or complete theory behind them, in any party-political or mainstream, social-scientific sense. As Philip Corrigan observed,

> Marx spoke often of how the working class demonstrated *future social forms in their current organisations of struggle* [my italics] – he saw the Paris Commune as a vindication of this, particularly with regard to precisely the question of the State. It is curious that nobody has made any attempt to found (historically and theoretically) a programme of (revolutionary) politics in Britain upon these insights.[105]

And, unlike statists, associationists do not collapse their project into their own assumption of power, as in 'we are the state', 'it' (*l'état*) as *moi*; or 'it', as in the case of collectivists, as rational 'us' rather than puerile 'them'. 'You don't know, do you (ah this human language)' writes Philip Gross, the poet and Quaker, whether this 'we' is the kind including 'you'.[106]

For associationists, millions, you, you, and you are involved – in the end every one. 'Society', as George Jacob Holyoake understood it, 'has been and is being improved by a million agencies and by the genius of a million minds'.[107] The associational 'we', as project and preliminary practice, of course includes 'you' and 'it'. E.P.Thompson urged, in the interests of European Nuclear Disarmament, that 'the Other is ourselves'. And as W.H. Auden imagined – in his case referring to the Incarnation – 'it became us'. And not in some other world or distant future, but here and now. Back to Mike Hales again:

> The challenge is to create counter hegemonic practices in which the possibility of deep difference can actually be *seen* and in which people can *actually* join and out of which truly different networks of living and working – systems of alternative forces of production, informed by changed relations of production – can *in practice* be articulated.

A productive – *making* – idea of *class* will help.

> Through my life as an activist I've always understood class as something to be *made*. That is, since any worthwhile politics is for liberation, the potential challenge is to *form* a class that actually is capable – here, now – of prefiguring liberated living and working systems.[108]

Twenty-six workers

At the height of the Greek economic and political crash in 2011, 26 workers took it upon themselves to occupy the plant where they worked in the city of Thessaloniki. The owners of the parent company had gone bankrupt and abandoned the site. This plant manufactured chemicals for the construction industry. Knowing that the alternative for them was poverty and unemployment, the workers decided to turn their working world upside down: no one as boss, no hierarchy, everyone on the same wage. Having consulted the local community about what they should make, they switched to making soap and eco-friendly household detergents. Staff also use the building as an assembly point for local refugees, the offices also being used as a weekly free neighbourhood clinic for workers and locals. The production line model where each person does one or two minute tasks all day every day has been abandoned.

'Here everyone gathers at 7 am for a mud-black Greek coffee and a chat about what needs to be done. Only then are the day's tasks divvied up.'

'Before, I was doing only one thing and had no idea what the others were doing. '

That is how Dimitris Koumatsioulis remembers the factory when he started in 2004. And now? 'We're all united. We have forgotten the concept of "I" and can function collectively as "we".' Another old timer, Makis Anagnostou, talks of how their factory is proof 'that an alternative economy is feasible'.[109]

My aim throughout the rest of this Note is to continue to overhear and supplement the voices of people articulating association(s) as 'world-changing' practices – the phrase that Holyoake preferred to the word 'utopian'. Their activities, past and present, will take us as near as we are likely to get in present circumstances to what Holyoake called 'the new art of association'. Such voices are often full of hope ... but surely, we might mutter to ourselves in today's (2018) world, also rather hopeless.

Associationism *is* more of a hoped-for socialism, a *not-yet* as well as a *has-been* socialism, than is the case with my other two -isms. It consists mostly of a patchwork of promising, sometimes very 'ordinary' presents, remembered pasts, and future possibilities, 'a maze of being', in Burnside's words, rather than a finished product. I recognise my associational self as naïve – wilfully utopian – but I 'own' it too, as fuel, as a necessary optimism of the will in dark times when, as Naomi

Klein argues in her 2017 book of that name: *No Is Not Enough*. Our associational selves could add up – now *have to* add up – to a utopianism of the present tense, and of the active rather than the passive mood. In today's global circumstances it has to be unlikely that anything like associational socialism will ever be given enough (make or seize enough) time to constitute itself as the Society that Owenites were invited to join in 1817: 'An Association of All Classes and All Nations'.

'Pluralism'? 'Community'? Delivered to, or made by, us?

Ambitious association has formidable foes in the market as well as in the state. Some of these act as apparent patrons, encouraging goals like individual self-help, voluntary organisation, the 'voluntary sector', 'the community', 'communitarianism', 'pluralism', and the 'Big Society'. Patrons, like vaccinators, advocate safe, state-aided, even compulsory, 'communitarian' doses of association, designed to prevent a general, more threatening outbreak.

Paul Hirst (1946–2003) – the most coherent modern socialist advocate of 'pluralism', of 'new possibilities of governance', and hence of 'associative democracy' – was more radical. In his *Associative Democracy* (1994), he recognised the vaccinators. He drew attention to 'the dangers of conservative decentralisation' and acknowledged that 'at present pluralism has become a policy of the state'.

Hirst's was a formidable socialist journey, from the theoreticist, mind-manacled, revolutionary socialism of the late 1960s and early 1970s which provoked the Social Movements and Political Action course at Sussex with which this essay began, to 'retrieving pluralism' from its twentieth-century advocates in the *festchrift* for Tom Bottomore in which my Three Socialisms first appeared.[110]

Hirst went on to spell out an 'associationalist' political

philosophy as challenging to Social Democrats and Marxists as it was to complacent liberals.[111] Recognising that democracy and representative institutions were in crisis before this became widely apparent, he sketched 'the architecture of an associationalist commonwealth'. This could be built, he argued in 1994, 'neither by revolution nor the building of a new society'. It required 'merely the extensive but gradual reform of the old at a pace directed by the realities of politics and the choices of citizens'. *Associative Democracy* (1994) was a brave attempt to state the 'principles of political organisation' which could inform 'associative democratic reform of existing forms of representative democracy'. At the same time – uniquely among thinkers or activists outside the Co-operative Movement since the pre-Bolshevik period – he recognised and regretted the neglect of the *working-class* associational *socialist* (but not anarchist) inheritance in Britain. His belief in and regret for that which could have been, and his statement of principles of what, he believed, could still, step by step, come into being, are both worth listening to again today. Lacking a convincing, persuasive, popular narrative, why, one wonders, did New Labour not attend to Hirst? [112]

Two points are striking. First, there is his sense of regret at the lack of acknowledgement from the labour movement as well as the Party, of latent, large-scale, working-class *socialism* among people who chose not to call themselves socialists. Old old, pre-1900 Labour should have been of much more interest to New Labour than the too easy, Parliamentary antagonist that it dismissed as Old Labour.

'Imagine', Hirst wrote, 'that Beatrice Webb had been convinced by J.N. Figgis of the virtues of the pluralist state':

> In that case socialists might have tried to build their socialism in civil society, whilst ensuring, through seeking politically

appropriate representation, a state at least not hostile to this enterprise. Such a socialism would have been based on mutual welfare through organizations like the Friendly Societies, on the organization of distribution through non-profitmaking stores, like those of the English Co-operative Movement, and on the organisation of production either through worker-owned co-operatives or labour–capital partnerships, in which workers took a part of their income through equity. Such developments were eminently possible, for the Friendly Societies and 'the Co-op' were very successful. Such a socialism would very likely still exist, since it would have been built in civil society and would have been relatively independent of the state ... Socialism in Britain, once so strong, so pragmatic and fundamentally humane, died though its dependence on the state no less than did the brutal Soviet state collectivist version.

Secondly, Hirst proposed 'three principles' of an associative democracy:

> (1) that voluntary self-governing associations gradually and progressively become the primary means of democratic governance of economic and social affairs;
> (2) that power should as far as possible be distributed to distinct domains of authority, whether territorial or functional, and that administration within such domains should be devolved to the lowest level consistent with the effective governance of the affairs in question – these are the conjoint principles of state pluralism and of federation;
> (3) that democratic governance does not consist just in the powers of citizen election or majority decision, but in the continuous flow of information between governors and the governed, whereby the former seek the consent and co-operation of the latter.[113]

These are excellent Principles. Just how generative – or useable – they prove to be, however, will depend on how associationists use them to inform their actions. How much associational, as opposed to statist or collectivist, weight does 'democratic' have in Principle (1)? Does 'democratic governance' mean SELF-management, by means of accessible, available, associational forms? In Principle (2), what is the weight of the passive mood: 'be distributed' and 'be devolved'? Who does it? Who is the subject and who the object of those verbs: 'distribute' and 'devolve'? 'Effective governance', yes, but effectiveness for what, and measured by whom? And in Principle (3), from whom to whom is 'the continuous flow of information between governors and the governed'? 'Guv'nor, who do you think WE are? Are we to remain, for ever, "the governed"?' How far does this move us beyond the collectivisms already characterised, for example, in the work of the Webbs?

'We shall have...'

Marx and Engels, in the *Communist Manifesto* of 1847–8, were more assertive:

> In place of the old bourgeois society, with its classes and class antagonisms, we shall have an association, in which the free development of each is the condition for the free development of all.

Later in the same Manifesto :

> When, in the course of development, class distinctions have disappeared, and all production has been concentrated in the hands of a vast association of the whole nation, the public power will lose its political character.

'We *shall* have ... a vast association of the whole ... the public power *will* lose ... '. Akin to the generation of novel means of production and exchange within feudal society, there is within capitalism, Marx observed, 'a movement going on before our own eyes'. Contrary to more philosophical interpretations of his work, Marx liked the immanent details of working-class practice. The working classes, he thought, 'must revise the relations between themselves and the capitalists and landlords, and that means they must transform society':

> This is the general end of every known workmen's organisation; land and labour leagues, trade and friendly societies, co-operative stores and co-operative production are but means towards it. To establish a perfect solidarity between these organisations is the business of the International Association.[114]

But 'perfect solidarity' is a difficult set of social relations – still less a 'system' – to write about in any convincing detail, however imperative it has to become if perfect barbarism is to be avoided. *We shall have*: such affirmation feeds the continued determination to achieve, in the face of what might otherwise prevail. As Marx anticipated, 'the common ruin of the contending classes' was to become an increasingly present, alternative possibility. As that possibility becomes more evident, at least we become more conscious of the scale of the struggles involved.

There are durable slogans: *liberty, equality, fraternity; by the people, for the people, of the people; the many not the few; the 99% not the 1%*. There are formulas: 'from each according to their abilities, to each according to their needs'; 'each for all and all for each'; 'a next system grounded in community, equity, inclusion and prosperity for all'; 'only in community is personal freedom possible'; 'organic' as opposed to 'mechanical' solidarity. And there are mantras around which members of associational movements have clustered: a coming time when 'mastery gives way to fellowship', 'a mutual state', and a 'solidarity economy'.

The project of associationism proposes an end to the fetishism of ownership, whether private or public. It is not so much about the transfer or 'capture' – of power, knowledge, or the means of production – as it is about the transformation of the categories themselves. The use of plurals in place of singulars is part of this: *socialisms, knowledges, powers, practices*. Writing about associationism stretches the limits of prose. In its conscious practice – no matter whether it does so in 'theory' – associationism raises the nature of the state (states) and of the market (markets). And it does so from a stance of changing the world as well as understanding it, and through the agency of 'the self-conscious, independent movement of the immense majority in the interest of the immense majority', 'the whole superincumbent strata being sprung into the air'.[115] An associational theory of state(s) and market(s) cannot but be a theory of associations (associating) in general which will be more than 'functionalist', 'pluralist', and 'communitarian'. It will have to be theorised from within and below rather than from above, as *souvey* rather than survey. *Whose* understanding, and changing, yes, but by and for *whom*?

The scandal of associationism

The scandal of associationism is that it proposes to put an end to monopoly. As a way of producing things (relations), it will be (would be) distinguished by an absence of the enclosure of any part of economic, political, or social reproduction. Ways will be found to undermine monopolistic holdings in the means of production, cultural and (as) economic: labour, information, communications, and capital. The conditions for (social) equality and therefore for (human) difference would thereby be established.

This *is* a scandalous aspiration. It takes the breath away, as *News from Nowhere* by William Morris still can. In Rudolf Bahro's *The Alternative* (1978), there is an extraordinary chapter, written from within the German Democratic Republic, called 'The present conditions and perspectives for general emancipation'. The chapter makes us mutter to ourselves (living in 'the West') 'it can't be like that ... that's not what people (human nature) are like ... unsustainable, utopian fantasy, no better than Gonzago dreaming away in *The Tempest*'.

A century before Bahro, Samuel Smiles put forward the revolutionary idea that 'all men might without difficulty become what some men are'. Bahro put social flesh on Smiles's gendered, individualist skeleton.

> Our present educational system wants the specialist whom official species' self-consciousness, itself specialised, can address to a single pigeon-hole. It says to him in Mephistopheles' words: 'Believe the likes of me: the single whole/Was fashioned for a god alone'.

'This era', Bahro suggested,'is coming to an end'. 'What is involved is rather the "basic training" of modern social man, who should be able to say without the devil's pact of privilege: "Whatever is the lot of humankind/I want to taste within my deepest self".'[116]

Such aspiration is, literally, incredible for most of us for most of the time: and yet it is also inherent within, or built into, capitalism, as possibility. Capitalism systematically dangles what the 1 per cent know that it cannot deliver to the 99 per cent.

Associationism contests the division of labour in the deepest possible way. It is obvious now that transforming the division of humans into the division of work – a formulation of John Ruskin – presents seeming impossibilities. In *Politics and Letters* (1979), Raymond Williams told his interviewers from the *New Left Review*, 'it is towards an unimaginably greater complexity – complex rather than simple co-operation – that an adequate socialist politics points'.[117] In *The Country and the City* (1973) Williams knew that the complexities included formidable internal or psychological structures of feeling, 'recesses within ourselves where what we want and what we believe we can do seem impassably divided':

> There is nothing now more urgent than to take the fundamental idea, the problem of overcoming the division of labour, to the tests of rigorous analysis, rigorous proposal and rigorous practice. It can be done only in new forms of cooperative effort. If what is visible already as the outlines of a movement is to come through with the necessary understanding and strength, we shall have to say what in detail can be practically done, over a vast range from regional and investment planning to a thousand processes in work, education, and community. The negative effects will continue to show themselves, in a powerful and apparently irresistible pressure: physical effects on the environment; a simultaneous crisis of overcrowded cities and a depopulating countryside, not only within, but between nations; physical and nervous stresses of certain characteristic kinds of work and characteristic kinds of career; the widening gap between the rich and poor of the world, within the threatening crisis of population and resources; the similarly widening gap between concern and decision, in a world in which all the fallout, military, technical and social, is in the end inescapable. And to see the negative effects, with whatever urgency, can be

to paralyse the will. The last recess of the division of labour is this recess within ourselves, where what we want and what we believe we can do seem impassably divided.[118]

A utopian, impossibilist nerve may be our only hope in a situation where despair is growing, at the possibility of mass, even total, human destruction. What are 'defence' and 'security' now? For *everyone* to be able to speak and act as if 'The Other is Ourselves' and not to project their enmities on to other persons or nations is now – with the weapons our rulers have – a huge psychic, spiritual, democratic, political task *and* a precondition of human survival. We will now get less and less without asking ourselves for more and more.

In his study of would-be-practical, earth-bound futurists from Goethe's Faust onwards, *All That is Solid Melts Into Air* (1983), Marshall Berman quotes first from the *Communist Manifesto*, and then from Marx and Engels' *The German Ideology* :

> the constant revolutionising of production, uninterrupted disturbance of all social relations, everlasting uncertainty and agitation, distinguish the bourgeois epoch from all earlier times. All fixed, fast-frozen relationships, with their train of venerable ideas and opinions, are swept away, all new-formed ones become obsolete before they can ossify. All that is solid melts into air, all that is holy is profaned, and men are at last forced to face with sober senses the real conditions of their lives and their relations with their fellow men.

'The humanistic ideal of self-development grows out of the emerging reality of bourgeois economic development': and yet 'only in community with others has each individual the means of cultivating his gifts in all directions; only in community, therefore, is personal freedom possible'.[119]

Through association, 'it is being done'

William Morris told the readers of the *Hammersmith Socialist Record* in May 1882, 'there is no royal road to revolution or the change in the basis of society, here is work enough for the most energetic; it is the work of patience, but nothing can take the place of it. And moreover, it is being done, however slowly, however imperfectly.'[120]

Personal freedom only in community; independence only achievable through a recognition of mutual dependence. Meanwhile there is some firmer, historical ground to stand on – even an emergent vocabulary. Hybrid terms like 'associational' – 'communionalist' was the clumsiest – were part of the emergent cluster of words from which the modern vocabulary of 'socialism' emerged during the late eighteenth and early nineteenth centuries.[121] 'Association', 'associated', 'associational', and 'associationism' were all words used by Co-operators from the early nineteenth century onwards, including George Jacob Holyoake (1817–1906). They were used to describe the practice of what we would call a co-operative form of socialism, but which they saw as critical of 'socialism' *tout court*.[122]

Among the radical journals of the 1820s was one called *The Associate*. This vocabulary continued to have currency in nineteenth-century Britain, emerging from Fourier and working its way through into Co-operation via the Christian Socialists. Edward Vansittart Neale used it as frequently as Holyoake. An early Webb phrase for 'collective bargaining' was 'associated bargaining'. The Co-operative Wholesale Society (CWS) magazine, *The Millgate Monthly*, founded in 1905, was 'A Popular Magazine devoted to Association, Education, Literature and General Amusement'. The subtitle of the *Co-operative News* from 1886 onwards was the *Journal of Associated Industry*.

The usage was not confined to co-operators: Marx used 'associated labour' as the stage which, he argued, had already started to succeed the era of 'hired labour'. Marx described the 'associated mode of production' at length in *Capital*, volume III:

> The cooperative factories run by workers themselves are, within the old form, the first examples of the emergence of a new form, even though they naturally reproduce in all cases, in their present organisation, all the defects of the existing system, and must reproduce them. But the opposition between capital and labour is abolished here, even if at first only in the form that the workers in association became their own capitalists, i.e. they use the means of production to valorize their own labour. These factories show how, at a certain stage of development of the material forces of production, and of the social forms of production corresponding to them, a new mode of production develops and is formed naturally out of the old. Without the factory system that arises from the capitalist mode of production, cooperative factories could not develop. Nor could they do so without the credit system that develops from the same mode of production. This credit system, since it forms the principal basis for the gradual transformation of capitalist private enterprises into capitalist joint-stock companies, presents in the same way the means for the gradual extension of cooperative enterprises on a more or less national scale. Capitalist joint-stock companies as much as cooperative factories should be viewed as transitional forms from the capitalist mode of production to the associated one. It is simply that in the one case the opposition is abolished in a negative way, and in the other in a positive way.[123]

Just how positive Co-operators could be – many of them would have been l(L)iberals – about the abolition of the opposition was evident in an editorial in a CWS magazine in 1917. The occasion was a Labour party conference in Manchester, the headquarters of the CWS. Here in full is the editorial of *The Producer, with which is incorporated 'The Consumer'*. It sets out Co-operators' view of a successful, associationist, and business-based socialism rather different from Labour's and from Soviet Communism as welcomed by the Webbs twenty years later:

> With all its teaching and agitation, its preaching and writing, its local and Parliamentary representation, the Labour Party does not yet seem to have realised that for the economic betterment of the common people, collectively-owned fields, factories and workshops are better than speeches and resolutions; they could, in fact, be made more effective in the economic welfare of the workers than almost any kind of legislation. When we are treading the paths of national legislation we are upon very uncertain ground, that is apt to give way at any moment. But when we acquire fields and grow wheat, build factories and manufacture goods, erect warehouses and distribute the contents one to another, we know we are getting on solid ground.
>
> The Labour Party does not proceed in this way. It calls for higher wages, and leaves those who supply the commodities of life to exploit the higher earnings by increased cost of living ... What is and always has been the failure of the Labour Party from a business point of view? It is that they have asked other people to do things for them rather than do things for themselves ... And when all has been said in favour of a high legal rate of pay, what does the term suggest? It suggests that the workers are still dependent upon other people for wages, as they are for the price of the means of life. They are between two oppressive

stools – one to keep down wages, one to inflate prices. How can they disentangle themselves from the position? We presume some would say by State action; perhaps by forcing the Government to own and control industry and the distribution of food. But how full of doubt, uncertainty, and perhaps corruption such a course would be. Would it not be better, and as quickly done in the long run, for the people to get hold of the machinery of production by co-operative means? Once that process was anything like complete the workers could then determine by collective action their own rate of pay, their own price of food, clothing and shelter. And co-operators would then be so numerous that they could walk into the Houses of Parliament and take over the reins of government without any further palaver. This is not a dream. It is simply a business problem.[124]

Associations and the liberal-democratic state

Associationism was a label which inheritors of co-operative culture, in particular, continued to reach for during the twentieth century. 'Is it not ... true to say that whereas members of the Labour Party are collectivists, co-operators are associationists?' asked T.W. Mercer in 1920, in one of the many articles at that time which urged co-operators to bring co-operation into politics rather than politics into co-operation.[125] Whether co-operators should form a mainstream political party was a matter of dispute within the movement from the early 1880s onwards until, in 1917, they finally did so.

A Parliamentary Committee was formed in 1880 to monitor legislation on behalf of the movement. This was one thing: a political party, whether allied with an emergent Labour Party or not, was another. It was prudent to put up a parliamentary umbrella to protect Co-operative businesses from unequal regulation and taxation. But many co-operators felt that their project was not to substitute state action for a drive towards hegemony by the members of a whole movement and its Societies, federated as they were in a Wholesale Society and in a Co-operative Union. At Co-operative Congress ('the parliament of the movement') in 1913, a Mr J. Young from the Scottish Section of the Union argued that there were only two ways whereby the working classes could emancipate themselves, namely by the strike and the vote. Against him, later in the same Congress, Mr Maddison drew delegates' attention to the sad fact that 'we have a Co-operative delegate who does not know there was another way ... the way of the Rochdale Pioneers'.[126]

Associations separate from the state, or 'states within the state' which had the ambition to form another whole state of affairs, were characteristic of nineteenth-century working-class culture. A London-based Co-operative Wholesale Society official, Ben Jones, saw the co-operative movement as a whole in this way, in his *Co-operative Production* (Oxford: Oxford University Press, 1894). And in 1889, a visiting Austrian Liberal, writing about *English Associations of Working Men* and ranging much more widely than the co-operative movement, saw England as a 'gigantic theatre of associated life', giving its culture a 'decisive stamp'. For the French historian Halevy, Protestant, particularly Methodist, associations were a distinguishing feature of nineteenth-century English social development. The American populist and journalist Henry Demarest Lloyd published a study of *Labour Copartnership* in Britain in 1898, in which he conveyed a sense of delighted possibility. He subtitled this work *Notes of a Visit to Co-operator Workshops, Factories and Farms in Great Britain. Country and the City.*

In the same year Ebenezer Howard effectively activated the Garden City movement with *Tomorrow: a Peaceful Path to Real Reform*.[127] On the way to realising the First Garden City in Letchworth in 1905, Howard founded the Garden City Association in 1899 and also worked as a lecturer for the Co-operative Union. *Tomorrow* ... was a sustained, practical, and self-conscious argument for combining individual and 'associated effort'. He aligned himself with 'socialistic writers' in their view that 'a very large part of the "wealth" forms now in existence are not really *wealth* at all. They are, in John Ruskin's term, "illth".' Howard could not see why socialists wanted to take over such forms of wealth 'which are not only rapidly decaying, but are in their opinion absolutely useless or injurious'. Associated effort was to be realised in a federation of community-owned Garden Cities, starting in Letchworth. This meant 'the sweeping away of (old) forms and the creation of new forms in their place'.[128]

Self-management – 'the general end of every known workmen's organisation' – and its enemies

As working people's consciousness of their own productive activity and the potential of their characteristic associational forms for replacing middle-class patronage grew during the last quarter of the nineteenth century, so the struggle against them, from above, also became more and more explicit. 'It is marvellous', Mr Horrocks wrote in the Amalgamated Society of Engineers' *Monthly Report* for December 1898, 'how many persons are desirous of controlling the affairs we ought to control ourselves'.

Constructive resistance to such persons was more class-conscious by the early twentieth century than historians have so far documented.[129] To cut a long story short, examples can be found across associations, from clubs affiliated to the Working Men's Club and Institute Union, to football clubs in the Football Association; from co-operatives in the

Co-operative Union, to trade unions in the Trade Union Congress; from Working Men's Educational Associations to land-reform movements, housing associations, and Affiliated Orders of friendly societies; from fields, farms, and workshops to areas for voluntary association such as religion and recreation. Capitalist forms were colonising more and more of these sites for association from the early twentieth century onwards.[130]

The size, ambition, and understanding of what they were up against; their detailed creativity or 'moral art' of association; above all else their sense of a future utterly different from what actually happened during the twentieth century in Britain, now need to be given back to them and to us as our useable past. To memorise the future in this way is to recognise the reality of a whole culture – for that is what it was – which has been neglected and side-lined, perhaps particularly by socialists. Contemporaries and foreign observers were struck by it more strongly than later Labour activists and scholars in Britain. And whatever their ultimate stance was, the Webbs were the most meticulous and prolific students of this culture. Their masterpiece, *Industrial Democracy* (1897), was used by thinkers as different from one another as Bernstein and Sorel, as well as by Lenin. There *was* an emergent working-class practice in nineteenth- and twentieth-century Britain which raised fundamental, even revolutionary matters such as the nature of the state from a class point of view. Could this be a more helpful way of seeing the nineteenth-century working-class culture of association than seeing it as less-than or *not* socialism, *not* Marxism, as 'mere' liberalism, voluntarism, or – an insult that Left theoreticians used at Sussex against associational heretics – 'humanism'?

Describing ellipses: 'a new age does not begin all of a sudden'

Recovering the history of 'association' and its *-ism* in no way absolves us from the difficulties of thinking about and re-imagining its most useable meanings now. These cannot but be messy, full of first-person singulars as well as collectives, beliefs as well as hypotheses, faiths as well as theories, laden with contradiction and marked by defeat.

Systematic and universal mutuality, fraternity, equality, 'a vast association of the whole nation' will have to consist of myriads of actual activities, links, productions, distributions and exchanges, modes of being, cells capable of multiplying ... in the public sphere. This sphere will have to be reconstituted through private 'civil' construction, thereby transforming the meanings of both 'public' and 'private': going through the countryside to the cities, in Mao Zedong's phrase. To abolish the political in a complex society – or to fold it back into the social – will mean so many horizontal lines that new vertical ones emerge: in a phrase, *democratic* centralisation. Some of these lines must be visible – 'a movement going on before our own eyes' – before all of them can be actual. They cannot all be drawn at a stroke, 'after the revolution'.

It is, to say the least, a difficult exercise – risking ridicule – to recover and re-present worn paths, overgrown gardens, traces and hints: pre-figurations within a rampant system which would prefer to obliterate all of them. As suggested already, poets can help: proceeding from image to image, from 'natural' breath to breath, fragment to fragment, line to (indented) line, association to (free) association may be how most human brains work and communicate best.[131] W.H.Auden's often-quoted line 'poetry makes nothing happen' was followed by the seldom-quoted line, 'poetry is a way of happening, a mouth'. Brecht, the pre-eminent Marxist poet of association, was preoccupied with the dialectic at work in transitional times, in poems such as 'Parade of the Old New', and 'Looking for the New and Old'. In 'New Ages' he wrote:

> A new age does not begin all of a sudden.
> My grandfather was already living in the new age.
> My grandson will probably still be living in the old one.
> The new meat is eaten with the old forks.
> ...
> From new transmitters came the old stupidities.
> Wisdom was passed on from mouth to mouth.

What is (would be) involved for labour is finding the forms – economic, political … no, cultural (material), and social – that can resolve, rather than abolish, a set of contradictions: novel cells or anticipations with the capacity to multiply. The question for labour is not *whether or not* the state, or how to talk in general about the administration of things replacing the administration of persons, but of what (changing) forms the 'vast association of the whole nation' (world) could consist.

By this I mean, again, constructing forms within which necessary contradictions have room to jostle, then move on. These contradictions need to be specified in as material a way as possible. This is a productive, creative, material task, rather than only an expository one, prioritising construction and production – social innovation – over criticism. Elsewhere I have tried to summarise the contradictions as the contradiction between locality (taking place) and the capacity for universalisation; between cheapness (affordability) and high dividends for labour; and the contradiction between autonomy and engagement, with allies and against enemies.[132] The distinction between 'abolition' of contradictions and finding forms within which they have space to co-exist productively is based on *Capital*, volume I, where Marx refers to 'the form within which contradictions have room to move':

> We saw in a former chapter that the exchange of commodities implies contradictory and mutually exclusive conditions. The further development of the commodity does not abolish these contradictions, but rather provides the form within which they have room to move. This is, in general, the way in which real contradictions are resolved. For instance, it is a contradiction to depict one body as constantly falling toward another and at the same time constantly flying from it. The ellipse is a form of motion within which this contradiction is both realized and resolved.[133]

Associated labour will have to describe and include such ellipses. Associations for labour, as opposed to those predominantly brought into being for capital – although these too are full of contradictions – provide forms in and beyond which these contradictions have to take (and change) place. The associational project cannot be achieved without uniting necessary contradictions in an active tension. This is hard enough in the head, and even harder to sustain in social practice through long stretches of time, in real locations. For associated labour there can be no real distinction between the problem of agency, or constituting an associated mode, and the problems of realising and living within and maintaining that mode itself. If the associated mode is to be actually and materially *for* labour rather than, say, for a new administrative, technical caste, all of its problems have to be solved to the extent that they are humanly soluble, away from and as a necessary preliminary to the *coup de grace*, the capture – which is also the transformation – of the state. They have to be solved – to use terminology widely adopted by Solidarity members in Poland in 1980 – by means of a struggle between 'the society' and 'the power', generating a movement which 'cannot be fitted whole into any of our existing political categories'.[134]

There is no way of making any of this simple. It is no longer possible to go backwards, towards small is beautiful. William Morris has sometimes been taken, quite wrongly, as an advocate of 'the simple life'. Nothing could be further from the truth: he even knew about the difficulties of representing his vision in words. 'Although we have simplified our lives a great deal from what they were', explained Hammond to the Guest in *Nowhere*, 'and have got rid of many conventionalities and having sham ways which used to give our forefathers much trouble, yet our life is too complex for me to tell you in detail by means of words how it is arranged'. No words but things or, rather, more (or less) *social* relations. In this respect Morris was a modernist. His utopia was a technologically sophisticated place, but it was also morally poised: full of detailed choices, available to everyone. The purpose of writing about it was to liberate further choices. The best known of these was the choice – inherited from John Ruskin – between 'useless toil' and 'useful work', 'illth' and 'wealth', in a setting in which 'work-pleasure' was to become synonymous with 'art'. And the questions 'whose?' and 'for whom?' are always the most radical ones. Whose work-pleasure? Whose use-value? In the longest chapter in *News from Nowhere*, looking back from an imagined 1950s, Morris described exactly how the great transformation had taken place, not all at once but stage by stage over two or three years, and such violence as erupted being engineered by those in authority.[135]

Back to where I began

This extended 'Note' on socialisms began, as I recalled at the outset, on a corridor in the School of Social Science at Sussex University where Tom Bottomore and I had offices during the first twenty years in the life of *The Idea of a New University: An Experiment in Sussex* (1964).[136]

This was a time when 'revolution' did not seem either impossible or inherently tragic, at least to a number of socialist students and staff in universities in Britain. I have cited Paul Hirst's patient, reformist work on behalf of 'associationalism' in his *The Pluralist Theory of the State* (1989) and *Associative Democracy* (1994). After an early, revolutionary, 'British Althusserian' phase during the late 1960s and early 1970s – epitomised in the journal title *Theoretical Practice* and lampooned by Edward Thompson in *The Poverty of Theory* (1978) – Hirst championed radical democratic renewal and constitutional reform in Britain. He chaired Charter 88 and advocated 'Renewing Democracy through Associations'. As a graduate student of Tom Bottomore during his revolutionary, but not yet Althusserian, phase, it was Hirst who encouraged a group of undergraduate activists in the Sussex branch of the Revolutionary Socialist Students Federation (RSSF) to agitate for an applied-political course – 'relevant' was the word used at the time – to be added to the Sussex curriculum for students in the School of Social Science.

A Working Party was appointed, and the course came into being as 'Social Movements and Political Action'. It lasted for almost twenty years.[137] The causes and effects, sociology and history, theory and practice of a number of social movements and forms of political action were examined in weekly seminars, fed by papers from students and lectures by practitioners from outside the university, as described at the beginning of this Note. The aim was to make a wide range of associational forms, their politics, and their contexts as understandable and as available for choice and change as we could make them. There was a strong emphasis on the present, and on critiques of dominant social-scientific assumptions, for instance on the allegedly 'iron laws' of organisational development.

This was controversial. I recall the Dean of the School of Social Science at one point proposing to replace the course with one called 'Social Policy in Modern Britain'. But in spite of such attempts by determinedly single-discipline academics in the School to re-cast the course, or to close it to students in particular disciplines – economics, social psychology, and political science among them – Social Movements and Political Action provided generations of Sussex students, alongside Tom Bottomore and myself, with alternative and sustained teaching and learning opportunities.

In the epigraph from Alick West's *One Man in his Time* (1937) which heads this essay, he reflects on his hesitation about using his own experience before concluding that 'it would be still more presumptuous to imagine that I was exceptional'. It would of course be wrong to claim even a small place in the social history of socialism for the University of Sussex, even in its early days when, led by Asa Briggs, it was radically self-conscious about the critical, interdisciplinary arrangements that the university made for the production, distribution, and exchange of knowledge among students and staff.[138] But the politics and sociology of knowledge has become a crucial component in any future-possible socialist construction: *whose* knowledge, *how*, and *of what?* [139]

The practical and theoretical issues at stake during those years are now widely acknowledged among all kinds of socialist. If we are few, these issues are many. They include the necessity of Hirst's 'new forms of economic and social governance' if even merely 'representative' democracy, let alone socialism, is to survive as a worthy successor to democracy's 'classical' antecedents. The practical and theoretical issues still at stake also include the importance of a plurality of 'voluntary associations' in any society worthy of the name, and the salience of conflicts within and between such associations – conflicts in which the 'from below' impulses and energies that they contain or express contend with those coming 'from above'. The sterility of 'all or nothing' socialisms, either 'in' or 'out of' power, for people who want some, at least, of socialism's attributes before they die is another critical issue. Then there are the energies that flow from holding together (socialising) real human differences within and between societies/associations working for 'the common interest'; and the need to multiply horizontal lines of federation between diverse associational forms, as against installing quick and easy, vertical chains of command. And, finally, how to incubate and strengthen the possibility of individuals (persons undividable from each other) *being* the change, that is to say constituting and re-constituting the *social* inside ourselves, as opposed to iterating the either–ors of 'the individual' versus 'society'?

An emergent, new social economy?

'I pondered all these things', William Morris ended his *Dream of John Ball* in 1886,

> and how men fight and lose the battle, and the thing that they fought for comes about in spite of their defeat, and when it comes turns out not to be what they meant, and other men have to fight for what they meant under another name.

But even in Britain, even in 2018, associationism is not all a dream. It has been practised and prefigured, with or without any socialist label, among many of the 'new social movements' which have roots in the 1970s. These include the women's movement, community politics, working-class writing and community publishing, producer and wholefood co-operatives, fair-trade initiatives, faith communities, Transition Towns preparing for climate change, social enterprises,'the new social economy', solidarity, e-petition and on-line resistance groups, and commons-based projects and workshops and networks of many kinds. Of all these, it is probably the 'new directions in municipal socialism'[140] as practised and theorised in London particularly by Robin Murray (1940-2017) during the life of the Greater London Council (GLC) to which he was Principal Economic Adviser, which have been, so far, the most fully realised.

Among many other initiatives, Robin was a founder of the Conference of Socialist Economists (CSE) and a key contributor to the economics content of the Penguin edition of the *May Day Manifesto* (1968). He was an inspiration to the groups of local activists which that *Manifesto* generated, and an analyst of global capitalist corporations at the Institute of Development Studies (IDS) at Sussex University between 1972 and 1993. He was also a lucid interpreter of 'post-Fordism', 'flexible specialisation', and successsive changes in the labour processes that define the modern global economy. Locally, Robin was one of the pioneers of QueenSpark in East Brighton, with its successful community campaigns for facilities to meet people's needs rather than generate privatised profit, its community newspaper, and QueenSparks books of local autobiographical and other writings.[141] Robin was a leading *animateur* of a range of anticipations or, in his terms, *creative cells* capable of generating an entirely possible – even emergent – Social Economy. These cells include a Third World Information Network (Twin). This is a trading organisation designed to ensure economic equity for producers in a global market. It helped to catalyse fair-trade brands such as CaféDirect and Divine Chocolate in order to realise post-commodity, imperfect but actual forms of production, distribution, and exchange.

For Robin, these anticipations – 'prefigurative forms' in Shelia Rowbotham's phrase[142] – included Fair Trade co-operatives and other arrangements for global and 'Equal Exchange' in a wide variety of goods and services. They also included practical steps towards a *Zero Waste* economy and society, beginning in East London. Working with The Young Foundation and the National Endowment for Science, Technology and the Arts, Robin also scanned the world for practical examples of *Social Venturing* and *Social Innovation*, while also producing successive drafts of 'Co-operation in the Age of Google' for Co-ops UK, the apex organisation of the co-operative movement in Britain.

> The early years of the 21st century are witnessing the emergence of a new kind of economy ... in many fields, including the environment, care, education, welfare, food and energy ... I describe it as a 'social economy' because it melds features which are very different from economies based on the production and consumption of commodities. Its key features include: the use of distributed networks to sustain and manage relationships, helped by broadband, mobile and other means; blurred boundaries between production and consumption; an emphasis on collaboration and on repeated interactions, care and maintenance rather than one-off consumption; and a strong role for values and missions.[143]

A model associationist, Robin Murray was as adept at theorising the three socialisms – first named as such in the Labour Process Group of the Conference of Socialist Economics (CSE) in Brighton – as he was at practising the minute particulars of associationism and knitting them together into a common movement. It was after he had worked at the IDS that he became chief economic adviser to the Greater London Council (GLC) in 1981, leading a team working for a democratic economy informed by – his phrase – Popular Planning. Democratic self-management and collaborative creativity were to instantiate socialism – in and against the systems and the -isms striving to contain and destroy it. Social enterprises in the interests of labour rather than of capital were to multiply NOW, most clearly in the form of co-operatives but in many other shapes and sizes as well, enabled by local and national states where possible.

The GLC was, notoriously and quite simply, abolished in 1985 by a Conservative government acting in the interests of a very different form of economy and state. But not before the outlines of an entire *London Industrial Strategy* became visible. This remains an extraordinary collection of documents, full of the details of the possibilities and practices of complex co-operation, voluntary association, and popular planning.[144] With its Enterprise Boards, Networks (a word also used by Solidarity in Poland), and 'restructuring for labour', the Popular Planning Unit at the GLC went a long way towards redefining what socialist 'planning' for labour could mean, and towards reaching beyond the simple polarity of 'planning *versus* the market'. By pooling the problems of everyday life and the skills and knowledge gained at work, people began to develop proposals for change. These were designed to be more durable than an approach dependent on expert plans based only on 'consultation'. For a time critics of statism and collectivism had a precarious base in large-scale associationist practice, or 'the politics of production'. To illustrate this moment in the history of associationism and because of its understanding of the state and of Fabian-style management by experts – and its grasp of an alternative mode of being – I will end this essay by quoting from Robin's 'New Directions in Municipal Socialism':

> The concerns with the quality of products and not just their quantity, with popular planning, with human centred technology, and with transforming the services and the administration of the state – all of these are also of central relevance to a new socialist economic policy at the national level. But perhaps most important is the consciousness that the state's power – locally or nationally – is quite limited in the face of the power of private capital. The traditional Fabian theory of the state as somehow set apart from classes, an instrument of power which needs to be patiently captured and then run by experts independent of sectional interests – this theory is in as urgent a need of revision as the economic theory. For when the state attempts to control and supersede private capital, the outcome of the ensuing battle will depend crucially on the extent of popular support any administration can command. It is one of the unintended results of the Government's abolition campaign against the metropolitan counties and the GLC that councillors and council workers alike are having to argue the case for their existence to ordinary people. This is a democratic process far more substantial than a four-yearly visit to the ballot box. It involves councillors explaining what they are doing, justifying it, and if they cannot justify it, dropping it in favour of something else. This is one aspect of the necessary link between a socialist administration and the people they represent.
>
> Another is the need to redefine the role of the state as the supporter of others' campaigns and struggles rather than as the universal provider. I discussed this in respect to state support for trade unionists. But it is equally true with respect to discrimination against particular groups of

working people – women and black people most notably. Local councils can help directly, through anti-discrimination monitoring of suppliers, and of their own practices. But any successful fight against discrimination will depend on the actions of those who are facing the discrimination, and it is one task of a socialist council to support them in their struggles rather than offer to replace them.

Power in short is not centralised in the state but decentralised [my emphasis]. A Labour administration has considerable power, but it is the temporary power of holding an important position on a wider field of battle. Its economic policies will affect the relative strength of others elsewhere on the battlefield. Mrs Thatcher has recognised this in using public economic policy as a means of a direct attack on the power of labour in production. It is important that the labour movement takes at least this lesson from monetarism and develops an economic strategy which will shift the balance of economic power back to organised labour.[145]

May Day 2018

---

*I would like to thank Paddy Maguire, Stefan Collini, Bob Benewick, William Outhwaite, and Jennie Shaw, as well as Tom Bottomore, for helping with this essay, and Robin Murray for inspiring it. The essay retains many signs of its times, and traces of its origins as a talk. The *Festschrift* for Tom was edited by William Outhwaite and Michael Mulkay: *Social Theory and Social Criticism: Essays for Tom Bottomore* (Oxford: Basil Blackwell, 1987 and Gregg Revivals, 1992), pp.83–114. Also in 1987, I published an essay which contained overlapping ideas and material: 'Notes on three socialisms – collectivism, statism and associationism – mainly in late-nineteenth- and early- twentieth-century Britain', in Carl Levy (ed.), *Socialism and the Intelligentsia 1880–1914* (London: Routledge, 1987), pp.219–271. In the 'Note' published here I have imported material from the second essay into the first, made some stylistic changes, and added insights and materials from work published since 1987.

PART II.
A NEW LIFE:
THE RELIGION OF SOCIALISM IN BRITAIN, 1883–1896*

Walter Crane, Cartoons for the Cause, *London, 1896*

In April 1897 Robert Blatchford introduced a series of articles in *The Labour Prophet*, the journal of the Labour Church Movement. He recalled:

> The Religion of Socialism is a phrase first used, I think, in 1885 in the manifesto of the Socialist League ... We have the right to refuse the name of socialist to those who have not grasped the economic truth. But an economic theory alone, or any number of economic theories will not make a religion. If you want socialism to be a religion, you must widen your definition of socialism. You must draw out all the ethical and spiritual implications of these desires and efforts for a juster social order. It is not for nothing that propertied people seek to overturn our whole system of property; nor does a workman seek to jeopardise his bread for the fun of the thing. Socialism is a step – a long step indeed, but still only a step – to the realisation of a new social ideal. The labour movement is but one sign of a new spirit at work in many directions throughout human affairs. A new conception of life is taking shape, to which it is affectation, if not folly, to refuse the name of Religion.

The religion of Socialism had indeed been referred to, although not for the first time, in the peroration to the 1885 manifesto of the Socialist League, written by William Morris:

> Let us strive, then, towards this end of realising the change towards social order, the only cause worthy the attention of the workers of all that are proffered to them: let us work in that cause patiently, yet hopefully, and not shrink from making sacrifices to it. Industry in learning its principles, industry in teaching them, are most necessary to our progress;

but to these we must add, if we wish to avoid speedy failure, frankness and fraternal trust in each other, and single-hearted devotion to the religion of Socialism, the only religion which the Socialist League professes.[146]

The phrase – and close cousins to it – were to come from many different lips during the 1880s and 1890s. Related notions were to linger in the British labour movement in attenuated forms for a long time after that.

My own attraction to at-first-sight surprising meanings attaching to socialism began during the late 1950s. This was when Raymond Williams was exploring class-contested meanings attaching to keywords such as *industry, democracy, art, class,* and *culture* in his *Culture and Society 1780–1950* (1958). By keywords Williams meant words with radical as well as reactionary potential, 'the problem of whose meanings are inextricably bound up with the problems they are being used to discuss'.[147] His work was part of a phase of values-based, morally informed socialist activism associated with the Campaign for Nuclear Disarmament, feminist praxis, and incipient community and cultural politics associated with the early numbers (1958–60) of the *New Left Review*. While the practice of this 'new left', small 'p' politics referred back to the pre-Parliamentary Labour Party, and the 'ethical socialism' and syndicalism of pre-1914 labour movements, my own experience suggests that we did not always travel under an explicitly 'socialist', still less a 'communist' banner. As was the case for Co-operators during the life of George Jacob Holyoake, too much statism and collectivism had attached themselves to those -isms to make us feel comfortable with them. Hilary Wainwright's *A New Politics from the Left* (Polity, 2018) is a direct descendant and revival of this critical discourse, having 'waited for it to become topical again'.[148]

During the 1880s and 1890s there were manifestly religious individuals and organisations practising a 'religion of socialism', such as John Trevor and the Labour Church. But spirituality was also evident in other, less obviously religious sectors of the movement. Eleanor Marx Aveling urged the Council of the Socialist League to have a Christmas tree in 1885. 'We cannot too soon make children understand that Socialism means happiness', she urged. Why shouldn't socialists adapt 'the beautiful old Pagan feast that celebrated the birth of light', just as Christians had done? 'Is not socialism the real "new birth", and with its light will not the old darkness of the earth disappear?' She was apprehensive about what some friends might think – 'I tremble a little at the thought of Bax' – but Belfort Bax of the Socialist League and Social Democratic Federation (SDF) collected essays under the title *The Religion of Socialism* in 1885. Katherine St. John Conway and John Bruce Glasier of the Fabian Society, Socialist League, and Independent Labour Party (ILP) did the same in 1894; Blatchford published a pamphlet called 'The New Religion' in 1892; branches of the Marxist/secularist SDF were sometimes distinctly 'religious' in flavour, George Lansbury later recalling:

> Our branch [he is referring to the Bow and Bromley SDF in about 1892] was about 40 strong. We were all in good jobs, all very enthusiastic, and convinced that our mission was to revolutionise the world. Our meetings were usually well attended and orderly. Our branch meetings were like revivalist gatherings. We opened with a song and closed with one, and often read together some extracts from economic and historical writings. These weekly branch meetings were held in the premises of a fine club established by Annie Besant for Match-girls after she joined the Theosophical Society ... every Saturday we ran dances – humorously telling our critics we

were going to dance into Socialism ... We ran an economics study class under Comrade Hazell and weekly struggled with *Das Kapital* and Engels' *Socialism Utopian and Scientific*.[149]

The purpose of this essay is to put such 'ways of happening' back on the map: to make them useable again in their own right – not as 'early or 'primitive' – but useable by people choosing among socialisms TODAY. This phase in the story of socialisms has, of course, been known about by historians for some time, and has been interpreted – or passed by on the other side? – from two, related directions of travel. On the one hand the religion of socialism has been seen as filling a gap left by declining 'orthodox' religion and serving to wean mainly Northern, nonconformist, working-class Liberals on to the harder stuff of secular, scientific socialism. On the other hand it has been interpreted as metaphor, or as the moralising dress worn by socialists because of the historical, post-Reformation peculiarities of British popular and middle-class culture.

In his *Marxism and the Origins of British Socialism* (Ithaca, New York: Cornell, 1973), Stanley Pierson interpreted religious fissures in British socialism as cracks into which Marxist ideology fell when it met class organisation in national culture. From the late 1980s onwards – impelled by the collapse of Soviet Communism, the rise of market fundamentalism, and the hobbling of social democratic parties and ideas – detailed work has been done on the intellectual and, to a lesser extent, the social history of socialism. In his *The Making of British Socialism* (Princeton and Oxford: Princeton University Press, 2011) Mark Bevir distinguished 'the Ethical Socialists' of the late-nineteenth and early-twentieth centuries from two opposed, but often overlapping strands in British socialism: 'the Marxists' and 'the Fabians'.[150] The presence of the religion of socialism during the 1880s and 1890s and the expectations of imminent change which were built into it were so substantial that they may well have had something to do with the large space subsequently occupied by the Labour Party in British socialism, and with the consequent small space available for creative thinking on the problem of *agency*. 'How the change came' is the title of the longest chapter in Morris's *News from Nowhere* (1890-1), a central text in this period of British socialism. The chapter begins with an old man reminiscing about an ideal Communist society. He asked the Guest: 'Does anything especially puzzle you about our way of living, now that you have heard a good deal and seen a little of it?' The Guest replied, 'I think what puzzles me most is how it all came about'. 'It well may', said the old man, 'so great as the change is. It would be difficult indeed to tell you the whole story, perhaps impossible.' He then proceeds to narrate the culminating years of a long revolution. Unfortunately, how the change is to come, rather than how it came, is the modern problem for socialists.

1. 'We have a glorious and inspiriting work in hand' (Tom Mann, 1894)

The period from the mid-1880s to the mid-1890s was no backwater in the history of British socialism. Not was it a mere tributary feeding into a supposed mainstream – 'the origins of the Labour Party'. The period had its own special dynamism which became a wistful memory soon afterwards, in Labour Party days. The tributary soon looked larger than the river. Hostile observers and active participants were agreed at the time about the explosive strength of developments in 1894. Robert Blatchford was excited that 'Five years ago there were not 500 socialists in Manchester. Now there must be 30,000.' As a critic put it in 1891,

> ... in 1883 a socialist movement seemed to break out spontaneously in England, the air hummed for a season with a multifarious social agitation, and we soon had a fairly complete equipment of Socialist organisations – social democrat, anarchist, and dilettante – which have ever since kept up a busy movement with newspapers, lectures, debates, speeches and demonstrations in the streets.

Or, as Morris and Bax put it in 1893,

> Ten years ago the British working classes knew nothing of socialism ... A socialist lecturer in those days almost invariably found himself in opposition, not only to the middle classes who might be present but also to the working men amongst his audience ... that is now so much changed ... there is no longer any hostility to socialism ... the socialist lecturer rather finds a difficulty in drawing out opposition to his views until he begins to deal with details.[151]

The dates stand out. In 1883 the Democratic Federation became socialist; by 1888 more than 40 branches started in England and Scotland; in 1884 the Fabian Society began; in 1888 Scottish Labour Party formed; between 1889 and 1892 there was a massive escalation of trade-union membership; in 1889 the Second International convened; in 1890 the first May Day celebrations were held; in 1892-3 the Independent Labour Party was formed. A Yorkshire weaver who in 1889-90 joined the Leeds Socialist Party and the Leeds Trades Council, and helped to start the local branch of the Gasworkers' Union, remembered how 'it was a very lively time ... nobody expected pay in those days. It was not alone a labour of love, but a labour of joy, for the workers seemed awake.'[152]

Thus, if 'religious' notions were at the centre of the socialism of these years, they were not, on the face of it, associated with passivity. A Nottingham shopworker, Alex Thompson, who went through the Social Democratic Federation into the Labour Party, remembered them as

> glad, creative days ... Even those of us who lived through them did not realise how happy and privileged we were ... Arid minded highbrows thought that it was trivial, the politically orthodox disliked it, Socialist doctrinaires declared that its economic basis was not sound, but the man in the street accepted its teaching to which he gave the intense fervour of a happy convert.

H. H. Snell, introducing Thompson's autobiography, thought that the *Clarion* newspaper, started by Blatchford in December 1891, 'helped to transform the early Socialist movement in Britain from a mere exercise in economic thinking into a crusade for a more excellent way of living'.[153]

Observers as cool as Sidney Webb and Engels, against their better judgment, were impressed by the potential of such a crusade. 'Just now', wrote Webb in his *Socialism in England* (1893 edition), 'the tendency is strong and it may perhaps carry us forward more rapidly than any politician yet foresees'. In his 1892 introduction to *Socialism Utopian and Scientific*, Engels was interested in the Salvation Army: 'the British bourgeois ... finally accepted the dangerous aid of the Salvation Army, which revives the propaganda of early Christianity, appeals to the poor as the elect, fights Capitalism in a religious way and thus fosters an element of early Christian class antagonism, which one day may become troublesome to the well-to-do people who now find the ready money for it.'

A Socialist crusade was not just an emotive cloak. An

exciting conjunction had been reached between deeply felt moral imperatives and an actual social agency which by its very nature would carry them into existence in a soon-to-be-realised social order.

The intensity of aspiration which characterised socialism at this time was most stark in the work of William Morris, whose revolutionary politics grew out of a detailed 'delight in the life of the world; intense and overweening love of the very skin and surface of the earth on which man dwells such as a lover has in the fair flesh of the woman he loves'. He felt 'the great motive-power of the change' as a 'longing for freedom and equality akin if you please to the unreasonable passion of the lover'. He hated capitalist 'civilisation' for its perversion of these passions. While working ceaselessly for socialism after 1883, in dark moments he preferred a cataclysmic plunge into barbarism.[154] Unlike some socialists, Morris hated capitalism more because it was morally repugnant and should change than because it was historically redundant and would change.

Deeply felt social divisions led to loving, cross-class, personal relationships such as those between Edward Carpenter and socialist workers and friends in and near Sheffield, or between Katherine St. John Conway and Dan Irving in Bristol.[155]

Some socialists' vision of the working-class man as hero could best be expressed in sexual terms. 'As a Woman of a Man' was the title of a poem in Carpenter's *Towards Democracy* (1883–1905). The poet stands in front of a man who represents the coming of democracy. 'O somber swart face, now thou art very beautiful to me!' He abandons everything in his own and his society's past to the new power, which is 'no longer a name' but a physical presence:

> Gigantic Thou, with head aureoled by the sun –
> wild among the mountains –
> Thy huge limbs naked and stalwart erected member,
> Thy lawless gait and rank untameable laughter,
> Thy heaven-licking wildfire thoughts and passions –
> I desire...

He vows:

> I stand prepared for toil, for hardship – this instant if
> need be start on an unforeseen and distant journey –
> I am wholly without reserve;
> As a woman of a man so I will learn of thee,
> I will draw thee closer and closer,
> I will drain thy lips and the secret things of thy body,
> I will conceive by thee, Democracy.

Such imagery was mirrored in the anguished lives of men like George Gissing, Oscar Wilde, or George Moore, who felt a comparable force and turned away in shrill revulsion for fear of being swamped by it, or who let it change their whole aesthetic. Moore did both. At the time of his *Confessions* (1886) his rejection was as firm as Carpenter's embrace:

> ... the old world of heroes is over now. The skies above us are dark with sentimentalism, the sand beneath us is shoaling fast, we are running with streaming canvas into ruin; all ideals have gone; nothing remains to us for worship but the Mass, the blind inchoate insatiate Mass, fog and fen land before us we shall founder in putrefying mud, creatures of the ooze and rushes about us ... The French Revolution will compare with the Revolution that is to come, that must come, that is inevitable, as a puddle on the road side compares with the

sea. Men will hang like pears on every lamp-post, in every great quarter of London there will be an electric guillotine that will decapitate the rich like hogs in Chicago. Christ, who with his white feed trod out the blood of the ancient world and promised universal peace, shall go out into a cataclysm of blood. The neck of mankind shall be opened and blood shall cover the face of the earth.

Whether experienced as threat or hope, the symbolic and real presence of 'the mass-people' as a coming force was electric. 'To myself', wrote H.W. Nevinson of the SDF in a chapter of his autobiography called 'Purgation',

> though I naturally belonged to the comfortable classes, the attraction of repulsion was very strong, and during those years (1885–1897) my shamed sympathy with working people became an irresistible torment, so that I could hardly endure to live in the ordinary comfort of my surroundings. Many of us felt the same.[156]

Such intensity was part of a wider 'late-Victorian revolt' among sections of the middle class. The revolt touched many areas other than politics, notably sex, poetry, fiction, and the theatre. It was identified in its early stages by Beatrice Webb as 'a new consciousness of sin amongst men of intellect and property', not a sense of 'personal sin', but a 'collective or class consciousness … a growing uneasiness amounting to conviction that the industrial organisation which had yielded rent, interest and profits on a huge scale, had failed to provide a decent livelihood and tolerable conditions for a majority of the inhabitants of Great Britain'.[157]

It was not only middle-class rebels who were in the fullest sense *converted* to socialism in these years. Such an experience was common. Beatrice Webb was worried that 'the working men are especially afflicted with the theological temperament – the implicit faith in a certain creed which has been "revealed" to them by a sort of inner light'. Conversion was indistinguishable from religious conversion as documented in William James's *The Varieties of Religious Experience* (1902). Indeed, James used John Trevor of the Labour Church as a case in point in his lecture on Mysticism.[158]

Poverty, religious eclecticism, unresolved guilt, domestic unhappiness, unfocused indignation, scattered activity, wealthy aimlessness, and social unease preceded conversions in different mixes in individual cases. A book then came to hand, or a salient meeting was attended, or an individual evangelist was met. The idea of socialism then presented itself as a certain ground for hope, a convincing analysis of what had gone before, a morally impeccable challenge, and an organised movement demanding commitment, sacrifice, and missionary activity by the newly converted. Previous tensions were released in joyful struggle. The choice was put fairly and squarely to John Smith of Oldham in 1894, in Robert Blatchford's *Merrie England*:

> This question of Socialism is the most important and imperative question of the age. It will divide, is now dividing, society into two camps. In which camp will you elect to stand? On the one side there are individualism and competition – leading to 'a great tirade' and great miseries. On the other side is justice without which can come no good, from which can come no evil. On the one hand are ranged all the sages, all the saints, all the martyrs, all the noble manhood and pure womanhood of the world: on the other hand are the tyrant, the robber, the manslayer, the libertine, the usurer, the slave driver, the drunkard and the

swearer. Choose your party then my friend and let us get to the fighting.[159]

'Lo! I was one of the band ... I was born once long ago; I am born again tonight' (William Morris, from 'Pilgrims of Hope', 1886)

There are three main sources for understanding the quality of conversion experiences. First, contemporary socialist/labour newspapers. These gave the facts, for example, of 'two converted Tories' in Liverpool in 1895:

> At a meeting in St. George's Street last Sunday these two sound fellows made their declaration of faith by rising in the meeting and telling of their conversion, brought about by Sam Hales. We have several instances of a similar character, but never publicly professed as these were.[160]

Occasionally they also convey something of the feel behind the facts. An SDF adherent, H.W. Hobart, recalled in 1894 how, during the late 1880s, he went to hear a lecture by Herbert Burrows on the 'Morality of Revolution':

> I had not at that time sufficiently shaken off my religious prejudices to consent willingly to give up an attendance at the Mission Hall where I used to sing in the choir, but after a sharp conscientious struggle I went. I listened with rapt attention to the new gospel and was transfixed with astonishment ... The arguments and the reasoning of the lecturer had convinced me of the truth of his gospel but the prejudice I had incepted from various sources seemed to hold me back from declaring my convictions. A second appeal from the Chairman had an electrifying effect. When he asked again whether anyone would like to join the branch I said, 'Yes I would'.[161]

Autobiographies provide the fullest accounts. Indeed, spiritual autobiographies or Confessions in the Augustinian sense were a characteristic genre in late-Victorian and early-twentieth-century culture.[162] Some socialist confessions were masterpieces, managing to combine a high pitch of emotional intensity with details of the intellectual change. Among many, four stand out: John Trevor's *My Quest for God* (1897 and 1908), Edward Carpenter's *My Days and Dreams* (1916), D. B. Foster's *Socialism and the Christ and the Truth* (1921), and Percy Redfern's *Journey to Understanding* (1946).

Some subjects described their conversions more briefly, but in revealing language. H.H. Snell, a Nottingham jack-of-all-trades and son of agricultural workers, told how 'the adhesion to Socialism of Mrs Besant had helped to sway my mind and in due course I made my confession of faith one Sunday evening from the platform of the SDF at a meeting in the Great Market Place ... once the decision had been taken I experienced a sense of relief which has remained constant throughout my life'.[163] Rachel McMillan, a middle-class girl living in Inverness, had a more dramatic experience. She read W.T. Stead's *The Maiden Tribute of Modern Babylon* (1886). 'If a bomb had fallen on the house it could not have caused a greater upheaval. She was fully awakened now to the existence of a dark world that ringed her sheltered life.' Then on a trip to Edinburgh in 1887 she met with socialism through John Gilray of the Socialist League. 'During the following week Rachel was a diligent attender at Socialist meetings.' After the trip, 'she was like a traveller who suddenly arrives at the turning of a narrow road at the edge of a valley and sees before her a new range of wild and wonderful country. She returned home a little bewildered but stirred into a new life.' Shortly afterwards she wrote a letter to a friend, explaining that she had had many pamphlets to digest. She had become certain that 'very soon when these teachings and ideas are better known people generally will declare themselves Socialists. They are "bound to do it" if they think at all.'[164]

Katherine St John Conway's Damascus Road was a fashionable ritualistic church in Clifton (Bristol) where she normally worshipped. One wet November Sunday in 1887 striking cotton workers staged a church-in. She was converted:

> I had been drawn into the High Church movement of the day and was at church in Clifton, when in they came ... lassies out on strike against starvation wages and for the right to combine. The church was crowded with a fashionable congregation ... I had been praying for a fuller consciousness of the Presence, and there they stood, sister-women, if the 'Our Father' were true – ill-clad, wet through with the driving rain, hungry ... 'They stand between me and the Christ.' So the thought smote me; so I see it still. Never shall any human being, so long as the world suffers wrong, know one moment's real communion with the mind of the Master till they have actually thrown in their lot with the poor and the oppressed.
> 'Inasmuch as ye have done it or not done it.' For the first time in my life I heard and began to understand.[165]

The next day she went to the Socialist Society's headquarters, a bare upper room above a local coffee house. There she was introduced to Carpenter's *England's Ideal* (1887), which awoke 'a new power of love and worship within me':

> It was as if in that smoke-laden room a great window had been flung wide open and the vision of a new world had been shown me: of the earth reborn to beauty and joy ... As I went back to my Clifton lodgings, I vaguely realised that every value life had previously held for me had been changed as by some mysterious spiritual alchemy. I was ashamed

of the privileges and elaborate refinements of which I had previously been so proud; the joy of comradeship, the glory of life, had been revealed to me, dimming all others.[166]

D.B. Foster's conversion happened *after* he had joined the Holbeck branch of the Independent Labour Party in 1894:

This vision of co-operative production and ownership of the means of life came to me as the dawning of the morning.
Here I saw the way to that Kingdom of God on earth for which I had prayed and worked so long. My joy was beyond words, because the revelation of life which I had seen in Jesus of Nazareth became clearer and more real to me every day.
I began to see why Jesus pitied the rich and said the poor in spirit possessed the Kingdom of God.
I saw why Love was the fulfilling of the Law, and why Love made men give to those in need.
The Fatherhood of God became to me the abiding conviction ... My outlook on life was fundamentally changed, and my relation to my fellows became altogether different. The men whom I employed became my comrades in life, whose needs constituted their right to wages rather than their ability to make profit for me.
I realised that the incoming of the Socialist ideal into my life had revolutionized my relationships with mankind.
I read Bunyan's *Pilgrim's Progress* in a new light. I saw that the New Jerusalem, the City of God, though a long way off, was a possibility, and the vision drew me with irresistible attraction.[167]

The third source for the quality of conversion experiences is literary. These were frequently written in order to recruit more socialists, although the fictional or semi-fictional account of intellectual/ spiritual change was another characteristic genre in the culture more generally.[168]

A fine example is Section V of Morris's poem 'The Pilgrims of Hope' (1886), written shortly after Morris himself had crossed his 'river of fire'. The hero passes through romantic exaltation to despair to realistic assessment of the horror of the life of the poor in London, contrasted with the ease or guilt of the rich. He is then invited by a workmate to a meeting, where suddenly, 'lo! I was one of the band ... I was born once long ago; I am born again tonight'.[169] The description of the meeting, the dingy room, the thirty attenders, their reluctance, the zeal of the speaker who called twice before the hero was converted and who got too 'hot and eager' to answer critics clearly, the exaltation of the convert is a quintessential account. There are also touches special to Morris, such as the realisation that socialism will not dissolve difficulty, rather it will enable hardship to be faced four-square and by everybody equally:

> Bitter to many the message but sweet indeed unto me,
> Of man without a master, and earth without a strife,
> And every soul rejoicing in the sweet and bitter of life.

Following conversion, being a socialist at this time involved a whole change in way of life. It was not just a question of being entered on a party's membership list and paying the first instalment of a monthly subscription. A separation from older jobs, friends, places, and habits was succeeded by acquisition of new ones. The process was more like joining a sect than a church, still less a political party. This was obviously true of dramatic individual cases such as those of Edward Carpenter in Sheffield or Katherine Conway in Bristol. But it is also true of undramatic cases such as Sidney Webb programming himself to 'self-deadness', in order to subordinate the individual self to the collectivist social whole.¹⁷⁰ And it was true for the rank and file as well, for whom membership (particularly in the SDF) was regarded as a privilege to be gained after struggle rather than a card sold on the doorstep.¹⁷¹ Foster hesitated after taking 'so great a step' as joining the ILP, while for Joseph Toole of Salford, joining the SDF led to his falling out with his parents, but 'joining the socialists was to me such a sincere and sacred thing'.

'The separation of politics and religion has ceased to be ... politics are henceforth merged in morals' (Belfort Bax, 1884)

Changes in ways of life associated with conversion have often been regarded as counter-political. The classic case is early-nineteenth-century Methodism, as interpreted in E.P.Thompson's *The Making of the English Working Class* (1963). On each side of the divide between Christians and socialists throughout the nineteenth and twentieth centuries there has been the difference between individual change and structural change. The two have characteristically been seen as antithetical. The antithesis between them was expressed in conventional ways by some socialists during this period, but in tones which suggest that synthesis was a serious enough possibility to be attacked.¹⁷² The antithesis was also argued at length from the opposite point of view by Christians. But again the tone was highly charged. General Booth of the Salvation Army was intensely preoccupied with the difference between 'The Socialism of Infidelity [which] says: Make the circumstances of the people prosperous and society will be prosperous', and 'the Socialism of Salvation [which] says: make the people good and their circumstances will be good'. In 1888 he was exclusively backing the latter; but, in an agonised re-think in the introduction to *In Darkest England and the Way Out* (1890), he conceded that circumstances had to be attacked directly in order to get through to individuals, who remained the real 'bricks of the social fabric'.[173]

In our period a temporary denial of the divide between structure and personal life or individual agency was much more characteristic. The denial was written on the tablets of the Labour Church, whose fifth principle was 'That the development of Personal Character and the Improvement of Social Conditions are both essential to man's emancipation from moral and social bondage' (1893). A conjuncture of detailed and general change was also experienced and expressed with a rare degree of honest intensity by Edward Carpenter at a time when 'Freedom and Equality came for the time being to control all my thought and expression'. *Towards Democracy* may indeed be read as a document of what it felt like to experience unity between things normally held apart in the culture, particularly between revolutions on a volcanic scale and change in the 'long-accepted axioms of everyday life'. Socialism to Tom Maguire had to be inside the self, not an opinion 'hung around'.[174] Temperance and even SDF or Socialist League socialism were not incompatible in this period, as the case of H.W. Hobart illustrates. H. Halliday Sparling was 'by historical studies drawn towards socialism and made public profession in 1880 while also advocating total abstinence'.[175] More far-reaching conjunctures were announced: 'in Socialism ... the separation of politics and religion has ceased to be, since their object-matter is the same'; 'from this day forward there will be no such thing as political differences ... politics are henceforth merged in morals'.[176] The later memories of those who shared the experience of such fusion provide poignant evidence of its earlier reality as they charted the effects on their being as well as on their consciousness of the re-opening of the divide. Choices which for a time had not had to be made between emergent meanings of 'politics' or 'socialism' and 'the rest of life', especially 'religion', had to be made all over again by people like Reade and Redfern after the mid-1890s.[177]

Such antitheses are so much a normal part of the mental furniture of many socialists that a time of synthesis is easily misinterpreted. It is tempting to dismiss socialists who spoke a moral language of evangelical exhortation as not-quite-socialists, as fuzzy, peculiarly British, soft, unrevolutionary socialists who could not quite moult their religious feathers. The difficulty is that there is definite evidence for this point of view. There undoubtedly was what E.P. Thompson has christened 'cosmic mooning' in socialists like T.J. Cobden Sanderson or R.J. Derfel. Until the mid-1890s, however, it is important not to be misled by the 'sermons' of Fred Brocklehurst, for example, into forgetting that although he was a classic ILP/Labour Church morality-monger, he was also advocating specific anti-parliamentary socialist 'lines of advance'.[178] Equally, it is important to remember that, as well as carrying on the style of his Good Templar, Evangelical Union youth, Keir Hardie was also at this time with more than half of himself (it became somewhat less than half) an optimistic revolutionary socialist.[179] In his pamphlet *The Religion of Socialism* (1894), Bruce Glasier's rhetorical socialism as 'our highest idea of the conduct of life' is accompanied by a harder identification of the roots of inequality in minority ownership and a commitment to making 'Land and Capital' 'common property'. Later, his rhetoric was used to mask blatant ILP opportunism. Trust in what Glasier called the 'reason and social intuition of the people' (even though 'social conditions' meant that 'the meaning of life itself has been lost'), confirmed by widespread rebellion in a seemingly fragile political/economic context, made the 'making socialists' option seem like a genuine line of advance. It was a line of advance because it was understood dynamically – 'to make life from within, *to keep on making it* [my italics] and to be men of action' was John Trevor's version of socialist religion. In the end 'all the human race' could be 'roped in'.[180] Stress on self-produced change was also part of working-class anti-statist thinking which, because it was anti-state, was not thereby anti-socialist. The supposed antithesis between state and initiative was a deeply rooted part of the larger dichotomy in the culture between structure and behaviour. When it was put by D.O. Burt to Keir Hardie (representing the Ayrshire Miners) at the Royal Commission on Labour on 11 February 1892, it had to be answered:

> D.O. Burt: Would you not say that it is rather a natural result that if you teach men to look to the state or to an outside power for their salvation it will happen that the spirit of self-help and of self reliance will be weakened.
>
> Keir Hardie: I think not. Socialism is not help from the outside in the form of state help, it is the people themselves acting through their organisation, regulating their own affairs industrially as well as otherwise … Socialism properly understood tends to organisation as a necessity rather than to the opposite.

'It was because the class war dogma led the workers to look outside themselves for the causes which perpetuated their misery that he (Keir Hardie) opposed its being made a leading feature in socialist propaganda.'[181] Similarly, Tom Mann wanted to answer those who drove wedges between individualism and socialism, in language which he would later jettison:

We have a glorious and an inspiriting work in hand, nothing less than the purifying of the industrial and social life of our country, and the making of true individuality. For, let it be clearly understood, we labour men are thoroughly in favour of the highest possible development of each individual ... I do distinctly believe in the necessity of socialism out and out, and that it is my duty to work for its realization. But I also know that something more than good machinery is necessary if really good results are to be obtained. I desire to see every person fired with a holy enthusiasm to put a stop to wrong doing. Before this is possible individuals must submit themselves to much and severe discipline. The baser sides of our nature must be beaten down that the higher and nobler side may develop. Regard for the brethren (brethren meaning all) must be the mainspring of our action, the development of the highest possible qualities in ourselves is undoubtedly a religious duty, but for this chief reason, that we may be of greatest service.[182]

'As the early Christians founded Brotherhoods and Sisterhoods, so in a sense must we if we are to convert the people' (Katherine St John Conway, 1893)
Such language could be mistaken for 'morality mongering' by those not used to hearing it from the lips of outstanding working-class revolutionary agitator-organisers like Tom Mann. In fact the call for 'severe discipline' and for suppression of 'the baser sides of our nature' was an authentic expression of much that was central to the socialism of these years. Puritan and revolutionary virtues have only recently been separated. They were separated deliberately in this period by Edward Aveling, but with unhappy results. Admittedly, asceticism was for many socialists a necessity at this time. Journeys which would later be described as morality tales, with titles like *From*

Workhouse to Westminster or *From Workshop to War Cabinet*, did not in their beginning have known destinations. The most usual consequence of setting out on the journey was the sack. John Burns (an engineer) was boycotted by employers in the mid-1880s simply 'because I was a Social Democrat'. In his own magnificent 'History Will Absolve Me' speech from the dock in April 1886 he pointed out:

> 'We have gained nothing by this agitation, on the contrary, we have lost what material wellbeing we had, and come before you, not as paid agitators ... but men anxious to change the existing system of society to one in which men should receive the full value of their labour.'

The threat of prison meant nothing to him, because

> '... through the present system of society, life has lost all its charm, and a hungry man said truly (as Isaiah said in the Holy Book) that there was a time in the history of our lives when it was better to die in prison or better to die fighting than to die starving'.[183]

Burns was proud of being an artisan. But he was careful to point out that he was in the dock with a remarkable sample of New Life Socialists. 'There must be some unusual agitation to prompt one of the idle classes like Mr. Champion, a skilled engineer like myself, an unskilled labourer like Mr. Williams and a middle-class man like Mr. Hyndman to stand in this box for one simple cause.' For the middle- and idle-class socialists, sacrificial asceticism was also on occasion a necessity – they too could be fired, for example if they became curates in the Church of England. But more often asceticism was seen as a virtue – a sign of socialist practice, among workers as much as among the privileged. Giving up all for the cause, including one's life (Caroline Martyn drove her missionary self to death in 1896, as had Tom Maguire), was what it would take to make socialism. This was partly the expression of a felt need for the Simple Life, and partly also the expression of how middle-class life had lost its charms for some, including many whose revolt did not take socialist forms.[184] But it must also be seen, most notably in William Morris, as authentic revolutionary discipline:

> By union I mean a very serious matter ... I mean sacrifice to the Cause of leisure, pleasure and money, each according to his means: I mean sacrifice of individual whims and vanity, of individual misgivings, even though they may be founded on reason, as to the means which the organising body may be forced to use: remember without organisation the cause is but a vague dream, which may lead to revolt, to violence and disorder, but which will be speedily repressed by those who are blindly interested in sustaining the present anarchical tyranny which is misnamed Society: remember also that no organisation is possible without the sacrifices I have been speaking of: without obedience to the necessities of the Cause.[185]

Morris had a deeper understanding of revolutionary necessities and possibilities than others. But other 'sentimental socialists' during this period meant business as well. Just as Morris called for organisation and subordination of fractions to the whole, so Katherine Conway called for pilgrimage:

> As the early Christians founded Brotherhoods and Sisterhoods so in a sense must we if we are to convert the people ... In the birth of the movement there is a great need of lives absolutely consecrated to the work with no home ties to bind them to one

spot more than another, and with no need of earning more than a bare subsistence wage ... It is a new band of pilgrims who are needed to go through the length and breadth of Great Britain.[186]

The period from the mid-1880s to the mid-1890s was delicately poised. The movement was active and growing, constituting a threat which would soon have to be diverted, but not yet a milch-cow to those who made careers out of it, a ladder to lucrative jobs, or engagement for intellectuals.[187]

Nor had the state yet opened itself in such a way as to make frank reformism appear penetrative. Indeed, such was the asceticism, there was even an unwillingness to see socialism as a struggle for material betterment or even as a struggle on behalf of a single class. Even *collective* self-interest was seen as a degradation of the noble cause of 'social redemption' or 'social salvation' (the titles of talks given by Tom Mann in 1892 and 1894).[188] 'It is a degradation of the socialist movement', wrote Hardie, 'to drag it down to the level of a mere struggle between two contending factions.'[189] 'My ideal', wrote Blatchford in *Merrie England* (1894), 'is Frugality of Body and Opulence of Mind'. Altruism was one of his favourite words in connection with socialism.[190] Such an enlargement of the socialist vision was by no means the exclusive property of the better off. A worker in a retail shop in Nottingham remembered going into the market place to hear speakers during the 1893 miners' dispute. There were two distinct kinds of socialism in his mind. 'Eloquent hands pictured the round cake of the national income. The workers made it; the capitalists and landlords took it. One slice only, a mere one-third, they gave back to the workers.' It was not this kind of speaker that attracted him. 'Marxian doctrine' and 'Fabian diagrams' were one thing, but Margaret McMillan came with a vision of health, joy, and beauty in working lives to be demanded and created by the people themselves. 'We listened with respect, touched by something vaguely, unattainably fine, and then we went back to the strike.'[191] The latent contradiction in socialist struggle between the ends and the means made necessary by a recalcitrant enemy was manifest, and opposed by activists at the time. An advocate of class war 'to the bitter end' had to start his argument in the SDF by saying, 'I know there are those in the movement who think this feeling of hatred amongst the exploiting classes, instead of being fanned and developed to its bitterest extent should be stifled out of existence as an unholy thing'.[192] There were many who agreed with Tom Mann that 'brethren' meant 'all', and not just the converted.

An altruistic language and style normally associated with 'religion' surrounded socialism in these years. The words 'evangelists', 'apostles', 'disciples', 'new birth', 'preachment', 'street preaching', and 'gospel' recurred in the discourse of anti-'religious' Morris as much as in that of the 'religious' Hardie. Morris spoke of 'the regeneration of the conscience of man' as much as Hardie spoke of 'regenerating the character of the democracy'. The author of 'The Red Flag' (Jim Connell) later recalled Herbert Burrows the Fabian as one who 'spoke in a semi-devout manner, as if he wished to convey that socialism was his religion'. In 1884 *Justice* published the first of a series of weekly instalments of J.L. Joynes's *Socialist Catechism*. This was much used, and in its penny pamphlet form had sold 15,000 by 1886.[193]

'Religion' usurped?

What this language and style meant in terms of any harder definition of religion is more difficult to determine. 'Each thought ... or secular social ritual is not "religion" because of the derivation of its symbols or forms.'[194] There are two preliminary obstacles to distilling the essence of what was experienced as a new religion during the late 1880s and early 1890s. The first is a smokescreen of organised Christian/labour-movement relations. The second is the variety of theologies and anti-theologies which went with 'the religion of socialism'.

Organised relations between the church and the labour movement were, on both sides, touchy at this time. There was mutual fascination which easily turned into aggravation. For example, Blatchford's well-known assault after 1903, by which time his optimistic enthusiasm had begun to wane, on 'the superstition and the ignorance, the self-righteousness and cruelty which in this country usurp the name of Religion' had been anticipated by some of his sharp pamphleteering in Manchester in the early 1890s. Only elitists masquerading as democrats made him as angry as Christians masquerading as Christians: religion was too important for such a 'rampart of the rich' to represent it. As he bit at it in the *Clarion* and in pamphlets, so denominations pecked back. And yet he was accused of having been captured by the 'High Church party' in 1895.[195] Even in its unreformed state, however, labour leaders like Tom Mann, Keir Hardie, and Ben Tillett showed considerable interest in denominational Christianity.

Such relations are of interest in their own right, and in individual cases were closer than later acknowledged. But they do not get us any closer to 'the religion of socialism' than do the widely varying scatter of individual theologies. Stanley Pierson was the first historian who took the socialist metaphysics of thinkers like Belfort Bax seriously enough to expound them clearly. Mark Bevir has now deepened the analysis.[196] Positions varied. They included systematic, metaphysical, and counter-christian stances (Belfort Bax); mystical, nature-based, eclectic appropriations of Christianity and other religions (Carpenter); William Morris's take on

Marxism; F.D. Maurice's Anglo-Catholic socialism and his disciples in the Guild of St Matthew like Thomas Hancock; Christ-the-working man back-to-the-plain-origins Christianity (Conway); baptising socialist demands with the name of religion (Glasier and Brocklehurst); rooting socialism in 'brotherhood of man, Fatherhood of God' language (Hardie); attempts to articulate and then to organise a new church arising out of, but not simply 'reflecting', labour-movement development (Trevor); and a religion based upon evolutionary determinism (Blatchford).

Across many of the positions the phrase 'the religion of socialism' recurred. The question of greatest interest now, perhaps, is not 'was it or was it not a religion?' – as if the word 'religion' stands for 'a single principle or essence'.[197] The question is rather, 'Does examining whether socialism at that time was doing a job for many people which more conventional religions have at different times done, help to clarify and explain some crucial – and powerful – features of that socialism?' Some of these features, on the movement rather than the individual level, will be examined in Section 2 of this essay. Even on the individual level, however, it is clear that in spite of collisions of formal belief, dominant directions of communication at this time were outwards from a felt common centre towards 'the great unattached' (a favourite Blatchford phrase), rather than internecine and fratricidal as in some other periods of socialist history. At least until the mid-1890s, when the period began to be seen as a whole and rejected even by those who had been part of it, there appeared to be a cluster of shared and dynamic commitment. In what did this consist, and does the 'collective name' religion help the modern, would-be socialist observer to understand it as much as it helped contemporary activists to sustain it? Towards the end of the second decade of the new millennium we do not speak from a position of strength: we cannot afford too much condescension.

In trying to explore a religious structure of feeling, experience, and articulation in the socialism of these years, illustration will have to be taken from the most vivid cases, rather than from every conceivable case. Six elements will be selected which, together, make it helpful to think in terms of 'the religion of socialism' at this time. First, the problem of theodicy or 'the experience of the irrationality of the world', which Max Weber singled out as the problematic which defined and promoted religion, was an active dynamo in the socialism of the day.[198] Second, a hidden hand was commonly thought to be at work. It would cut through the theodicy problem, offering salvation. Third, the times were thought to be special times in relation to this hidden hand. Fourth, some people, or *the people*, were thought to be special vehicles or mediators of the hidden hand. Fifth, there was an absolutism about commitment which was expressed as doctrine rather than prudential tactical discussion. Sixth, in spite of Bax, who argued against unnecessary frills of this kind, there was a 'cultus' – beyond but including the Labour Church, as wide as the movement itself.[199] Alongside these elements there was also an awareness of the way in which material conditions affected what was possible in *any* religion or any form of association, including the religion of socialism. It is not often remembered, for example, that the book that affected many activists in their immediately pre-socialist period – Henry George's *Progress and Poverty* (1879) – had an important section showing how the rescue of political economy made possible the rescue of religion as a progressive force.[200]

The irrationality of the world was experienced as the unequal distribution of life's cultural and material goods. 'Why are some men not like us?' was the insistent question.

'Why are the many poor?' was the question answered by H. Sharples of Blackburn at an SDF meeting in 1893.[201] From the young Keir Hardie's sight of his employer's breakfast table to William Morris's sight of workers walking past his window in Hammersmith,[202] remembrance of poverty, insults, and degradations, resentment of hypocrisy and callousness, came back again and again in working-class autobiographies. Indignation changed people's lives, into those of settlers as well as socialists, into new styles of fiction as well as into politics.

Morris articulated the feeling most clearly. The Guest was happy in *Nowhere* because 'here I could enjoy everything without an afterthought of the injustice and miserable toil which made my leisure; the ignorance and dullness of life which went to make my keen appreciation of history; the tyranny and the struggle full of fear and mishap which went to make my romance'.[203] Although professedly 'careless of metaphysics and religion', Morris was convinced that 'the aim of socialists should be the founding of a religion, towards which end compromise is no use, and we only want to have those with us who will be with us to the end' (1883).[204] Socialism for Morris was 'emphatically not merely a "system of property-holding", but a complete theory of human life, founded indeed on the visible necessities of animal life, but including a distinct system of religion, ethics and conduct which ... will not enable us to get rid of the tragedy of life ... but which will enable us to meet it without fear and without shame'.[205] The context of his religion of socialism he explained clearly in a letter of July 1883:

> ... in looking into matters social and political I have but one rule, that in thinking of the condition of any body of men I should ask myself, 'How could you bear it yourself? What

would you feel if you were poor against the system under which you live?' I have always been uneasy when I had to ask myself that question, and of late years I have had to ask it so often, that I have seldom had it out of my mind: and the answer to it has more and more made me ashamed of my own position, and more and more made me feel that if I had not been born rich or well-to-do I should have found my position *un*endurable, and should have been a mere rebel against what would have seemed to me a system of robbery and injustice. Now it seems to me that, feeling this, I am bound to act for the destruction of the system which seems to me mere oppression and obstruction; such a system can only be destroyed, it seems to me, by the united discontent of numbers; isolated acts of a few persons of the middle and upper classes seeming to me (as I have said before) quite powerless against it: in other words the antagonism of classes, which the system has bred, is the natural and necessary instrument of its destruction. Nothing can argue me out of this feeling which I say plainly is a matter of religion to me: the contrasts of rich and poor are unendurable and ought not to be endured by either rich or poor. Now it seems to me that, feeling this, I am bound to act for the destruction of the system which seems to me mere oppression and obstruction; such a system can only be destroyed, it seems to me, by the united discontent of numbers; isolated acts of a few persons of the middle and upper classes seeming to me (as I have said before) quite powerless against it: in other words the antagonism of classes, which the system has bred, is the natural and necessary instrument of its destruction.[206]

It seemed for a happy moment as though the contrasts of rich and poor would be intolerable to sizeable enough sections of both classes to end them. There were 'unmistakeable signs', thought Bax, of a recognition by the working class of their 'true interests'. Total cure was available within the power of man in organised association. It could be explained in an evening meeting.[207] To attend such meetings, to join an organisation which promoted them, to participate in the range of activities sponsored by the organisation – such actions enabled men to be identified with the cure. Conversion to doctrine based upon a particular understanding of history, plus organised effort, could not only achieve specific changes within elected bodies, but could effect liberation from 'the curse of poverty [which] is to the modern world just what that of slavery was to the ancient'. The word 'poverty' and the facts of poverty were for a time omnipresent in the culture. 'Happiness was not a dream. It was a thing contrary to the hell of unemployment and poverty, of work made penal, of homes brought down to slums, of disease and early death, of life frustrated and denied. To reverse all this and to do so by the organised will and intelligence of the suffering masses: this is what we wanted.'[208] What mattered about socialism was the 'conviction that the social problem could and would be solved'.[209] 'That aspiration after complete equality which we now recognise as the bond of all happy human society' seemed capable of being broken into through the theodicy tunnel. A Battersea boy with daily experience of overcrowding, lack of sanitation, unemployment, and 'the desert of poverty which encompassed me' came to 'refuse to accept it as being just or inevitable'. He 'read voraciously all books I could borrow', tramping to spend hours in the Westminster Public Library. He devoured Carlyle's *Past and Present* and *Chartism*, George's *Progress and Poverty*, early Fabian Tracts, SDF pamphlets, and Kropotkin's *Appeal to the Young*. It was the latter that finally pushed him into 'conversion to a gospel embodying a great purpose'. Before joining the Battersea branch of the SDF, 'in these modest publications I found what I had sought:

the causes of inequality, penury, and the resulting suffering and moral and material degradation, and, what was more precious, the way out to a higher, nobler, and more dignified form of society'.[210]

The hidden hand working 'Towards Revolution' was nothing less than History. The story, or so it felt, had reached a climax, mediated through the working class, 'the people', or even 'the masses'. Throughout the movement there was a foreshortening of time and a sense of epochal change, with comparisons to the rise of Christianity.[211] A long poem published in *Commonweal* in 1888 and reprinted in *The Labour Annual* for 1895 caught the mood:

> I tell you that all that has gone before has been but a preparation for this,
> That all the early savagery, fierce hunger and thirst, tribal feuds, despotisms,
> All the oppressions and exactions of kings and nobles, the wars, civil wars and popular insurrections,
> Have had no other object for their existence than to render this finally possible.[212]

Socialism and Democracy were connected to a number of versions of inevitability. Either because of a Marx-derived view of the imminent collapse of the economy under the weight of its contradictions; or because of a softer set of assumptions about this being the 'age of the people' (assumptions going back to the 1867 'leap in the dark' speculation, but sharper now); or because of an evolutionary view with these years as a qualitative leap; or because of a widely shared sense of crisis in the political and party machines, socialism was going to happen. 'Socialism will come, of that I feel sure', wrote Blatchford in *Merrie England*. He made others feel the same.

In spite of subsequent efforts to rewrite their early history in order to ratify later developments, even the *Fabian Essays* of 1889 should be looked at in this light. 'Explosion points' and the view that 'so unstable a state of things cannot last' were as central a part of these essays as the example of Fabius Cunctator.[213]

Bernard Shaw later mocked this phase of socialism. But in a speech on the Eight Hours question in May 1890, he said that the strength of the workers' movement lay 'in the numbers, its aspirations, in the justice of its cause and in the certainty of the triumph of that cause in the long run. Aye, in the long run, but the question is, how long is that run to be? Everybody agrees that the millennium will come some day ... But we are in a hurry I hope.'[214] Belief in the instability of the current political system and of dominant forms within it such as Parties was perhaps the most important immediate factor making it possible to think in terms of sudden change.

The Parties, especially the Liberal Party, were not going to survive. There was therefore going to be a cleaner confrontation between capital and labour, or, as often expressed, between selfishness and humanity. Socialists would stand against Party and Politics to represent an utterly different but forthcoming world. As Frank Smith, the ex-Salvation Army, ILP member, put it in Andrew Reid's *New Party* volume in 1894, 'party politics will be known no more and principle in the place of policy [will] be the guiding force'. Or, as Sidney Webb thought, 'the lines of battle are being shifted. The issue cannot long remain between one capitalist party and another. The political conflicts of the near future will necessarily take place between the party representing property and economic privilege on the one hand, and the party of wage earners on the other. The fundamental principles of the one will be individualism, that of the other will be collectivism.'[215] 'There are many of us who have entered into the socialist movement because we are tired of party politics', wrote a correspondent to the *Workman's Times* in 1892, 'and we are born again into a new life and hope that as Labour-men Conservative and Labour-men Liberal we bury the hatchet of old party squabbles and march on shoulder to shoulder under the banner of the brotherhood of labour.'[216]

'It is self-evident', wrote Keir Hardie in 1895, 'that our present industrial system is nearing its end'.[217] Hyndman's 'Thoughts on the Coming Time' in 1892 were that overproduction was leading to a revolutionary crisis.[218] 'In conclusion,' wrote T. Ellis, reporting on the Clerkenwell branch of the SDF in 1890, 'I should like to point out what seems to me the bright prospects for revolutionary parties in the near future ... Everywhere there are indications of another commercial crisis coming upon us ... It is for us then to go back with renewed vigour and determination to spread the glad tidings of Social Democracy, so that not only in Clerkenwell, but throughout the country and the civilized world, the wage workers will sweep away this system of oppression and injustice and on its ruins will be that of the co-operative commonwealth, which means freedom for the worker.' [219]

'The people' were the special agents of certain and imminent change. On one level – in the view of middle-class enthusiasts – this was the discovery of a tangible rescuing agent, 'no longer a name', which Matthew Arnold had almost allowed himself to find in the 'populace' in *Culture and Anarchy* (1869). The intensity of this love affair during these particular years is well registered.[220] On another level 'the people' themselves had a long tradition and memory of their role over centuries. As the dockers' leader and later Labour politician, Will Crooks, put it in his Sunday morning addresses by the East India Dock Gates (known at the time as 'Crooks' College'):

Labour may be the new force by which God is going to help forward the regeneration of the world. Heaven knows we need a little more earnestness in our national life today, and if the best-born cannot give it, the so-called base-born may. We common people have done it before. Who knows but that it is God's will that we should do it again.[221]

On another level there was a theology which suggested that the people were the Body of Christ on earth; Thomas Hancock of the Guild of St. Matthew was the most coherent exponent of this view. John Trevor also veered towards such a view, substituting the class movement for the people, and God for Christ. So did others, with varying degrees of Pauline and Maurician learning. 'Instead of a state-church it is possible that we may have again a church-state …THE PEOPLE ARE GOD'S CHURCH. It is with the multitude Jesus left his Gospel. It is they who will become the voice of God in the future.'[222] No. 1 of the *Workers' Cry* on 2 May 1891 began with a poem by Fred Henderson called 'The Cry'. It identified the workers with Christ,

Whose brows, like His, have sorrow for their crown,
Who bear the world's great burden and its frown, –
Gaunt Christs, whose thorns are not yet hid with bays.

The Second Coming was to be a material event – the doctrine of the Kingdom being secularised, but thereby being restored to the pattern of its original exposition by Christ.[223]

Given such an exciting conjuncture of problems and answers to problems which religions of other varieties have also addressed, it is not surprising that there was a doctrinal flavour about socialist ideas at this time. This was noticed by those who disliked it as much as by those who expressed it. If there was the felt problem, the active will to resolve it, the agent to hand, and propitious times – what need for compromise, or for tactical discussions, or for going round about (for example through Old Age Pensions) to socialism? There was no fracture between means and ends now, because ends were guaranteed. It was a matter of 'The Social Revolution and How to Prepare for it', not how to manufacture it.[224] In such a context, it was just as well to hold to one's central beliefs and aspirations religiously: there was no need to pawn them to pay for the revolution.

2. A single social group? *'I belonged to all these bodies, neither caring much for the dissensions'* (Ben Turner)

Before moving away from individuals and into the movement proper, it may be helpful to ask whether we are dealing with the experience and problems of a single social group, class, national organisation or cult.

There are difficulties in answering these questions. First, there is no clear-cut number of people involved, defined for instance by membership of a single organisation. There were contemporary socialists, like H. Quelch, H.H. Champion, and F. Rogers, who defined 'sentimental socialism' by attacking it, and who clearly can be excluded. But there is also doubt about figures like H.M. Hyndman, who claimed a religious basis to his socialism, but only later in his *Further Reminiscences* (1912).[225] Secondly, biographical information – from autobiographies, biographies, or movement records (the socialist press, *Labour Annuals*, etc.) – is necessarily biased towards those who would be more likely to write about themselves or be written about, or towards those in leadership positions. Quantification is therefore bound to distort the sociology of the 'movement'.

This essay did not start with *the* religion of socialism, neatly on its shelf with prophets, priests, buildings, rituals, doctrine, members ... ready to be cut up in the manner of an institutional study in the sociology of religion. Rather I was led by the language and experiences of varieties of socialism during the 1880s and 1890s to see whether the idea of a 'religion of socialism' might help to understand what was going on at that time, and might, for that matter, still have some political importance. So it would be appropriate to look for generalisations from as large a group as possible of those who were part of such a formation for at least a portion of their lives, though without attempting to be comprehensive. Questions about gender, class background, geographical location, early work experiences, pre-socialist affiliations, and age on joining the movement were applied to the lives of 46 individuals.[226]

Numerically it may not seem significant that there are eight women in this list. In fact, however, one of the most striking features of this phase in socialist history was the overwhelming popularity and presence of four of these women: Margaret McMillan, Katherine St. John Conway, Enid Stacy, and Caroline Martyn. At branch level too, women were integral to the movement.[227] There is a preponderance of white-collar, professional, and business backgrounds in the list – at least 28 out of 46 definitely fall into this category. To take the first five as examples: Blatchford's father was an actor, Brocklehurst's a journalist, Burrows' a Methodist preacher, Glasier's a farmer/butcher, Conway's a Congregational minister. This is not incompatible with what little we know about the sociology of, for example, the core of the Socialist League.[228] And as research proceeds it is likely that it will be discovered, with an air of mock surprise and a real feeling of satisfaction among some historians, that the ILP, or the SDF, or whatever were 'not working class'.

But before it becomes interesting or significant to conclude, as Pierson does about William Morris's following, that it was 'not from the working classes, but from the indeterminate social strata just above or outside' or 'from the lower middle classes', some cautions should be offered. First, it is a common pattern of political argument to suggest that radical demands are 'not representative': 'the people as a whole' were quite satisfied, it is implied. Admittedly this does not make the argument untrue: it merely locates it. Second and more important, given the sparse resources of money, time, and other cultural goods available to most of the working class, it was extremely difficult to be part of anyone's following in a continuous and organised way while remaining working class – at least in a way which would present itself to the historian a century later, complete with names and biographies. Acquiring visibility by paying outside speakers or by sending delegates to conferences was often more than socialist groupings could manage 'from the workers' own pennies'.[229] People in our list would often be appointed as acting delegates at ILP conferences for areas with which they had no geographical link. Branches without patrons or a penumbra of non-political money-raising activities found sustaining a continuous existence problematic. It would certainly be illegitimate to use post-conversion occupation as a significant indicator of the material basis of the socialism professed. But since the sack was a frequent result of politicisation, a job had to be found, either within the movement (partly accounting for its rapid bureaucratisation) or relatively independently (such as Tom Mann's shop, or Tom Maguire's newspaper vending and photography enterprise). Having sold his small business, as part of 'the final struggle with Capitalism in my own life', D. B. Foster

> quickly looked round for a job, and finding nothing better I undertook travelling for a tea firm on commission. I was very dissatisfied and wished more than ever for an opportunity to work as a wage-earning producer. Fortunately, this period of anxiety only lasted a few months, it being ended by an offer, which I accepted, to organise the Labour Party in the City of York.[230]

Thirdly, parental background is not necessarily a good guide to formative pre-socialist work experience. Thus, Blatchford's actor-father died young. Blatchford then lived a precarious life, in a lithographic printing shop as an apprentice brush-maker (seven years), then as a run-away recruit to the army, and finally as a clerk in an engineering firm before he became a journalist and then a socialist. Hannah Mitchell's parents were tenant farmers. With just two weeks' schooling, and after a brief apprenticeship to a dressmaker she ran away from home aged 14, and thereafter worked as a maid, a dressmakers' assistant, and in various clothes-making jobs before, self-taught as an avid reader and writer, she began to read the *Clarion* and attend Labour Church meetings. This was in her mid-20s. And Glasier's experience over many years of a poor Glasgow home is not conveyed by 'father: farmer/butcher; became an architect, 1878'. It would be misleading indeed to refer to a socialist like Leonard Hall as 'son of Dr. Spencer Hall', given the fact that he was 'cast on his own resources' aged 13 and worked as a railway porter, a deck-hand, and in the United States as a farmhand and docker before returning to Manchester in the late 1880s. Perhaps the fact that there *were* notable working-class (by origin) figures even in our list where we would least expect to find them (for example, Hardie, Smith, Irving, Maguire, Meek, Snell) when added to evidence that will be considered later is more remarkable than the fact that there were not more.

Indeed it is what Sanders of the Battersea SDF recalled as 'this diversified band', or what John Burns referred to as the 'remarkable sample' aspect of the religion of socialism in these years which stands out. There appears to be no obvious geographical clustering, although contact with a metropolis such as Bristol, Glasgow, London, or Manchester was important in the socialist lives of many in the list. Nor was there a clustering of age at conversion. There were cases of conversion in people's late teens (Maguire, Sanders, Redfern), early twenties (Glasier, Conway, Meek, Bax, Martyn, Mitchell, Lansbury), middle-to-late twenties (Leatham, Trevor, Reade, Mann, Snell, Hall, and Sturt), thirties (Blatchford, Burrows, Hardie, Smith, Besant, Thompson, Foster), and forties (Morris, Carpenter, Hartley). We are dealing with a phenomenon which is not usefully reduced to a single sex, class, religion, or age.

Pre-socialist affiliations were equally scattered. For many, Henry George's *Progress and Poverty* was a milestone, and preoccupation with the land question, the drink question, or the Christianity question (through secularism) was a precursor of conversion to the religion of socialism. There were clear cases of abandonment of strong adherence to orthodox Christianity. John Trevor's *My Quest for God* is terrifying testimony to the experience and after-effects of a Calvinist upbringing. But right to the end he wanted a religion 'as spiritually intensive as the one in which I had been brought up'. The journey was not always one way: Hardie went away from free-thinking parents into Evangelicalism. Nor was socialism always a staging post on the way to no recognisable religion at all. Reade, for example, went through it into Christianity. It is not clear how a label like 'secularisation' helps in the understanding of the religion of socialism, or how it may be taken as evidence of a waning of the religious impulse – unless one subscribes to an evolutionary view with religion on the way out, in which case every active religious manifestation becomes a death throe. An active quest for meaning through organisational or associational affiliation certainly characterised many on our list. They all shared an eagerness to *join*. Caroline Martyn joined everything political that she could find in Reading during the late 1880s, being at the same time in the Primrose League, the Fabian Society, the Radical Club, and the Women's Liberal Association. The early lives of men like Mann, Snell, Foster, and Reade were eager journeys through Christian, temperance, food-reforming, charitable, astronomical, literary, and other associations.

It would be wrong to conclude from such a scatter of biographies that we are dealing with maverick practitioners of the religion of socialism, eccentric to the main movement. On the contrary, they were for a time at its centre. So much so that a simple explanation along the lines of 'this is what people liked and demanded when it was possible to have it', seems as appropriate as explanations which start with the assumption that the religion of socialism was a strange anachronism needing unique causes such as the relative earliness of the English bourgeois revolution.[231]

The 1880s and 1890s were, as already suggested, a time of great associational creativity. This was particularly manifest in terms of the religion of socialism. Not only was there a Labour Church, but a large number of 'allied social movements' – including Socialist Churches, the Labour Brotherhood, Brotherhood Churches, and the Labour Army (with its periodical *The Workers' Cry*, and its renegade

Salvation Army/ *War Cry* prophet, Frank Smith – with whom Keir Hardie felt a close affinity). Journals with titles like *Seed Time* and *The Link* mushroomed alongside organisations like the Fellowship of the New Life. In February 1888 *The Link* sought no less than 'the temporal salvation of the world and the establishment of a New Church dedicated to the service of man'.[232] Groups gathered to follow prophets – Whitmanites in Bolton, Tolstoyans in Purleigh, Ruskinians in Liverpool – giving a grounding in reality to Katherine Conway's purple vision of a socialist guru in her *The Religion of Socialism*.

The sheer scale of activity needs stressing, particularly to modern socialists accustomed to working on stonier ground and tempted to patronise the 1880s and 1890s as the 'origins' of their own rational, grown-up placidity. Edinburgh 'Labour Day' in 1894 was addressed by Bruce Glasier, Katherine Conway, and Fred Brocklehurst. Seventeen bands took part in the parade, 37 organisations, 10,000 marchers, and an estimated 120,000 spectators.[233] Glasgow socialists were mounting 30 meetings a week in mid-1895; at an ILP picnic there in the same year were 1,000 participants.[234] In the same city, 'our propaganda was carried on in the finest theatres and picture houses ... Nine large meetings were running simultaneously every Sunday evening in the Metropole, Olympia, Palaceum, Seamore, Victoria, Prince's, Gaiety, Lorne, and Pavilion theatres, and in Govan Town Hall. In addition to these, the large St Andrew's Hall was on many occasions packed with great audiences, and smaller indoor and outdoor meetings were organised by branches in ten different districts untapped by the theatres.'

Haddow's opinion in the early 1940s was that 'unless we return in some measure to these enthusiastic days, we shall never make real progress'.[235] Keir Hardie was at a Manchester Labour Church meeting with 3,000 attenders in January 1894: two months earlier, Bradford ILP reported a paid membership of 2,000: three months before that, Enid Stacy drew a crowd of up to 4,000 people in Blackburn.[236] In late 1894 it was reported from Huddersfield that the Glasiers had spoken 14 times in a week. Caroline Martyn's letters during the early 1890s are those of an exhilarated revivalist preacher, moving from Oldham to Liverpool, to Rochdale, to Newcastle in an excited flurry of enthusiastic receptions. Within eight months in 1892-3, 44 ILP branches had been started without the benefit of official organisers. The Labour Church in Bradford in 1896 had a 'membership of 300, a local "weekly" with a circulation of 5,000 and *no debt'*.[237] For a time the Labour Army even managed to penetrate a town as difficult for socialists as Reading. During an open-air meeting in August 1891, 'Officers, including secretary and treasurer were appointed, and many new members enrolled amidst much enthusiasm. The Reading branch is going up, and already in the town five centres are engaged in the work of enrolment and organisation.'[238]

The release of energy in individual lives following conversion was matched in the movement more generally. 'The men and women who were its members and workers were not moved by envy of those who were richer than themselves; they were in the grip of a new and compelling faith. It appealed to the emotional side of their natures and they became, in imagination, citizens of a new and better world. The ideal of a co-operative commonwealth, the possibility of creating a social environment in which men would live "with the light of knowledge in the eyes" released in them hidden stores of moral energy.'[239]

At this stage of the movement, as in any revival, the circle of involvement was much larger than the numbers formally organised. This on occasion led to hectoring, for example of the 200 *Clarion* readers in Jarrow who obstinately refused to get organised.[240] But more usually, and especially with Robert

Blatchford, it was a boast that the flavour of contemporary socialism was particularly palatable to 'the great unattached'. This was his special constituency, just as, among the attached, *Clarion* was the special mouthpiece of independent socialist societies not affiliated to a single apex-organisation. The fact that the religion of socialism could appeal to layers untouched by other varieties was stressed.[241] One observer of Labour Church meetings in Manchester in early 1894 found 'at least a thousand men present'.

> Every variety of type was represented, the shrewd stunted weaver, the powerful labourer, square and set with heavy toil, dapper intelligent men who might be clerks and shop-men, men with strong earnest faces – one whom I knew to be a popular journalist – quiet, depressed men, and men with discontented burning eyes. Steady attention, riveted on the speaker, was common to all alike, and the one expression I failed to note was that of sarcastic mockery, which so often characterises the keen-witted democrat in any sort of religious assemblage. Each man seemed, as it were, to be off his guard, and to have given in his allegiance. Applause and laughter had their way freely, and every telling point was caught up. They were leaning forward in the seats below, hanging over the rails in the galleries, heads resting upon hands, brows knitted, eyes anxiously strained. Close to me one night, sat a mean, ill-grown worker with sad eyes, to which at certain words of the preacher he furtively lifted his worn hand again and again to clear away the tears.[242]

Descriptions of such intense occasions are common. They often related to readings, providing evidence that works like *Towards Democracy*, *Merrie England*, and *News from Nowhere* were gulped into the consciousness of groups of workers, and were used as integral parts of socialist life. There would be silence, demand for more, and then 'reading on their own account by the listeners'.[243] Similarly, collections of labour hymns, songs, and 'Chants for Socialists' showed that poems escaped from books, or the newspapers which printed them, into collective use. Views of contemporary evangelists are, to a modern, soured sensibility, embarrassing in their romanticism. But they leave no doubt about the reality of demand among working people for what was then being supplied. For example C.T. Cramp, later Industrial General Secretary of the National Union of Railwaymen, remembered Carpenter thus:

> The first time I saw him he was speaking in a small and dingy room in Sheffield to a little body of men and women one Sunday evening. His subject was 'The Simplification of Life', and as one listened to the man one mentally sloughed off the conventional husks which seemed to encase one's spirit and confine one's outlook as a result of modern industrial conditions. In a curious way he seemed to take one both forward and backward; forward to a freer and less care-worn world, yet backward to something which all of us had lost. One lost the sense of the grimy city with its jostling thousands living under a pall of smoke and earning their scanty livelihood by sweating at mill or forge, amid sulphur and gases. One lost the sense of those small worries and oft-time ridiculous conventions which oppress the soul and make of life a weariness. One saw a reconquest of the green and beautiful England by a happy and healthy people ... At this time he lived at Homesfield, situated in the peaceful Cordwell Valley in Derbyshire, and his house was a rendezvous for all sorts and conditions of men, particularly at week-ends. The Sheffield cutler, engineer, miner, or railwayman met poet, musician, or dramatist beneath his roof and were all made to feel one of a great family.[244]

A 'workman' described a lecture on 'Art and Labour' by Morris in Bristol in 1885 thus:

> The hall was crowded, and Morris walked on to the platform in the manner of a university professor, alone, and without a chairman. He wore the familiar dark blue serge jacket suit and pale blue cotton shirt and collar. His head was massive, lionllike. Rather beyond middle age, his shaggy, dark curly hair and beard showed traces of greyness. He looked into our faces, but his penetrating eyes seemed to suggest far away thoughts. Sturdily built, he appeared both fearless and conscious of his own strength – the nearest living approach I had ever seen to my ideal human. A wonderfully inspiring figure – and the vision remains.
>
> The two sections of the audience were poles asunder – the literary folk who were 'curious' and perhaps apprehensive, listened attentively and without emotion until the end, then dutifully joined in the applause of thanks; while we workmen, somewhat shy and painfully conscious of our unusual surroundings and shortcomings, soon realised the presence of a champion, forgot ourselves, and frequently burst into rounds of applause.[245]

One who heard Caroline Martyn in 1894 in Eagley said:

> I knew nothing of the subject of Socialism, and did not care to learn much about it, but for curiosity's sake I took my seat on a tree-stump that Friday evening when Caroline Martyn came to Eagley to speak in the open air. In company with some two or three hundred people I listened to an exposition of Socialistic principles, illustrated and interspersed with the sayings and doings of the Carpenter of Nazareth. My wonder at what seemed to me the intrepidity and courage of a young

and defenceless woman grew and changed to amazement at myself that I had never seen these things in this light before. She had spoken as no woman ever spoke before in my hearing. Scales fell from my eyes, and ere long I was a Socialist. Though I have never had the good fortune to hear Caroline again I have found it to be a cause for thankfulness that once I heard her, and that her ethical treatment of her subject, her intense religiosity, plainly manifest to me in that one short address, was my first introduction to Socialism.

Two years later she was present at a demonstration at Hardcastle Craggs:

> Then from a dais-like, heath-clad rock, around which the choristers had stood, arose our Carrie Martyn. Truly, no Diana of old was ever more godlike than she, as she stood before the background of waving green, and with the wind gently moving her flowing gown into graceful folds, spoke from her noble heart words of burning fervor and truth, which it were well that the whole world upon that day should hear and heed.[246]

The more this phase in the social history of socialism is documented, the more understandable its wide acceptability becomes. It can speak for itself. If one could, even if only momentarily and in consciousness rather than in structure, experience the new life in the old, why not go out of one's way to do so? If there was the assurance of what General Booth referred to as 'the great overturn', why not participate in the life of those preparing for it? 'If I could but see a day of it', he said to himself; 'If I could but see it.' Nostalgia for a period in which this seemed possible, and there was much of it from the early 1920s onwards, was appropriate rather than soppy.

Only because of certain assumptions among modern, secular Marxists does the phrase 'religion of socialism' seem odd. If, for example, it is held that religions are essentially other-worldly in orientation, and that they are being displaced by natural or social process, or natural or social science, then a this-worldly religion such as the religion of socialism is a masquerade or an anachronism, on the way to being no religion at all. Incidentally, such a judgement would have to apply to many versions of Christianity. Or if it is held that the working class and/or the labour movement are, first, inherently 'secular' in tendency or, secondly, destined to conceive socialism immaculately through intensified self-interest (wage pressure, strikes, etc. - always distrusted even by the anti-sentimental SDF in this period) or 'usual channels' political activity, then religion of socialism beliefs and activity were at best 'primitive'. Or if it is held that there is no necessary link - on the contrary, that there is a necessary rupture - between the means chosen to bring about socialism and the ends; or that morality, ethics, and religiosity can only serve as culture-specific stiffeners to universal, 'basic' working-class struggles; or that labour movements develop inexorably towards 'mature' organisational models, just as children become adults - then what we are looking at is at best quaintly incidental to mainstream labour-movement development and at worst false consciousness functional to the continuity of capitalism but not to the advancement of socialism.

Underlying these assumptions is a view of this period in the social history of socialism as transitional to something higher.[247] This essay offers a contrary emphasis. The religion of socialism did not just degenerate: it was also destroyed. As the engineering trade unionist G.N. Barnes recalled at the end of his journey *From Workshop to War Cabinet* (1924), 'we were passing through a fanatical time ...Those were indeed exciting days. *They were in fact too exciting to last* [my emphasis].'[248] Socialism could still be a contagious *working-class* hope and practice during the last two decades of the nineteenth century because of the relative absence of factors which later bore down upon it. These can be listed. They will acquire more meaning when we return to the specifics of the movement from the mid-1880s to the mid-1890s.

Socialism at that time had not yet become the prisoner of a particular, elaborate party machine – a machine which would come to associate its own well-being with the prospects for socialism. One of the most important (and unwritten) parts of the history of the mid-1890s is precisely the shaping of the ILP into such a machine against much resistance from below. But as yet labourism had not found a large institutional seat. As a corollary of this, dominant forms of activity in the movement were not yet (although again this was happening in the early 1890s) of an expensive kind, like electioneering, which would prohibit their being the property of local associations of the working class, or else force money-raising, goal-displacing activities on to those associations. It was financially difficult to keep typical 1883–1896 associations of socialists going, and the difficulty pervades the records. Furthermore, socialism had not yet been faced with a distorted reflection of itself in the mirror of welfare legislation, and a rapidly enlarging State. Nor had it yet become the ideology of social engineers: socialism had not yet become confused with superior understanding by experts.[249] Moreover, socialist associations, and indeed working-class associations of all kinds as users of leisure time, had not yet been faced with the competition of a fully developed capitalist mass leisure industry, not only competing for time, but standing for diametrically opposite, passive ways of relating to society. The continual tendency within capitalism towards division of labour and specialisation of function between associations was at work during our period. But there was still space, as we shall illustrate below, for local nexuses of leisure/ educational/ political/ welfare/ social/ religious life, standing for a unity which socialists of the time wished to realise into a whole social order. Finally the doctrine of Socialism in Another Country had not yet taken hold. That is to say, the ultimate barrier between the self-activity of the working class and socialism, which would be erected by feeling constrained to state that the best road to socialism is to defend the Soviet Union or support 'Third World' revolution, had not yet been erected.

Such constraints were absent or not yet dominant between 1883 and 1896. As already suggested, it was also a time of economic and party-political plasticity. Even if 'the new life' was not inevitable, at least the old one looked fragile. There was also 'the coming century', and the remembrance of what had happened in France at the end of the previous one, to give a sense of epoch. Finally, and in terms of the late-Victorian revolt not accidentally, there were also present some exceptional advocates. Propagandists like Morris, Carpenter, and Blatchford do not appear in every generation. However favourable the general context, *News From Nowhere* had to be a special work of genius to produce the effects that it did:

> ... in the Albion Halls last Sunday, owing to the unavoidable absence of William Nairn, Mr. J. Bruce Glasier reviewed 'News from Nowhere', an ideal of socialism by William Morris. The meeting was one of the strangest I have seen since the lectures began. Quite a religious feeling seemed to pervade the hall, and you could have heard the proverbial pin drop while Comrade Glasier was reading some of the passages from the book. Not that the meetings have been noisy hitherto, but the silence at the last one was so still and death-like that it shows a wonderful power in the book.[250]

Nowhere was a compellingly attractive place. Even when the 'black cloud rolling along to meet me, like a nightmare of my childish days' had broken the Guest's vision at the end, bringing him back to 'dingy Hammersmith', he was left undespairing. There was a voice urging him to 'Go back again, now you have seen us, and your outward eyes have learned that in spite of all the infallible maxims of your day there is yet a time of rest in store for the world, when mastery has changed into fellowship – but not before ... Go back and be the happier for having seen us, for having added a little hope to your struggle.' If *Nowhere*'s attraction for socialists at that time does not need elaborate explanation beside the vision itself, the subsequent effect of such visions on the movement does need exploring. The religion of socialism led to a concentration on the movement – joining it, being a socialist within it, getting others to join it – and this strength had its own important weakness. It is always a danger in socialist vision, as it is in labour history, to let the movement become a cult, eclipsing the as-yet-unattached members of the class.

There were occasional socialist funerals: on a day when Hyndman talked at 11 a.m. on 'Socialism and the Family', and at 7.00 p.m. on 'Glories of the Coming Time', he talked at 3.00 p.m on 'Death and Social Democracy'. Leeds Labour Church considered seeking a marriage licence in 1894. John Trevor tried hard to keep prayer as part of Labour Church life: and Katherine Conway's imaginary socialist guru in her pamphlet on *The Religion of Socialism* (1887) gave the young man sitting at his feet advice about baptism, marriage, burial, and 'gatherings for worship ... [to] gain even clearer visions of full and perfect life, and vow ourselves yet again to its service, and through the brotherhood of man gain a real faith in the fatherhood of God'. But the absence of conventional ritual, liturgy, and sacrament was much more striking than its occasional presence.[251]

Opposing a suggestion made at the 1903 ILP Conference that they might institute a socialist burial service, Glasier said 'neither in life nor in death should they seek to separate themselves from their fellow citizens'.

The cult was the movement itself. 'Up at the League', chapter one of *News from Nowhere,* begins: 'there had been one night a brisk conversational discussion, as to what would happen on the Morrow of the Revolution, finally shading off into a vigorous statement by various friends of their views on the future of the fully-developed new society'. It was a small meeting – only six people present – but, 'those present being used to public meetings and after-lecture debates', it was a discussion full of mostly good-tempered disagreement. From the meeting, the first person of the story goes home 'discontentedly and unhappily', but yearning for the post-revolutionary society. He had lost his temper and (a typical Morris detail) had forgotten some of the best points that he had wanted to make. 'If I could but see a day of it,' he said to himself, 'if I could but see it.' The rest of the book is what happens when he does. Such inspiration from such forms was the stuff of the movement in those years. For modern participants in comparable forms it is difficult to step outside and see that political commitment to political socialism need not and does not – in the same degree in comparable cultures – take the form of regular attendance at branch meetings whose basic purpose is listening, talking, and affirming. The aim was to congregate, to be and become better socialists, to strengthen belief and commitment, 'teaching the root doctrines of socialism to everyone we can reach, enrolling in the socialist body everyone who genuinely accepts these doctrines; making our voices heard as socialists on every opportunity'.[252] Morris added, 'holding ourselves aloof from every movement which has not the furtherance of socialism as its direct aim'. Not everyone in the ILP, Labour Church, Labour

Army, SDF, Clarion, Socialist League, or independent socialist societies would have agreed with the last instruction. But in the early years it is not possible to separate meetings or the organisations themselves from the problem of socialist *agency*. They were themselves, they thought, the means.

> Its desire is, in the words of John Trevor, 'to emancipate Labour from the bondage of the Landlord and the Capitalist; the individual from the power of evil wishes and passions; Woman from Economic dependence on Man; the Nations from Aristocratic, Autocratic, or Foreign Government; and the Religious Life of the People from Superstition, Tradition, and Priestly Control. Hence, to develop the Religion of the Labour movement, to destroy all forms of Slavery, to work for true Comradeship, and to fill the hearts of the people with new confidence in themselves, in each other, and in God, the Labour Church has come!'[253]

Trevor's ideal order of service for his meetings 'will vary according to local requirements of customs' but was as follows: '(1) Hymn (2) Reading (3) Prayer (4) Solo or Music by the Choir (5) Notices and Collection (6) Hymn (7) Address (8) Hymn (9) Benediction'.[254] He feared that people might leave after the Address, and that 'perhaps the Benediction will be deemed too formal a matter'. It should therefore be kept brief, simple, and 'a real thing', with words like 'May the strength and joy of God's presence be with all who love their brethren in sincerity. Amen'. In practice Labour Churches filleted such an order, leaving the bare bones of singing, reading, and talking. Trevor called it 'Free Religion'. The meetings were certainly less formal than, say, a Catholic Mass. More interesting is the fact that so many meetings of such a wide variety of formal organisations, within a felt sense of a common movement, shared the form at this time.

The Bristol movement was particularly keen on 'this new comradeship of song'. They had their own 'workman composer', their own song sheets, and later a Song Book which went through several editions. 'As Socialism was a movement inspired by art as well as of [sic] economics', explains an early minute, 'readings, recitations and music were introduced to the weekly *circle* thus completing and making it *whole*.'[255] The frontispiece of their song book was an archetype of the movement: a handsome, strong young man sowing seeds by hand in a perfectly furrowed field curving away towards the rising sun, the sower having reached the shade of a ripe apple tree. Collections of poems and songs were numerous, from Carpenter's *Chants for Labour* (1888) to Wm. Reeves's *A Song Book for Socialists* (28 songs for one penny), to Maguire's *Machine Room Chants* (1895), Mr and Mrs Trevor's *Labour Church Hymnbook*, and Morris's *Chants for Socialists* (mostly written for *Justice* or *Commonweal* between 1883 and 1886). Fred Jowett of Bradford recalled:

> Sometimes in summer-time the joint forces of Leeds and Bradford Socialism tramped together to spread the gospel by printed and spoken word in neighbouring villages. And at eventide, on the way home, as we walked in country lanes or on river bank, we sang –
>
> What is this, the sound and rumour? What is this that all men hear,
> Like the wind in hollow valleys when the storm is drawing near,
> Like the rolling on of ocean in the eventide of fear?
> 'This the people marching on...'
> And we believed they were![256]

William Hines, the Oxford chimney-sweep, herbalist, and radical-orator-turned-socialist, liked singing at his open-air meetings in the 1890s. He brought his daughter along to start it, and compiled a collection of *Labour Songs for the Use of Working Men and Women*.[257] J.Hunter Watts, an SDF agitator who used his job as a traveller in paper-dyes to visit socialist groupings all over the country and lead 'open-airs' for them, did without. He would end speeches with poems, like Ernest Jones's 'Sharpen the Sickle'. He believed in instant testimony. Passing through the Bull Ring in Birmingham one night and 'seeing a number of people about, he ... suddenly made a stand and started to harangue them. Smilingly he told us that when he shouted the preliminary word "Friends" the people nearby turned as if someone had been hurt and was uttering a cry of distress'. The Aberdeen Socialists liked to arrive on the railway platform in good time on their return from a picnic, to give time to 'sing till our train came in'. The Newhall socialists, having been ousted from Lichfield Cathedral one day for making too much noise, 'revenged ourselves by gathering outside singing "England Arise" '. The typical song, for example Will Payne's 'Welcome' (sung to the tune of Jerusalem the Golden), spoke of joining a band of workers, hope, forward movement, righteousness, self-confidence, strength, integrity, and the inevitability of a future of which one had to be worthy in the present.[258] Many speeches had similar themes, which is why, when an orator like Ramsay MacDonald later went on making them, further and further out of context, they read like so much wind. The movement itself was the vehicle. It was the assurance, in a common phrase of the day, that 'we shall arrive' – sometimes, as in the case of branches celebrating their birthdays or annual teas, that we *have* arrived.[259]

Unities: 'making it whole'

Edward Carpenter thought that those who lived their lives in the 'cold' outside the movement could never understand the glory of the 'hot' inside.[260] The heat generated three particular strengths, apart from the sheer pleasure of fraternity which Carpenter tried to convey. Each had to do with union or unity, 'making it whole', paralleling individual experiences of unity. 'If it weren't for the hope of a realised "oneness" of life in socialism', Hannah Mitchell recalled apropos of a lecture by Katherine Conway in 1892, 'I don't know what I should do sometimes.'[261]

The first organisational 'oneness' was between rival parties, federations, or societies within the movement. This led evangelists to recruit indiscriminately to the SDF or the ILP, sometimes at the cost of their job, owing to vested indignation at headquarters.[262] Organisational affiliation was an accident of time, place, or convenience. Like Ben Turner of the ILP, SDF, Fabian Society, and other organisations, many in the movement could have said, 'I belonged to all these bodies neither caring much for the dissensions'. It also led branches to be able to turn easily into affiliates of another organisation; to be able to campaign for joint candidatures or organise a joint club; and to be able to exist as socialist societies or socialist unions independent of any national grouping. Between 1893 and 1899 there were at least 46 such societies, three of which continued until 1909.[263] Within rival membership organisations there was also considerable demand from below for ecumenism, blocked initially by the SDF, and then by the ILP. *Clarion* and the Labour Church were particularly keen on unity. The *Labour Annual* was created in 1895 by Joseph Edwards to promote federation. Blatchford urged multiple membership of Clarion Scouts in order to promote 'One Socialist Party'.[264] During the 1880s and

1890s, as in early nineteenth-century co-operation/ socialism, federal sectarianism flourished, demanded from below. The advantages of tightness of inner commitment were combined with a capacity to recognise as comrades those taking a different track. It is not possible to say that it was 'religion' making this possible, since religious sectarianism can be as exclusive and uncomradely as the political variety. But socialist religion did seem able to operate, in a participant's words, as 'Religion the binder without Theology the Separator'.[265]

The second unity was between means and ends. Agencies of socialism represented a prefiguring of the society desired. Hence the 'primitive democracy' in the ILP at the grassroots level, particularly in *Clarion*-inspired sections. This was identified and deplored by the Webbs in their strategic theoretical rejection of this phase in the social history of socialism, *Industrial Democracy* (1897): 'The old theory of democracy is still an article of faith and constantly comes to the front when any organisation has to be formed for brand-new purposes.' But gradually a group interested in bureaucratic consolidation gained a commanding administrative position in the ILP. Hardie, Snowden, MacDonald, and Glasier dominated after the mid-1890s. But they did not have an easy ride on the backs of those whom Hardie was pleased to call 'the rank and file' at an ILP Conference in 1899. Democratic pressure from below lasted well into the twentieth century.

'Primitive democracy' was also characteristic of the SDF at branch level. 'We were punctiliously democratic according to our lights', in the Battersea branch, 'and therefore had no permanent chairman. The proceedings were conducted by anyone who happened to be nominated and elected to the chair at the time.'[266] Although the SDF, like the ILP, acquired an ambitious leadership, there was a strong anti-leadership bias.[267] This was, in a way, surprising since within the Marxist

SDF, if anywhere, new thinking on class and democracy might have been expected to emerge. New thinking, not necessarily 'Leninist', but addressing the problem of trying to be disciplined but democratic and representative of members too, was going to be necessary during the twentieth century. The impulse in the thinking on discipline of men like Morris and Bax ran away into academic 'social engineering' elitism in twentieth-century Labour politics, rather than into serious thought on democracy and representation from a working-class point of view. It is less surprising that democracy had a firm base in the Labour Church, where Trevor had a crippling, almost pathological desire to avoid 'leadership' positions. He had a conception of 'priesthood' which meant human solidarity and co-suffering, a hatred of hierarchy, and a commitment to process rather than procedure or, as he put it, to 'organism' rather than 'organisation'. Evelyn March-Phillipps in her *Spectator* article on the Labour Church in 1894, quoted earlier, noticed the strength in this. There was 'a real sense of brotherhood ... a consciousness that each one bears a part in *a great moral order* [my italics], and can take an active share in the management, from the organisation of a labour demonstration, to the clearing of tables after a "social evening" '.

The third unity was between activities normally kept separate. Such unity was in some aspects only momentarily achieved, and it can be watched breaking apart in the accounts of contemporary witnesses. But it was striven for. There were four principal aspects to it: unity between socialist politics and socialist leisure, socialist religion, socialist welfare, and socialist day-to-day organisational/ financial activities. H.W. Nevinson of the SDF recalled how

> the next few years – say from the last month of 1891 to the third month of 1897 – were for me, as for so many people

in that variegated age of English life, a period of strangely vivid interests and strangely diverse pursuits. We were simultaneously, and almost equally, attracted by the soldier, enthusiastic for the rebel, clamorous for the poor, and devoted to the beautiful. Some of us were moved most by one of these incitements, some by another; but many, like myself, were moved by all four together, and *we recognised no contradiction in the objects of our admiration or desire* [my italics]. The apparent contradictions were reconciled in a renewed passion – a glowing intensity – of life.[268]

Social activities in a branch were sometimes started as a way of avoiding the felt conflict between socialist politics and family life. They then took on many functions, The Bristol Socialist Rambling and Propaganda Society had summer picnics, combining games, literature distribution, singing, fly-posting, 'quiet talks by the way on intricacies of economics and sociology, the development of communal interest in each other' – all with the added advantage that 'it brought old and young members into closer contact'.[269] The *Clarion* was a society as much as a newspaper, a clearing-house as much as a commentator. Until the mid-1890s, with the formation of the Clarion Scouts (1894) and then the Clarion Fellowship (1900), there were no vested interests acquiring their own momentum and pulling apart recreation from socialism. Originally a separate identity for Clarion cyclists (including a badge) was adopted not to further bicycling as such, but because, as was explained in *The Scout* in 1895, members of the organisation needed to know each other and realise that they were not 'a mere aggregation of atoms, but an integration, an organic whole, … bound together as never an army before under a common banner, grappled together soul to soul by the sheet hooks of devotion to a great idea and confident … that our cause must inevitably conquer'.

South Salford SDF had an orchestra in 1894, the Liverpool socialists had a brass band, Bolton ILP a cricket club, and Halifax, Hull, and Keighley all had glee clubs in 1895. On 28 December 1894 Heeley ILP held a Grand Tea, on the 29th their Cinderella Club entertained 155 poor children, on the 30th they had a lecture, and on the 31st a dance.[270]

Unity between socialist politics and religion was, in one respect, no problem. Trevor often had to point out that it was not that the movement needed a 'religious' department, it was that the movement *was* a religious phenomenon. The 'First Principle' of the Labour Churches began by stating 'That the Labour Movement is a religious movement'.[271] Until the movement was seen as religious, thought Trevor, there was no hope for it, even in its material aspects. 'If we are to command life, we must be in league and co-operation with the commanding power of all life, which is God. There is no other way.'[272] God was not at work through the 'Historic Churches': he was active through the labour movement. 'All life is of a piece'; man had to learn through his own development, which at the present stage of history could be achieved only collectively. 'The real revelation of God is to be found in life itself, and in man's continual growth in relation to the world around him.' That growth could only happen through the labour movement.[273]

Unfortunately adequate institutional expression of the unity between socialist politics and religion was fragile. After all, as R.H. Tawney traced in *Religion and the Rise of Capitalism*, the division between 'religion' and the rest of life was the first major division of labour. Trevor's theology was controversial.[274] Those who agreed with him found the Labour Churches increasingly stony ground after the mid-1890s, after he himself had left it.[275] And those in other organisations who had managed to unite their spiritual preoccupations with labour politics found a similar gap widening in the same years.[276]

Modern socialists grew accustomed to the fracture between social work and socialism. But during the late nineteenth century it was not so obvious that the sealed train bringing socialism to future generations would run along different tracks from the ambulance wagons bringing relief to present generations. Frank Smith tried to bring them together through his work in the Salvation Army Darkest England scheme, and then in the *Workers' Cry*. His closest political friend – Keir Hardie – never abandoned his interest in ambulance work. As far as Hardie's socialism was concerned, particularly before he became an MP, programmatic and personal work were not *either–or*s. And 'Cinderella' work for poor children was an integral part of the *Clarion* circle. In a typical week in 1893 Ashton-under-Lyne Cinderella Club fed and entertained 250 children, Stalybridge made a hot-pot for 300, Bradford served their weekly dinner for 689, and Salford gave supper to 500.[277] Cinderella Clubs had been started by Blatchford in 1889 when he was working on the *Sunday Chronicle* in Manchester, and they reached their peak between 1897 and 1906. ILP branches and even the SDF in places like Battersea, Clerkenwell, and South Salford were not afraid of direct charity work as part of their socialist presence in the locality.[278] It was a question of looking after one's own. Croydon Socialist Society had their own medical officer, and when a member's widow in Marylebone SDF branch fell on hard times a concert was put on for her benefit.[279]

Finally, there was a unity between day-to-day organisational/ financial activities and politics. Such a unity has been so lost in political machines like the Labour Party that a time when there was at least an awareness of its possibility seems strikingly different. Goal displacement through raising money to pay debts in order to raise more money to pay bills for elections already fought has become as common in political organisations as it has long been in churches (in their case to pay for bricks and mortar). Similar means, particularly bazaars or jumble sales, have long been favoured. In the New Life years, a series of 'Merrie England' bazaars were held in 1895. There was a noted bazaar over the New Year holiday in Glasgow in 1895–6. 'Coming home late one night from a branch meeting, wearily tired and dejected, I had just been informed by our Treasurer that the Factor was dunning him for the rent and he hadn't any money to meet the demand. On telling my tale of woe to my wife she said "Why not hold a Bazaar? If poor churches can raise money by this method, why can't you?" I answered "Why not?" '[280] Hardie, Blatchford, Edward Francis Fay (The Bounder of the *Clarion*), Enid Stacy, and others spoke on different days. Caroline Martyn wrote to the organisers apologising for her absence, and wishing financial success. But she saw success in terms of 'a new bond of comradeship, all its necessary social meetings conducting to a closer sympathy'.[281] A temporary balance between what it was necessary to do in order to keep going, and socialist politics, seemed possible:

> Thus at Barrow-in-Furness …a group of unaffiliated working men managed to pay the rent of a large building, and to bring speakers from a distance, greatly helped by the letting of their big hall for a Saturday-night dance at £1 a week. Besides this hall they had in the building a reading room, billiard room, and a trading department of which the mainstays seemed to be tea and boots!
>
> Wigan also ran a Saturday night dance. At Burnley the big St. James's Hall, leased by the branch, was used for meetings, and they paid Dan Irving a wage as branch secretary. Besides conducting a trading department, he had the letting of the hall on week-days to, say, an occasional commercial traveller for a display of drapery or fancy goods. The portrait of Karl

Marx would look down from the wall upon a part of the process which he had analysed with mordant logic. In those days one regularly met a bigger crowd of Socialists at Burnley than anywhere else in Britain. They claimed a membership of 1,200.[282]

Where the balance between socialism and funding seemed to be upset, as in the ILP's turn to business modes of organisation (including trading in tobacco) in order to raise a £20,000 election fund during 1894, there were still arguments against it.[283] Unheeding institutional growth had not yet taken over. It was not, and is not, the case that any practical activity is bound to disperse inspiration and vision. It was, and still is, a matter of attempting to name – and from a socialist point of view – the precise openings and closures characteristic of a particular moment or phase in and against the development of capitalism. This involves specifying the material choice available to the movement on 'the knife edge of the present', and for which the movement is, in part, responsible because of what it does or fails to do.

3. Failure or defeat?

'The times were in fact too exciting to last.' Barnes went on to recall the directions that individual comrades took after this 'fanatical time'. He listed three: employment in trade union offices (himself); work on 'administrative bodies' like the London County Council (John Burns) – these two he called 'practical work'; and small-scale leisure business. 'Our erstwhile chairman, Harry Johnson, … gave up the Labour platform altogether and became a prosperous publican, in which calling he no doubt found it much easier to deal out pots of beer than chunks of poetry to his unimaginative fellow-workers. Poor Harry! He has probably long ere now gone the way of all flesh.'[284]

In microcosm these *were* the main directions in which the religion of socialism was contained. To trace them adequately would require another essay. But following them through in outline, and where possible through the articulated experience of those who went through them, leaves no doubt that it was not a wholly voluntary process. As always, it is the dialogue between agency and structure, aspiration and containment which historians interested in socialist movements past and present need to overhear.

The business mode penetrated the movement as well as being an outside alternative for individuals who, through no fault of their own, could not last the course. It could be nicely subordinated to other purposes, as in Burnley, with Marx looking down from the wall on activities necessary to keep the wall there. Or it could lead to conflicts. The bazaar in Glasgow over New Year 1895-6 ended unhappily. It took a year of preparation, with a Committee meeting every Sunday. The Press was fed with 'news', 'sometimes highly coloured, which they freely used and so helped to advertise our venture'. A Liverpool firm was given the contract for the bazaar decorations. Hundreds of pounds were raised, if not the £1,000 originally wanted for their Parliamentary Election Fund. But 'as "money is the root of all evil", so it was that our success led to much discussion within the Party'. The election of 1895 'came upon us sooner than we expected. We were committed to run six candidates in Glasgow – and we had no money in the exchequer.' A wine merchant came forward with an offer to finance the election, provided that the money from the bazaar was paid to him. None of the candidates was successful. After the defeat 'the cry got up that Pearce's [the wine merchant's] loan was obtained from the liquor trade, and was therefore "tainted money"'. He then offered to give the money without any conditions. 'But the party would have none of it and at the final meeting of the Bazaar Committee which broke up in disorder, the Treasurer was instructed to pay back every penny of the bazaar surplus.'[285]

The story might have been different if the six candidates had won. Indeed the assumption on which the electoral tactic made sense was either that its purpose was educational or that it would be relatively quick and easy to win. Glasier thought during the early 1890s that it would be a matter of five years before they captured power. Once it began to look more difficult after the 1895 election, problems became more obvious, particularly financial ones. The terms upon which it was going to be possible to operate electorally were exacting. During the 'making socialists' conversion phase, electoral work seemed a long way off. The phase was so exciting that it did not prove possible for socialists to step back and see what was coming. A sustained electoral challenge required money. Money would have to come from people who had it. This meant either business patrons (the ILP used George Cadbury, Joseph Fels, and James Allen among others) with all that the client relationship implied, or money from the membership. But subs were hard to collect and hard to find among people with limited surplus. Or there was a characteristic way of collecting large sums from the working class – through small, almost unnoticed amounts gathered in from enormous numbers. This was the way forward for the Co-operative Movement. In the end it was to be the trade-union levy and trade-union donations that financed Labour electoral politics. But, on the way, subordination to rich individuals, and indeed (through electoral pacts with the Liberals) to another major Party, was to be the means of growth and survival.

Before this, however, business modes were tried, with displacing effects. Tom Mann described them in a worried letter of the late 1880s to John Burns. He had been organising for the SDF in Lancashire, and had got into trouble of a kind which led the Council of the SDF to ask him to resign. He was anxious to justify himself to his friend. The details of the episode are not clear. As Mann presents it, it was a sorry tale of economic difficulty leading to more economic difficulty, with a final result that when Mann left Lancashire he owed £15, which he had to pay off at 2/6d. a week. The idea had been that he was to run a tobacco shop as 'a source of remuneration to me' as Lancashire organiser, along with 25 shillings a week guaranteed to him by the Lancashire Branches. The first three months were all right. Then,

> troubles began, by a section of the Branch [in Bolton] headed by one Matt Phair deciding to start a Socialist workshop, called by them the Co-operative Commonwealth. This proved to be a very great hindrance to the progress of the Branch and in a short time, partly owing to a less vigorous propaganda, resulting from the members devoting time to what they thought was the practical side of Socialism, the membership began to decrease, considerable dissensions arose in the Branch, and at nearly every meeting quarrels took place.

The tobacco shop then began not to pay its way, because a promise of a £20 float towards stock was not delivered. Loans had to be obtained, no rent was saved, and a vicious circle of decline set in, with Mann using the 25 shillings a week to feed his family. Then colder weather came. The Branches could no long raise 25 shillings a week and, reading between the lines, it seems that Mann was forced to use the sales of *Justice* to maintain himself. He then began to trade in other movement papers and got into trouble with the SDF. The trouble was obviously owing to the shortage of working-class money, rather than to any moral failing on the part of Tom Mann.[286]

In November 1893 the ILP nationally turned to business modes. An ILP Cooperative Society was launched in order to help finance candidates. The man behind it, B. Billcliffe, admitted contradictions. To further ILP political ambitions, socialists would have to do business in an unsocialist way. They tried to avoid gross contradictions, for example by inspecting the factories in which the tobacco they wanted to sell was produced.[287] But they were aware all the time of inconsistencies. At the local level other priorities made electioneering impossible, and vice versa. Thus by October 1894 the problem in the Bradford Central Independent Labour Club was how to gain members – at the rate of a member a day – to help pay for their premises, and in Carlisle 'the ILP have decided not to contest this year, thinking they have enough on hand in the work of furnishing and fitting the new club premises'.[288] On the other hand, Pete Curran of Manchester complained at the 1894 ILP Conference that heavy expenditure on municipal candidatures was preventing branches from being able to afford even to come to Conference. Choices imposed by constraints on working-class associational life were extremely specific. Left hands have an awkward habit of being affected by what right hands do. When a trading department was formed in Bradford, it led to heated controversy over whether they should offer interest on money that they needed to borrow. Trading departments, started in order to prevent other activities collapsing, would then collapse. Greenwich ILP was forced to discontinue Sunday lectures in 1896 until they had found the time and energy to promote a social evening to clear the debts.[289] Such situations were not specific to labour movements. They were part of a whole context for working-class organisations, or for organisations aspiring to come from below. The Salvation Army, for example, also faced the displacing effects of the business mode.[290]

In the end, in the socialist movement, the exigencies of electoral politics led to a large and cautious machine being constructed, careful not to offend. The directory of ILP members on public bodies, published with the Conference Report for the first time in 1897, began to lengthen. After a time, to go back would have been more difficult than to go on. But to go on necessarily involved the softly, softly approach and 'practical' political realism. 'We have turned politicians', announced S.G. Hobson in two strategic articles in the *Labour Leader* in 1896.[291] In the same year the National Administrative Council of the ILP sent out a circular. They had reached the end of the era of 'wholesale denunciation', they affirmed.

> To our knowledge tens of thousands are looking towards us more or less kindly disposed. It must be our aim to enlist those under our banner, not by any sacrifice of principle, but by avoiding unnecessary offence.[292]

In 1898 Trevor wrote of

> the extreme narrowness of the Labour Party and the growing difficulty as it settles into organisation of a generous breadth of mind being developed within it ... the ILP must of necessity appear to be attempting the salvation of the world in an appallingly cheap fashion.

Many years later George Lansbury, saddened as he was by twentieth-century developments, tried to 'recall the early pioneers' who 'never for a moment thought Socialism possible of achievement without the conscious cooperation of the working classes', and who 'had no intention of creating a huge party organisation controlled from the top, but were true democrats'.[293]

The development of a large State dispensing social politics from above was both a cause and a consequence of electoral Labour politics, which was in turn a cause and a consequence of goal-displacement in the socialist movement. Alongside the large state, changing business modes in leisure and communications were also experienced by socialists as antagonistic to the belief in working-class collective self-activity which distinguished the socialism of the 1880s and 1890s. Individual adherents of the religion of socialism were jostled by the changes into new roles, or out of politics altogether. Some began to blame the 'apathetic masses' for changes which were in fact systemic, and to join in a powerful twentieth-century chorus of disillusion. An Eastbourne socialist like George Meek was driven out of the movement by the changes.[294] Sanders from Battersea, as also Snell, saw socialism in the later 1890s as a 'political or economic tendency', 'slowly and cautiously worked out by experts in administration'.[295] Redfern noted 'a growing incapacity to think of any social good to be done except through a state or municipal authority'. 'Everything which I loved personally called to me as a free person; but on another side I was being moulded in spirit to a complete dependence on collectivist aims and plans, especially as to be authorized by the state. The two attitudes could not continue to co-exist.'[296] In his life they did indeed split. Redfern went towards mysticism, combined with humdrum co-operative administration. James Leatham from Aberdeen disliked state 'pauperism'. 'It would be no wonder', he wrote during the 1940s, 'if there were a decline of enthusiasm for democracy and a rise of Fascism among people who neither want to sponge nor to be sponged upon.' He also identified the leisure and communications industries as agencies alienating crucial areas of self-production. He recalled how in Aberdeen 'as elsewhere in those days', during the 1880s and 1890s, with four daily and half-a-dozen weekly papers catering for a local public, unorthodox views and people could command more space than now'. Later in the twentieth century the press for the working-class became dominated by expensive sports coverage.

> To working folk the value of free speech can hardly be exaggerated. They have practically no press, and they have been so doped with sport news that they will not support a journal which does not contain a large quantity of it, provided at great expense. If grown men find gratification in kicking a ball, let them kick; but what rational pleasure can there be in looking on? The world is at the moment busy destroying that which has taken centuries of time, labour, and skill to create, and one potent predisposing cause behind the imbecility of it all is the absence of free, well-informed discussion and the substitution of deadly alternatives for it – drill, marching, and obedience in Germany, sport and betting in Britain.[297]

After leaving Bradford finally in 1902 Margaret McMillan opened a Child Welfare Clinic in Deptford in July 1910. The terms in which her sister described her adaptation are interesting. She saw how

> this is the place of the deep ford, very deep and soft it is, the soft black greedy mass under the black waters of poverty. At every step one goes down and down. At first it looked as if service would be joy. But it was not so. My sister saw very well that school clinics were needed. But she now understood their limitations. She learned that this was not to be a triumphant crossing – that here was no crossing at all in fact, but a tying of staves in the mud.[298]

'A tying of staves in the mud', even if this is what post-'welfare state' society has chosen to remember the McMillans for, was a very different type of activity from that of Bradford in the early 1890s, when a 'triumphant crossing' seemed imminent.

In May 1895 a Bristol ILP socialist, Hugh Holmes Gore, wrote the front-page lead in the *Labour Prophet*. He called it 'The Rule of the Road', and used it to look back:

> Socialists who are ten years old can recall their avidity in studying Marx and his expositors. They will remember how clear it all seemed, and how foolish it was of the civilised world to delay its journey to the co-operative commonwealth. We saw, as it were from the mountain top, the Socialist state; we realised its desirability and we chafed at the delay in its advent. Ten years ago ... we were very busy in expounding in the parks, at street corners, in upper rooms (unfurnished) of coffee-houses, what the Socialist state will be, and how it differs from the present commercial anarchy; so very clearly, indeed did we understand the position that we prodded the proletariat, we (not I) sang them Pisgah-songs, we drew vivid pictures of the Promised Land, and enjoined them to hurry up and journey thither.

Looking forwards, he was troubled:

> What exercises the minds of some of us, however, is a kind of consciousness that we have not considered the road at all. We have pictured the ultimate condition of Society, we have urged the wisdom, even the necessity, of its accomplishment, but we have failed so far to explain the rule of the road thither. Hitherto the work of the Socialist has been to explain the Socialist state, and kindle a desire of its accomplishment. This is the first necessary step. We must know what we want and

where to get it. The next step is to go and fetch it. It is here that we fail; we have not defined clearly the road, nor even realised that there is one.

Thus was the central problem of the religion of socialism stated as early as 1895: the power of the vision and the problem of agency. It was to be stated over and over again during subsequent years, in tones varying from nostalgic to tragic. Years later H.G. Wells still wanted to understand the failure of socialism to grow into a theory competent to 'direct' the modern world. Although he had identified growing forms of early-twentieth-century socialist elitism in *The New Macchiavelli* (1911), his own way out was an elitist one. He came to regret the 1890s linking of socialism with working-class aspiration. He came to blame the religion of socialism, and came to blame 'them' for its failures. '"Let us have a new world", they said, and they called it Socialism ... What we saw as in a vision was a world without a scramble for possession and without the motive of proprietary advantage gripping every intellectual and creative effort. A great light had shone upon us and we could see no more!'[299]

H.H. Gore's own position in Bristol, forty years nearer the great light, showed how right Wells was. By 1895 Gore's way out, informed as it was by the impulses of the previous ten years, was already part of the problem rather than part of the solution. He was a local activist, including successful electoral battles for a place on the Town Council and on the School Board. He even fought a by-election, not wanting to win, but because of 'the absence of a Socialist to protest against the worship of Wills' (the tobacco firm). But his main rule of the road, stated in 1895, was to go back and make unsatisfactory travellers fit for the journey. The 'making socialists' option was already joining forces with the moral interpretation of alienation, blaming the class's inadequacy for their inability to transform capitalism. His socialist priority was to work in a Boys' Club and make socialist citizens one by one. 'I am firmly convinced that it is greater to have infused into even five boys the spirit of Human Brotherhood than to win a seat in the name of Socialism in the Imperial Legislature.' He appealed to other socialists to take up the same work. But the bathos of his plea left him, and the whole approach that he represented, vulnerable to Wellsian or Shavian attack:

> I would ask the Socialist accountant to work out the following proportion sum: 'If it takes five years to make ten typical English boys into good citizens, how many Socialists will have to undertake the task to make England a Socialist state in 100 years?'[300]

This, for him, was an argument for going back 'amongst "his boys" at the Dings Club', rather than for changing strategy. No wonder Shaw was soon to have such fun at the expense of a position that he had also once shared. 'Their programme was', he mocked in a lecture on 'The Ideal of Citizenship' in 1909, '"We will explain our good intentions and our sound economic basis to the whole world: the whole world will then join us at a subscription of a penny a week; then, the whole of society belonging to our society, we shall become society, and we shall proceed to take the government of the country into our hands, and we shall inaugurate the millennium."'[301]

Evaluating the religion of socialism from a mid-twentieth-century socialist perspective is a matter of trying to strike a delicate balance between its positive and negative features. Positively, socialism *was* being practised. It was being preached by people who, after all, would die long before, if ever, it became universal. Some experience of socialism, particularly on the scale of these years, was better than none for those who could not have it all. Socialism was gaining ground fast. It was popular, inter-class, creative, and capable of releasing joyful energy. And British capitalism *was* ripe for transformation. It had already been warrened by extensive burrows of working-class self-organisation over the previous half century and was widely admitted not to be healthy at 'base' or 'superstructural' levels. All that is being said about it now was being said in 1900. Since then it is not fanciful to suggest that, from the point of view of 'society', let alone 'the economy', British capitalism has become rotten ripe. Like an apple tree starved of light, E.P. Thompson once suggested, it has begun to 'shoot at the top'.[302] Practising socialism, working for and anticipating a new life in early stages of this decay, was a reasonable and hopeful response.

Grinding counter-attacks were launched on working-class self-organisation across a wide front from the mid-1890s. These included attacks on trade unionism, co-operation, Friendly Societies, and other vehicles through which working-class aspiration was capable of being expressed, such as School Boards and Working Men's Clubs. The story of this counter-attack has as yet been told with reference only to trade unionism, and this because of interest in 'the origins of the Labour Party' which was only a partial response to attack in this area.[303] The rest of the story cannot be told here. But some of its contours have been outlined. They included new developments in the scale and nature of business organisation, new areas of penetration for those business modes such as leisure and the means of communication, increasing emphasis upon consumption and distribution of goods, and State-enlarging 'social politics'. As a result, the practice of the religion of socialism in local associations, and the whole 'making socialists' option, began to prove more difficult and, where continued, to look forlorn.

The strengths of the practice when it flourished most, the very size of its presence, made more difficult the urgently necessary development of responses adequate for a changing context. There had always been a weakness in the religion of socialism about what precisely practitioners should do, other than to *join* with socialists and *be* socialist. As Jim Connell complained in 1904, 'for over twenty years we have been trying to convert people to socialism, and we found that to keep them we must reconvert them 365 times each year'. It had been all very well to say that 'the Socialist-labour movement has always been of an essentially religious character ... It has invariably had the power of appeal, not only to the intellect of man, but to his very soul. On the one side it offers him an ideal, the ideal of a new humanity; on the other it shows him the advantage of taking a definite step towards the realisation of that ideal.'[304] But the 'definite step' tended to be, in the words of Will Payne's 'Welcome',

> Are you a British worker?
> Then come and join our band;
> The cause is yours and needs you.
> Lend God a helping hand.

The expression of demand *now* for fellowship, unity, participation, fraternity, together with the partial embodiment of that demand in actual associations, left a reservoir of local aspiration and practice which, while it was still there to be drawn on, enabled participants to ignore the contradiction between their local ideals and the national policy of a Labour Party which had annexed their associations. A serious socialist *programme* did not emerge.[305] Practitioners of the religion of socialism can help us to understand why. At the height of it, hard-headed Shaw had the faith of soft-headed Glasier at his worst:

When the empty assent to a lecturer's propositions is replaced by a genuine vital faith in human equality then the workers will have a real religion for the first time and *out of that religion the policy and party organisation of labour will spring spontaneously* [my italics].[306]

Rather later (in 1916) Carpenter could still feel that 'the real value of the modern Socialist movement' did not lie 'in its actual constructive programme'. Good! But with innocence like this, what hope had the movement of responding adequately to its new, twentieth-century enemies?

Even the electoral tactic was not pursued in a self-conscious way. During the height of the 1880s and 1890s phase it was pursued with happy optimism. A characteristic *Clarion*-backed electoral campaigner, E.R. Hartley, 'believes in converting the electorate first, so did no canvassing, issued no posters, and ran no carriages, but relied on good literature and plenty of street-corner meetings'.[307] Blatchford hated electioneering. Organisation was rudimentary. Euphoria was sustained by the widespread phenomenon, much noticed at the time, that public meetings were much larger and more enthusiastic than the numbers going to the polls. 'Those were the days of the great moral victories. They could not be anything else, for there never was any organisation until within a few days of the poll.'[308]

It was, perhaps, significant that original, twentieth-century work on class, organisation, and democracy, for example by the Webbs in their *Industrial Democracy* (1897), went with a dismissal of what came to be seen as ILP 'soft' or 'sentimental' socialism. Key practitioners of the religion of socialism like Blatchford and Morris *did* face hard questions during the height of the New Life phase of socialism in Britain. Blatchford called Letter XIV in *Merrie England* 'What are we to do?' and began it by asking: 'The question is, how can Socialism be accomplished?'; but he then went on to 'confess that I approach this question with great reluctance. The establishment and organisation of a Socialistic State are the two branches of the work to which I have given least attention.' He stressed the need for a 'Socialist Party' and listed demands that it should make. But the leitmotiv was, as always with him, making socialists. 'When your Public understands Socialism and desires to establish it, there will be no difficulty about plans.' Morris's 'How the Change Came', in *News from Nowhere*, was an extraordinary piece of writing, unusual in socialist literature in its detailed attention to the stages of socialist revolution.[309] But it is not helpful in specific organisational or programmatic ways. As the old man explains at the beginning of his exposition to the Guest, 'doubtless all the time the most of men looked on, not knowing what was doing, thinking it all a matter of course, like the rising and setting of the sun – *and indeed it was so*'. In a late lecture on *Communism* in 1893, Morris suggested some useful ground rules for advance:

> Well, since our aim is great and so much to be longed for, the substituting throughout all society of peace for war, pleasure and self-respect for grief and disgrace, we may well seek about strenuously for some means for starting our enterprise; and since it is just these means in which the difficulty lies, I appeal to all socialists, while they express their thoughts and feelings about them honestly and fearlessly, not to make a quarrel of it with those whose aim is one with theirs, because there is a difference of opinion between them about the usefulness of the details of the means. It is difficult or even impossible not to make mistakes about these, driven as we are by the swift lapse of time and the necessity for doing something about it all.[310]

* I would like to thank the Davis Center at Princeton University, the University of Sussex Arts Research Support Fund, Alan Pond, André Le Duc, Elaine Rassaby, and Neil Killingback. Above all others, I thank Dr Merfyn Jones. While an undergraduate at Sussex he wrote a dissertation – for his 'Poverty and Society, 1880–1914' Special Subject in History – which discovered and documented the religiosity of much socialism during this period, and which I inadvertently failed to acknowledge at the time of publication of the original version of this essay in *History Workshop, a journal of socialist historians,* Issue 4, Autumn 1977 pp.5-56. As do many others, I owe much to the selfless and patient editorial work of Anna Davin on *History Workshop Journal* over many years.

PART III. SOCIALISM, THE STATE, AND SOME OPPOSITIONAL ENGLISHNESS

for Philip Corrigan, without whom I would not have had the courage or the wherewithal to write this essay

A Co-operative Wholesale Society invitation, from The Producer
(April, 1927)

Preface

The first version of this essay was published in *Englishness, Politics and Culture 1880–1920*, edited by Robert Colls and Philip Dodd (London: Croom Helm, 1986). That book was reissued with a Postscript by Will Self thirty years later (London: Bloomsbury, 2014). This setting explains the essay's preoccupation with 'Englishness', together with the fact that much of my material was drawn from the late nineteenth and early twentieth centuries. My continuing uncertainty about any idea of 'Englishness' during Brexit days is the reason why from time to time I have put it between inverted commas. It also explains why I often hesitate before writing 'England' or 'English', in spite of the original setting of this essay, and have moved to 'Britain' in cases where it is clearly more appropriate.

I want to enable this essay to be read on its own, although published here alongside 'The Three Socialisms' and 'A New Life'. This explains my decision not to eliminate all overlaps and repetitions between the three pieces. To have removed every quotation used in the preceding essays would not have helped readers minded to read only this one. I am aware that the continuing interest in 'Englishness' in this culture is at least as strong as any remaining interest in socialism.

Here in England, we have a fair house full of many good things, but cumbered also with pestilential rubbish. What duty can be more pressing than to carry out the rubbish piecemeal and burn it outside, lest some day there be no way of getting rid of it but by burning it all up inside with the goods and house and all?
William Morris, 'Art, Wealth and Riches' (1883)

'First point,' began Mr Smollett. 'We must go on, because we can't turn back. If I gave the word to go about, they would rise at once ... Now, sir, it's got to come to blows sooner or later ... We can count, I take it, on your own home servants, Mr Trewlaney?'
'As upon myself,' declared the squire.
'Three,' reckoned the captain, 'ourselves make seven, counting Hawkins, here. Now, about the honest hands?'
'Most likely Trewlaney's own men,' said the doctor; 'those he had picked up for himself, before he lit on Silver.'
'Nay,' replied the squire. 'Hands was one of mine.'
'I did think I could have trusted Hands,' added the Captain.
'And to think they're all Englishmen!' broke out the squire. 'Sir, I could find it in my heart to blow the ship up.'
Robert Louis Stevenson, *Treasure Island* (1883)

The adventures of Toad, Mole, Ratty and Badger are those of grown men sufficiently rich and leisured to spend their days messing about in boats and their evenings muttering about the scoundrels in the Wild Wood.

Scholars have long speculated about the identity of those scoundrels. The literal answer is that they're the weasels and stoats who swarm out of their dark, rooty realm, break into Toad Hall and trash the place. Reading biographically, it's impossible to overlook the fact that in 1903 Grahame was ambushed in his office at the Bank of England and shot at by a madman with a gun. The fact that the would-be assassin identified himself as a socialist placed him firmly on the side of chaos, along with the anarchist, suffragettes and the increasingly belligerent Kaiser. For a mid-Victorian like Grahame, it must have felt as if the world was coming undone....

It's crucial that we should see the narrative of The Wind in the Willows *for what it is – not so much gently recuperative as anxiously stagnant. For what has actually changed by the end? Toad*

Hall has been returned to its bombastic owner, the defeated stoats and weasels slink back to the Wild Wood, and the four heroes are free to continue planning their picnics. This isn't growth, merely a return to stasis.
Kathryn Hughes, review of Peter Hunt, *The Making of the Wind in the Willows* (Oxford: Bodleian, 2018) in *The Guardian Review*, Saturday, 31 March 2018

To articulate the past historically, Walter Benjamin said, 'means to seize hold of a memory as it flashes up at a moment of danger.' For several decades we have been living through a continuous 'moment of danger,' so that our history and past culture presents itself to a danger-alerted mind, searching for evidence of democratic endurance and resources of cultural strength and growth. And some part of that cultural inheritance cannot but be 'national' in character, with its own particular pressures, resilience and idiom; this must constitute not only some part of what we think and feel about but also some part of what we think and feel with. These resources are unusually large and complex in this island; they are, by no means, always resources of strength, but ... If a future is to be made, it must be made in some part from these.
E.P. Thompson, Foreword to *The Poverty of Theory and Other Essays* (London: Merlin, 1978)

In all probability England will go first – will give the signal, though she is at present so backward.
William Morris to William Allingham, 26 November 1884

Keep smiling through

It is tempting to begin with a smile. We would situate ourselves, say, in a recent English 'radical populist' moment between 1940 and 1948 when a series of *Britain in Pictures* books was produced by Collins. G.M. Young's *The Government of Britain*, Neville Cardus's *English Cricket*, Edith Sitwell's *English Women*, and Edmund Blunden's *English Villages* were among the books in the series. George Orwell's *The British People* was announced, but published as *The English People* (1947).

Alongside such books we would smile on many things English, including Socialism. The 1940s were a time when 'Englishness' and Britain 'under siege' seemed to carry with them all kinds of radical possibilities, as in the *British Way and Purpose* booklets issued by The Directorate of Army Education between 1942 and 1944; and as in J.B. Priestley's 1940 'Postscripts', broadcast to large audiences on the BBC. These were full of Priestley's beloved, homely, Yorkshire Englishness.

The smile might be somewhat condescending: it would certainly blur the distinction between England and Britain. Going on about England in a British State which had long been annexing other nations has been a favourite form of mystification here. Behind the myths of 'Englishness' lies the reality of Imperialist Britain. One third of the *Britain in Pictures* books had 'English' in their titles: Priestley came straight out with it: 'and when I say "English" I really mean British'.[311] Nevertheless we would be assenting to a range of things. These include a leaning towards the countryside, crafts, and well-guarded skills; a *penchant* for 'getting things done' rather than ratiocinating for ever; middle-class angst, charm, irony, and self-deprecation; working-class (sturdy) independence and self-help, preferably in continuous associations of working people consisting more of men than women; the voluntary rather than the compulsory; variety rather than uniformity; and an openness to the Romantic critique of capitalism and Protestant invention rather than towards scientific authority or any would-be *magisterium*.

All very real, and all capable of articulation in positive ways during positive times. We would also be assenting to that which English/British culture pitted against Fascism during the 1940s and to some of what George Orwell, for a time, articulated. His subtitle for *The Lion and the Unicorn* (1941) was 'Socialism and the English Genius'.

In present times – as already explained, this essay was written in late 1984 and revised in 2017-18 – such a smile would scarcely be sufficient.

Flesh and blood, in the cupboard

Would a grimace be more appropriate? In one of the 1920 Home Office *Reports on Revolutionary Organisations in the United Kingdom*, 'attention is called to the opinions of working men taken at random on the subject of revolutionary agitation'. Under the heading 'What the Working Man thinks', we find the following assertion:

> A correspondent who has conversed with workers selected at random in various London industries finds that they all have a hearty dislike for the alien and are inclined to resent the dragooning methods of Trade Unions. A linoleum layer remarked that he hated the Unions – they were the bane of the country. England used to be a free country but now, thanks to the Unions, the life of his class was tyranny. He would like to see powder and shot used freely amongst the Labour leaders and the Jews.[312]

Enter Henry Hyndman, leader of the Social Democratic Federation, Britain's pioneer Marxist organisation, himself grimacing. 'I am', he said in 1883, 'quite content to bear the reproach of Chauvinism in regard to what I say about the English-speaking and Teutonic peoples ... We have to base the first real Socialistic combination upon the common interests and affinities of the great Celto-Teutonic peoples in America, in Australia, in these islands, and possibly in Germany.'[313] Winds changed over the next thirty years. Hyndman's face was somewhat fixed. In 1910 he upheld 'the right and duty of this nationality to maintain its independence, even under capitalism ...There is no mistake about that. If this is to be a jingo, then I am a jingo; if this is to be a bourgeois, then I am a bourgeois.'[314] By April 1916 Hyndman found himself forming a National Socialist Party no less, against those in the British Socialist Party who stood for internationalism.

Enter Ben Tillett, speaking at the founding conference of the Independent Labour Party in 1893: 'he would sooner have the solid, progressive, matter of fact, fighting Trades Unionism of England than all the hare-brained chatterers and magpies of Continental revolutionists'.[315]

The grimace might turn to sad laughter as we watched the genius of the *Clarion* newspaper, Robert Blatchford, confess in October 1899 that perhaps he too was, after all, a jingo. He had felt obliged to answer Tillett in the *Clarion* in 1893. But in 1899 he gazetted orders to his daughter 'to play Rule Britannia every night while the war lasts'.[316] The blimp had always been one of Blatchford's many faces. John Smith of Oldham, the 'practical working man' to whom the letters expounding socialism in *Merrie England* had been addressed in 1894, had been told:

> This, then, is the basis of Socialism, that England should be owned by the English, and managed for the benefit of the English, instead of being owned by a few rich idlers, and mismanaged by them for the benefit of themselves.[317]

By the time of *Britain for the British* (1902), nationalism had bitten deeper into the substance of Blatchford's socialism. There was a lot of such 'Englishness' in labour and socialist circles during the late nineteenth and early twentieth centuries.[318]

As examples accumulate, however, it is easy to forget what they are examples of, namely the imbrication of late-nineteenth and early-twentieth century English socialists in a culture which was indeed xenophobic, and in which the 'nation' – a term usable by earlier patriots for radical purposes – had now been partly lost to imperialism.[319] It could never be finally lost: Orwell, Priestley, and the radical populism of the early 1940s are inexplicable without the felt possibility of its still being salient.[320]

Socialists, unless isolated, *do* take on the colour of their surroundings. Nationalism does penetrate socialism to the extent that the latter is located rather than flown in from the outside. Such facts tell one, maybe, about nationalism and socialism, but nothing much, in these bald forms, about Englishness – in its specificity – and socialism.

It is also easy to forget that the intention and sometimes the function of labour and socialist *organisation* – rooted in its host culture as it has to be –is, precisely, to produce the possibility of alternative colouration. Thus, one of the reasons for the Socialist League's break with Hyndman in December 1884 was his 'attacks on foreigners as foreigners or at least sneers at them: coquetting also with jingoism in various forms'.[321] Against this William Morris educated, agitated, and organised around an exemplary combination of love of place (mainly bits of England) with principled resistance to Nation and to State. Morris loved where he lived. He wished to transform it so that everybody could share his affection, finding in *place* – as another poet, William Carlos Williams, did – the 'true core of the universal'. 'I am not ashamed', he wrote in *Early England* in 1885, 'to say that as for the face of the land we live in, I love it with something of the passion of a lover.' And Ben Tillett's outburst in Bradford in 1893 did not go unanswered at the time. Keir Hardie called on Edouard Bernstein, the German fraternal delegate, to reply from the platform.[322] Nor did Blatchford's buffoonery pass unrebuked. Photographs of him were defaced in many socialist club rooms after 1899.[323] Hyndman's quotation from 1910 (already cited) went on, 'if this is to be an opponent of organised socialist opinion, then I am an opponent of organised socialist opinion'.

Having distanced the modern reader from Second International English Blimpery, which got even uglier between 1914 and 1918, the argument could end by confirming that of course nation-hood, and in particular this England's nation-hood, has nothing to do with the socialist project. We could easily repeat the commination that socialism is international, nowhere unless everywhere, nothing if not everything, never if not always … This could slide into saying that socialism is, was, and ever will be elsewhere, but not here. With disdain resembling that of Matthew Arnold writing about the 'Hebraism' of English nineteenth-century nonconformist culture, we would contrast twentieth-century continental 'Hellenisms'/ Marxisms with 'the failure of British society to generate any mass socialist movement or significant revolutionary party in the twentieth-century – alone among major nations in Europe'. 'In England a supine bourgeoisie produced a subordinate proletariat.'[324]

Before the idea of 'Englishness', England, and its State

Walking against that particular run will be helped by rehearsing some of the orienting facts about England that have emerged from less absolute, less disdainful historical work. Such facts, particularly as they bear upon the public realm or state, cannot but affect 'Englishness', as well as socialism more generally. After all, the 'public' has been, for the most part, socialism's chosen sphere of operation. As Edward Thompson (quote above) wrote: facts about our inheritance 'must constitute not only some part of what we think and feel about but also some part of what we think and feel with. These resources are unusually large and complex in this island; they are, by no means, always resources of strength, but ... If a future is to be made, it must be made in some part from these.'

'Facts' make it sound too simple: Engels' phrase 'a contradictory state of affairs' might be more appropriate. Writing in 1892 *On Certain Peculiarities of the Economic and Political Development of England*, Engels was exasperated:

> By its eternal compromises gradual, peaceful political development such as exists in England brings about a contradictory state of affairs. Because of the superior advantages it affords, the state can within certain limits be tolerated in practice, but its logical incongruities are a sore trial to the reasoning mind. Hence the need felt by all 'state-sustaining' parties for theoretical camouflage, even justification, which naturally are only feasible by means of sophisms, distortions and, finally underhand tricks. [325]

Logical incongruities and underhand tricks are all too familiar in today's Britain. Engels' irritation followed the 1840s in Britain and Europe – when things had grown starker, more hopeful. By the end of that decade, compromises looked like being less eternal. But 'sore trials to the reasoning minds' of socialists are not lacking in the twenty-first century, particularly perhaps to people of my generation (b. 1939) when, as we grew up in 'the golden years' between the mid-1940s and the mid-1970s, progress seemed more predictable.

Four connected points may serve, if not to cut through the inner exasperation at least to turn it outwards. I will make them in a summary way first, before illustrating them from a range of recent writing.

First, in England – along with a great deal else – the State, often with the capital letter I will give it in this essay, is very *old*. Second, even in its modern or capitalist forms it goes back a long way: constituted not by a single event but developing in the shape of a 'great arch'.[326] Third, 'it', *the* State, is not really an it or a thing, separate from all other social relations, but has been integral to the development of those relations even in their modern or capitalist forms. The capitalist 'private' likes to contrast itself with, or pretend to do without, the State, or 'public' realm. But the two – in their modern forms – are two sides of the same coin. Fourth, there have been formidable pressures working against simple propositions like these three becoming apparent. These include the very age of the State itself, making it easy to reify or abstract it. The pressures include capitalist apologetics which suggest that capitalism is a 'private' or 'economic' affair, promising 'freedom from' the 'public'/ 'political' realms. These pressures have been breaking up fast in recent years. But the consequences for socialism of giving in to them – and thus working with an idea of 'the State' as a stable and easy ally – have been formidable, and are still very much present. It has come as a considerable shock to contemporary English socialists to realise that the 'public' State can be as much of a problem for them – as much a site for creative reconstruction – as is the 'private' firm.

To enter into more details on each of these propositions: England had been a State and a Nation for some centuries before the 1880s, the era of the socialism which called itself 'modern' in order to jettison 'primitive', pre-'scientific', 'utopian' ideas and methods.[327] If all that this essay can do is to put in place, in England, a particular State – at a time when there are formidable pressures to say that it has been weak, on the wane, aristocratic and thus less than bourgeois, not a problem for socialists, not an instrument for capitalists – that may be a contribution worth making.

As a Nation – 'a body of people kept together for purposes of rivalry and war with other similar bodies' – England was building on a domestic empire from at least the thirteenth century onwards. As a State – 'that is, the nation organised for unwasteful production and exchange of wealth'[328] – an English apparatus of modernity (written record, coherent sovereignty, common currency, reliable revenue, lawed property, sanctified contract) was infusing relations of production from about the same time. Things (relations) happened early here. So here there was a lot, and for a long time, to have ideas of Englishness *about*.

This is particularly important with reference to the State. The definite article is itself indicative: *the* State rather than a state or some states – slips easily on to the page, here in modern England. Socialists, like many other people, have tended to reach for the definite article, as if to hold the object constant: an 'it'. '"It", in short,' wrote Doris Lessing in a terrifying study of the disintegration of all relations between citizens and State, 'is the word for helpless ignorance or of helpless awareness. It is a word for man's inadequacy.'[329] It helps us to deceive ourselves with the notion that some Thing, a fixed entity, can be called upon to redress the wrongs of private capital. That capital can get away with calling itself 'private' is part of its achievement in keeping the private capitalist. It took the crises of the 1980s and 2010s to encourage socialists – Margaret Thatcher and the thinkers behind her got there first – to articulate the distinctively English and then the capitalist forms of the public, or State sphere. The public did not, in Britain, completely eclipse the private: indeed in their modern senses they were exceptionally interdependent. Not to see this is to allow ourselves to reach for a hand-me-down Thing (not seen as a changing set of more or less productive relations) called The State; to miss a whole epoch of active capitalist formation; and thus to expect The State to be an easy ally in a future non-capitalist project.

One encouragement to such reification or abstraction has been the age of the thing (set of relations) itself. England has an 'extraordinarily centralised monarchy'. Britain has been described as 'the oldest centrally organised state in Europe', 'a royal state unrivalled in its authority and efficiency throughout Western Europe'.[330]

> A national economy is a political space transformed by the State as a result of the necessities and innovations of economic life into a coherent, unified space whose combined activities may tend in the same direction. Only England managed this exploit at an early date.[331]

No matter whether it was ever finished, it was in 1279 that Edward I could begin a survey, the stated purpose of which was to settle questions of ownership once and for all:

> Commissioners in each county were instructed to list by name and have written down in books all villages and hamlets and every type of tenement whatsoever, whether of the rich or the poor, and whether royal or otherwise. ... No enquiry by any medieval government ever exceeded this one in scope or detail.[332]

Philip Corrigan has described successive 'long waves' in the formation of the modern English State from the thirteenth century onwards.

In his 1965 essay on 'The Peculiarities of the English' Edward Thompson used Marx's metaphor of a 'great arch' of bourgeois civilisation in England, in no way springing from industry alone: he invited us to think of that linguistic mess but coherent force in England, a rural bourgeoisie, in active dalliance with political power not just at 'moments' but over a whole epoch.[333]

The distinctively modern idea of the State as 'a form of public power separate from both the ruler and the ruled, and constituting the supreme political authority within a certain defined territory' emerged in England, when traced through language, in 1535.[334] Not surprisingly, such longevity has discouraged analysis and imagination from playing upon the object's past or future absence.

Since capitalism is all too often associated with industry rather than with agriculture or with finance, the old clothes that the English State possesses and delights in taking out whenever 'state occasion' offers an excuse may also serve to conceal its distinctively *capitalist* nature. The usual camouflage is the objective 'modern'. But 'this is an old European country': 'a substantial body of professionals who were directly employed by the state ... and whose vocational justification lay entirely in serving the state's needs, as opposed to [sic] private needs' has been noted before 1730.[335] As phrases about efficient government machines, homogeneous governing classes, 'improvement', and exceptionally revered states are pushed back to refer to the late- seventeenth and eighteenth centuries or before,[336] we have to keep pinching ourselves. This is the site of 'free' capitalism being talked about. This is England, not some Caesarist, State Socialist, Asiatic, Prussian, Other Country. For a long, long time, here, a particular state or form of state has been imbricated in freeing freedom for those who most call themselves and others 'free', including free labour and its freedom to 'move'. The attachment of Liberty to Property has depended upon a particular construction of the State. And it was so slow-cooked here that it can easily be *assumed*. Contrary to an ideological rather than historical view of Adam Smith – reinforced by neo-liberal ideologues in the Institute now bearing his name – his vision was underpinned by such a firm assumption.[337] So was the work of 'more modern capitalists':

> By the end of the Napoleonic Wars, the more modern capitalists in the towns had already achieved considerable strength on the basis of their economic achievements which, as modern historians now stress, had a long history behind them. Under the leadership of the landed classes, much of the road had been smoothed for them. The English capitalists in the nineteenth century did not have to rely on a Prussia and its Junkers to achieve national unity, tear down the internal barriers to trade, establish a uniform legal system, modern currency, and other prerequisites of industrialisation. The political order had been rationalised and a modern state created long before.[338]

Even when the definite article goes ('a modern state'), the adjective 'modern' can still obfuscate things (relations). Because essentials of the modern state *were* inherited or seen as 'granted' by post-Industrial Revolution policy leaders, there have been formidable pressures for Modern Socialists to take it for granted. Mists have surrounded it, as they do antiquity, suggestive of illusions like the following: the state played very little role in the making of 'private' capitalism anyway; the English state has been aristocratic and therefore less than fully capitalist; and the British state will evolve into something suitable for socialism organically, without deliberate class reconstruction or indeed much human agency.

Formidable work by historians with a global reach and a sense of capitalist crisis detectable from the early 1960s has been dispelling such mists. Immanuel Wallerstein traced 'the emergency of capitalism as a *political* [my emphasis] phenomenon' on a world scale:

> The sixteenth century witnessed the creation of a system of geopolitical states within whose borders production, consumption, and taxation occurred and economic and demographic phenomena played themselves out. ... In this sense, then, the emergence of the state was as important to the development of capitalism as the loans and advances of the bankers and traders were to the survival of the underfinanced, corruption-ridden states. ...The formation of nations legitimised, first, the survival and, later, the hegemony of the capitalist system.[339]

It did not need modern socialism to assert the primacy of politics. In a comparative study of 'The State and the Industrial Revolution' in 1973, the editor of the *Economic History Review*, Professor B.E. Supple, inclined to stress the role of 'the market' in England. Almost against himself, however, he came to a sharp theoretical understanding of the State:

> The state becomes an institutional device (perhaps the most important institutional device) by which groups seek to secure ends which, in other circumstances, they might conceivably secure by private means. ... And the important point to remember is that the state enters the arena of industrial development not as an arbitrary and unpredictable force, but as the agent of 'old' or 'new' forces or classes within

society, acting either in their own self interest or in pursuit of an ostensibly national purpose, within which their role can be rationalised. The state, like the entrepreneur, or the labour movement, is a social phenomenon.

In Britain's case, Supple conceded that 'the very characteristics of the market environment which distinguished Britain's position from that of other European countries' – for instance 'an unmatched degree of political stability and social harmony' – were 'in large part a function of state action'.[340] Such imbrication of capitalism in the state, it is now widely realised, puts the problem of *a* state – and therefore what kind of state – squarely back on English socialist laps. It requires us to try to break up old and comfortable structures of thought and organisation. This can be disturbing, whether done from the Left or the Right:

> To regard the state as a potentially (let alone necessarily) democratic form representing in some sense the public as against the private interests is to succumb to ... the 'fetishism of representation'. For if we recognise that capital from its inception always had two spheres of social economy – the market/private property (or commodity) economy on the one hand, and the levy bounty (largely state) economy on the other ... then it will be clear that the distinction between public and private is a distinction of two forms of capitalist economy ... the state is no more 'democratic' or 'representative' of the exploited classes than is I.C.I. – albeit that one represents itself as public and the other as private.[341]

Cut to 1984 and The Modern Leviathan

How much there is, in Britain, to go beyond! But what a lot there still is to go beyond with!

As an English representative at an Italian Socialist Party (PSI) historical conference on 'Trade Unions and the Working Class in the Second International' in Turin in 1981, I found myself being interviewed, towards the end of the event, by a correspondent from the Communist Daily, *Unita*. Like so many of its social democratic/ labour party equivalents in European and other nation-states, thirty-seven years later, the PSI scarcely exists as a serious political force.

The Conference had been disappointing. Not only was it about the Second International period, but it was enclosed within its categories. It was also lavish, feeling like a demonstration by the PSI that they too could put on prestige cultural events – just like the then Italian Communist Party. The journalist pressed me to criticise it. He had a Communist Party axe to grind. Wanting to criticise but not wanting to grind the same axe, I had little time to think. Rather than retreating into the specialist topic of the paper that I had brought to the conference, I came out spontaneously with something which met with blank incomprehension from him, as it would have done from any PSI people at the affair. I said that when we found ourselves discussing large forms as pregnant with possibilities of another epoch as things (relations) such as Medici banks had been in pre- and early capitalism, and debating their preliminary performance and future possibilities, we might be getting somewhere towards the goals we said we shared. I said that, maybe, trade unions (the subject of the Conference) were such forms, recalling Marx of 1866:

> Unconsciously to themselves, the trade unions were forming centres of organisation of the working class, as the medieval municipalities and communes did for the middle class ... they are ... important as organised agencies for superseding the very system of wage labour and capital rule.[342]

If so, they were certainly not being discussed in such a way. Where, I asked, were our 'organised agencies' with which, at such a conference, we might be comparing historical notes as to their roots, the opportunities and obstacles facing them? I asked him whether he thought that actually-existing Soviet socialisms were, or contained, such forms? Or the Italian Communist Party itself, in all its hugeness?

I did not know and nor, it was obvious, did he. All I did know, on reflection, was that I was thinking in these ways not spontaneously (as Sheila Rowbotham has it, 'spontaneity requires a lot of organising') but because of a whole spate of recent writing and practising in England which was re-presenting socialist politics. Attempts at theorising and practising (in the double sense of that word) 'the transition' were being made in new ways. Their specific gravity in the culture was greater than their actual size. Focusing on the details of the division between mental and manual labour, conception and execution, men and women; on *class* and *labour processes,* and on what a grounded socialist politics of complex co-operation might look like; on the politics of use values from labour's point of view, rather than on exchange value from capital's point of view; on the details of the *experience* of particular associational forms, their *stories* as recounted by themselves; on the meanings and possibililties of 'private' labour as opposed to 'private' capital; on restructuring by and for labour, going through society to the state ....All this was making it possible to ask questions about how to educate, agitate, and organise in new places and in new ways. The Robin Murray quotation on the state used above was part of all this, as was a whole cluster of initiatives stemming from a formation known as the New Left.

A renewal of thinking on *a* state, or *some* states (of affairs) in this specific context is central. If it is socialist to think in epochal terms – in terms of a future epoch other than barbarism, but as different from capitalism as capitalism's predecessors were – there are, to put it mildly, considerable transformations to make, or to discover. And in England there is a lot of State, as it were, to go beyond. What are or would be socialist forms of State: of commensuration, of private and public relations, of centralism, of locality, law, contract, history, production, making things (relations)? To think like this is to live, in England during the second decade of the twenty-first century, with a profound sense of defeat. I felt it painfully, through a rising sense of personal insignificance, as I put in writing the anecdote about the PSI conference used above.

England is, after all, the place where 1984 could be conceived as such, and not as a commentary only on Cold War communisms but also on advanced – even English – metropolitan capitalism. Winston Smith's nightmare has a very English location. It never was all about the Soviet Union. And we are now beginning to get a clear, conscious, articulation of the nature of the modern leviathan coming first from the Right – privatisation, the free market, globalisation and neo-liberalism – and, slowly cooking, from the Left.

The weight of *Our Island Story* (the history book by H.E. Marshall which was my own childhood introduction to the subject) has indeed been considerable, enough to get anyone stuck. If not as jagged as an alp on the brains of the living, it has at least the dull, depressing presence of a line of downs. In its national or Whig version, the story is presented with so much deliberate continuity that results tend to eclipse processes. How dissident it now is (all over again) to see 'our' (*The*) State as an association or union, to be dissolved and returned to its members (us) for reconstruction.

That was Tom Paine's vision, in his case of a 'people' or 'nation'. Against him, a pasteurised version of Edmund Burke has won the argument down to today, with the counter-revolution of his *Reflections*. Each generation, he proposes, is responsible not to itself but to a future buried in a past, to the dead and the unborn as well as to the living. 'The frame of our commonwealth *such as it stands*' is in trust to us, rather than our tool. 'The very idea of the fabrication of a new government is enough to fill us with disgust and horror.' In the name of such fear and novelty, the English State – and then the frozen details of its actual institutions – have been reified as part of 'the great primeval contract of eternal society'.[343] In such a permanent contract all breaches are to be hidden, past as well as future-possible. Partial truths and un-truths get told, as 'jubilant celebrations of English political continuity' and in big, imposing books. They include versions of the Norman conquest as restoration, and 1688 as an example of continuity rather than change. As late as the 1870s William Stubbs thought that the seventeenth century should not be taught to undergraduates: it was too close to contemporary politics. So myths appear on town hall walls, in Almanacks and in statues of Victoria and Albert dressed as Anglo-Saxons, as well as in the work of Eminent Historians.[344] The function of such elegant fibs has been to make the nineteenth-century 'transition to democracy' appear to retain – and to an important degree actually retain for 'the Englishman' – some continuity with 'His [sic] Past'.[345]

The mystifications have been profound. This English-man can still remember the satisfaction on the face of his Head of English, and the puzzlement in this thirteen-year-old brain, when the schoolmaster said two things in an 'English Literature' lesson. First that 'we', in 'our country', were fortunate enough to have no Constitution. Lesser nations had those. But secondly, the Monarchy was there to take over from the Commons if extremists threatened to win control. Twenty years later, in 1973, the Kilbrandon Report was the result of a body with the promising title of a Royal Commission on the Constitution. But it turned out to be about the technical and political consequences of different schemes of 'devolution'. The constitution, in the sense of the sovereign (Parliament) and 'the essential unity of the United Kingdom' remained as givens – an unquestionable inheritance. The State in the UK has been allowed to hide behind a sacrosanct Crown-in-Parliament ('Be it enacted by the Queen's most excellent Majesty, by and with the advice and consent of the Lords Spiritual and Temporal, and Commons'), and democracy hides behind 'Parliamentary democracy as we know it'.[346] As Seeley complained in *The Expansion of England* (1883), 'the temptation of our historians is always to write the history rather of Parliament than of the State and the Nation'.[347] And as Nevil Johnson found when he went *In Search of the Constitution*, almost a century later, 'there is probably no other country in which Parliament occupies such a special place in the political structure and in the language of politics'. 'There are many in Britain who profess to believe that only the British Parliament is a genuine species of the genus "Parliament" ... the English often refer to Parliament when other people might talk of the law, or the people, or the State.' More recently the Government 'of the day', like the Emperor in the Hans Andersen story, tries to put on the fine robes of the state ('from time immemorial'), and few subjects now dare to laugh in the streets.

The English revolution now gets seen as a 'settlement', adequate for 'Englishmen'. Thus *The Times* in 1979:

> the difference so stubbornly insisted upon in Ulster concerns the most fundamental of all political issues: allegiance, national identity, the legitimacy of the State, matters which Englishmen had settled for themselves by the end of the seventeenth century.[348]

Historians of the extraordinary rupture in human history represented by the 'modern' (capitalist) world also now emphasise that, in the English as in so many revolutions, what came after was cousin to what went before. In his brilliant *Lineages of the Absolutist State* (1974), Perry Anderson knew what 'deep and radical reversal' of the most characteristic traits of prior feudal development 'there was in the transition to the capitalist epoch' in England. But he also showed how 'a centralised monarchy ... produced a unified assembly'.[349] The degree of centralisation which exists in the English and British polity is now widely recognised – and firmly insisted on from its centre against all comers, and against strongly surviving myths of localism. An Act of Parliament which subtracted planning powers from local people and locally elected Authorities was passed into law by a Coalition government in 2011 and called – in Orwell-speak – the Localities Act. Jokes against the French centralised educational system look less funny in England in 2018. A centralised state emerged in the modern era in Britain, even allowing for 'devolution', in which the omnicompetence of the sovereign (Parliament) was to become as clear an impediment to constellations of popular power as the divine right of kings had been:

> The sovereignty of the British state is not in the British people as in most electoral democracies but in this special definition of 'Crown in Parliament.' British adults are not citizens but, legally, *subjects*, in that old term derived from absolute monarchy.... in terms of the actual constitution it may not be the House of Lords but the House of Commons that is anomalous.[350]

Parliament is not, of course, omnicompetent. Without referring to it, as William Morris did, as the Westminster dungmarket, it is widely felt not to be very competent.

That is not the point. The point is that its alleged writ runs everywhere. Every other Board, Nation, Public Corporation, Authority, local government unit, union, civil servant, branch of the judiciary derives its authority from it in the end, and sometimes disturbingly near to the beginning, And not even from it (Parliament). Lines of power called 'responsibility' go direct to Ministers, whose authority is in turn subordinate more and more to the Prime Minister.[351] Nevil Johnson found Ministerial Responsibility to be one of the main sources of what he saw as uniquely British centralisation. Personal rule prevents other clusters of (constitutional) legitimacy, and Ministers get very hot under the collar about 'the British constitution' when they feel it might be being usurped. For a Secretary of State for Defence to appear on television face-to-face with the leader of the Campaign for Nuclear Disarmament was seen as 'unconstitutional' by Michael Heseltine in 1983. It took a German king of England, George II, to grasp the realities here. He once murmured to Lord Chancellor Hardwicke, 'Ministers are Kings in this country'. 'That' observed Nevil Johnson (by no means a left-winger), 'is the core of it all.' 'Furthermore', he went on, 'Britain is distinguished from most other comparable societies by having no genuine concept of public law, and thus no proper public law structure which defines powers and by so doing creates barriers.'[352]

Politics (and with it 'Democracy') as part of all this has been increasingly confined to licensed, dominant, official forms thereof: to forms of association which legally cannot or do not threaten to take away their legitimacy. Forms of delegation and direct democracy which have been elementary components of English, voluntary, working-class, liberal practice for two hundred years get pilloried as populist interference with the rights of representatives – even as 'Stalinist'. They become the cause of seismic splits within the culture, breaking apart the Labour Party. One major cause of the Social Democratic Party rift was precisely these issues, in a tragi-comedy of Shirley Williams saying 'Burke' to imaginary Paines. There was an uncanny anticipation of such splits in February 1906 in the report of a Special Committee of the Fabian Society 'appointed to consider measures for increasing the scope, income and activity of the Society'. I have already quoted this in 'The Three Socialisms', but it is worth citing once more:

> Democracy is a word with a double meaning. To the bulk of trade unionists and labourers it means an intense jealousy and mistrust of authority, and a resolute reduction of both representatives and officials to the position of mere delegates, mouthpieces and agents of the majority. From this point, Democracy would find its consummation in a House of Commons where, without any discussion, divisions were taken by counting postcards received from the entire population on questions submitted to the people by referendum and initiative.
>
> Because the Fabians have given no countenance to this attitude they have been freely denounced as undemocratic and even Tory. Fabian democracy is in fact strongly opposed to it and certain to come into conflict with it at almost every step in the practical development of socialism. We have always accepted government by a representative deliberating body controlling an expert bureaucracy as the appropriate public organisation for Socialism. When asked where government by the people comes in, we reply that Government has to be carried out by division of labour and specialisation as much as railway management has; and what Democracy really means is government by the consent of the people ...

Between these two conceptions of the elected person as representative doing the best he can according to his own judgement after full discussion with other representatives of all shades of opinion, and as a mere delegate carrying out previous instructions from the majority of his constituents, there is a gulf which will sooner or later become a party boundary, and this gulf unfortunately cuts the Labour Movement right down the middle.[353]

In a long crisis of democratic theory and practice, 'representation' in the sense of 'making present in continuing and interactive ways those who are ... represented' has given way to other, more professional, managerial, expert, and symbolic senses of the word.[354] Burkean notions of the autonomy and 'freedom' due to an elected representative have been used to hide scepticism about popular, democratic representation as such: 'making present in continuing and interactive ways those who are represented'. Political re-formation – 'the fabrication of a new government' – in any 'from below' way gets classified as dissident, revolutionary, subversive, illegal, terrorist ... the use of industrial, educational, broadcasting or wider cultural power for political ends. In 'democratic' theory as well as in practice in twenty-first century Britain, the citizens have become the governed. Herbert Morrison's *Parliamentary Government in Britain* (1949) was unashamed to describe 'How Britain is governed' rather than how British people might, with a Labour government with an enormous majority, learn to govern themselves. People, they, we ... have become consumers rather than producers of 'policies' displayed intermittently as four-yearly 'packages' in a political market place to which only well-funded suppliers have the resources necessary for effective access. Democracy becomes a set of actually existing institutions to be defended – if necessary at the cost of killing everyone in a catastrophic war – rather than a process or struggle with a future. 'Parliamentary' as a qualifier for 'democracy' is now 'in effect an excluding adjective to indicate that there is only one real kind of democracy, which operates through the procedures of a parliament'.[355] So, from the Right we get diagnostic phrases like 'elected dictatorship' and from the Left the 'election of a Court'.[356]

If it has now become clear how many spaces have been closed down, the extent to which parts of 'the Left' have been an agent in their closure has also become uncomfortably visible. This will be a major theme in the remainder of this essay. To anticipate, the Labour Party in particular may be seen as party to this process of closure. During the twentieth century the Party has almost entirely retreated from civil society, and from organising 'private labour'. Unions are its sources of funds but also, from the leadership's point of view, its main (electoral) embarrassment. Autonomous action by unions (or even by Regions, or Scottish, Welsh, or Irish nations) is seen as a problem or threat. The Labour Party has ignored Co-ops, Friendly Societies, Clubs, and other associations OF or FOR Labour for too long, leaving them in the warehouse until they go rotten. Even its own movement or party or constituency is seen as problem rather than as opportunity. 'Voluntary action' has been seen by the Party as a contrast to its Politics, rather than a component of them. And in the public, political sphere the Party chose very early on to conform to actually existing, dominant forms of Politics. Keir Hardie was open about it, in his advice to the ILP in 1901. Their party, he urged, 'aimed at becoming a great political power in the land'. 'To enable it to do so it must conform as nearly as possible to the political institutions already in existence with which the public mind is familiar.'[357]

PART III SOCIALISM, THE STATE, AND SOME OPPOSITIONAL ENGLISHNESS

To complicate the story once more, it is important not to moralise any of this. Large constraints – systematic determinations – are involved, going way beyond ideology, intention, or simple condemnation by socialists like me. As a result of developments beyond Labour's control, the most available choice to Labour *has* been to conform. It is through such delicate, agonised, tactical conformity (including electoral pacts, accepting minority power, and then the role of His Majesty's opposition, and attempting to become 'the natural party of Government') that the Party has built up its strength. It has indeed become a precondition for one kind of success (electoral, official, legitimate) of Labour Politics that it should accept such confinement. And the rewards have been considerable. The Party *has* governed, better than other Parties. Through the existing State it *has* 'delivered' (the word is much used and well chosen) necessary reforms to working people. These have included securities of many tangible kinds: job protection; welfare; health away from work; health and safety at work; growing awareness of gendered and race-related inequalities; teeth and spectacles; council housing; commitment to (now much disdained) universal human rights and political correctness; independence from empire; 'national' responsibility for key industries; the possibility of 'popular planning' as well as planning from above; statutory minimum wages … such a list could go on. Sweated trades would never have retreated spontaneously, and, to the extent that Labour is weakened, such trades and ways of working – the precariat, zero-hours contracts etc. – will (are) advancing all over again.

But, but … for some time now it has been a difficult argument to mount within the dominant forms of Labour *and* socialist politics that it is the *forms* of State and politics that must be challenged before 'policies' have any hope of being fought for in a sustained way, and by the people in whose interests the policies have been formulated. To argue for political *forms* rather than *policies* is to sound obscurantist. But *who does what* will have to have as much to do with the agency of 'ordinary people' as *what is to be done*. During the second half of the nineteenth century, Liberals went further in challenging emergent forms of capitalist politics than Labour has done since then. They worried about representation, party machines (including the details of canvassing), politics and the manufacturing of opinion more than twentieth-century Labour has done. Defeat can easily feed despair: a sense of loss of the future, once falsely guaranteed by attaching an evolutionary idea of Progress to socialism, can easily contribute to a sense of loss of *any* future. As sub-nations within the United Kingdom have been outmanoeuvred in the last two decades, and then sub-state associations for labour like trade unions, and then sub-national units of ('local') government, it does seem tempting to conclude that we have entered the New Leviathan's cage. Is it all we can do to regret, with Nevil Johnson, 'the absence of any alternative tradition of how to constitute political authority'?[358]

Yeast was in that dough

To recall that futures other than that hugely dominant present have been available within the English past is the historian's special opportunity. 'Nor should you', as Brecht advised, 'let the Now blot out the Previously and afterwards.'

'Such a peculiar mixture of yeast and dough,' remarked John Fowles of the English middle class in *The French Lieutenant's Woman*, 'we tend nowadays to forget that it has always been the great revolutionary class; we see much more the doughy aspect.' What was the quality of the yeast? How available has it been, and is it still there for other baking projects, other class projects?

It is striking how much material which could be integral to socialist construction was already here in England long before Modern Socialism, within and against capitalism.

More generally

To follow such an assertion through, even at a high level of generality, is not easy. This is because *contradiction* is involved – back again to Engels' exasperation at a 'contradictory state of affairs' in England. There have been long moments in this country replete with what E.P. Thompson called 'co-existent opposed possibilities'. Contradiction is always hard to represent at any level of generality. To realise and to articulate contradictions is to look for the spaces within which they move, rather than to get impatient and simply negate or 'abolish' them. In *Capital* volume 1 Marx made this *historical* point with great clarity. He used the form of an ellipse as his metaphorical ground:

> The exchange of commodities implies contradictory and mutually exclusive conditions. The further development of the commodity does not abolish these contradictions, but rather provides the form within which they have room to move. This is, in general, the way in which real contradictions are resolved. For instance, it is a contradiction to depict one body as constantly falling toward another and at the same time constantly flying away from it. The ellipse is a form of motion within which this contradiction is both realized and resolved. [359]

In much of the best writing about the transition to modernity/capitalism in England there is this sense of articulated contradiction, of dialectic, of *not-only-but-also* rather than *either/or*. There is a sense of long construction, long revolution, and of one social formation depending on, but capable of emerging as an entirety through and from, another (antagonistic and therefore threatened) formation. There is a sense of prolonged and intermittently violent, epochal change rather than all-at-once, at a stroke, revolution. Capitalism is a dynamic system which discloses (and depends for its dynamism upon disclosing) possible successors, especially, perhaps, in its early moments: and the more prolonged its 'rise' (as in *Religion and the Rise of Capitalism*) the longer the disclosure of latent successors. As capitalism turns the world upside down, for however brief a period before restabilisation, its underside is exposed, its 'prostitute realities laid bare' in Marx's way of putting it. Paths are cut, then quickly overgrown for things (relations) to turn again whoever, by then, may be on top. It is, as the saying goes, a topsy-turvy world. To the extent that capitalism depends upon breaking relatively simple, customary relations of power, of inherited domination and subordination, it offers the possibility of displacing its first beneficiaries or owners – which is why from very early on, but latterly with more viciousness and haste, STOP signs, for counter-revolution, are (have to be) put up. From the point of view of the security of the existing holders of wealth and power, many people (the many not the few) need to be discouraged from taking too many of capitalism's promises too seriously. It is the burden of the existing holders of wealth and power that each of the vehicles they use to clear their own steep and rugged pathway can (must? anyway, in England *did*) carry other, antagonistic social possibilities. The very idea of a 'transition' to socialism as something (some relations) to have different ideas about – to have debates in the labour movement about – comes, in idea and in fact, from the transition to capitalism from previous modes. It is this earlier transition which 'must constitute not only some part of what we think and feel about but also some part of what we think and feel with'. Law, reason, 'freedom' all promise to go beyond exclusivity, from the few to the many. The commodity as the 'first citizen of the world' constantly threatens to walk out, beyond nations, states, and individual owners – and to become available for socialising in new ways. Alienable 'private' property, 'freely' disposable, is volatile. However often the adjectives 'bourgeois' or 'middle class' are thrown at 'democracy', that noun is never completely obscured. 'Democracy' always seems capable of escaping its existing limitations. Falling into excluded hands, it remains capable of transformation, being enlarged or realised more fully.

The possibility of desirables – 'goods' in both senses of that word – being made more public or even universally available is inscribed in their enclosure or privacy. Indeed, in the hands of the bourgeoisie or middle class on its long, English march, these goods characteristically promise, at times, in the end – in that much favoured capitalist distance, the long run – to include everyone, to become universal. And the *dimensions* (social length, depth, and width) of capitalist construction here, in England, made this double-edgedness doubly evident. The moments of co-existent opposed possibilities here in England have been many and long. The bourgeoisie, as it were, hung their goods out for all to get a good look at, use – ' yes, we'll have a bit of that' – and see beyond. Much which elsewhere in the world, and well into the twentieth century, had to be produced, hothouse fashion, by post-capitalist regimes, already had deep outdoor roots in England by the late nineteenth century, the era of Modern Socialism. Much which, in Other Countries, had to be produced by socialist regimes could, here, have been socialism's tools, useable as its inheritance.

This includes some of the ingredients of *any* revolutionary State. These were present very early in England, for example *class* and class struggle. According to one authority at least, there was a *class* of capitalist farmers in England by the end of the sixteenth century.[360] To use a colloquialism, a class is a grouping capable of getting its act together: materially able at least to *attempt* to construct or to defend ways of making things (relations) which can inform a whole social formation and thus produce (make) a 'society' – most likely anticipated in prefigurative cells or Co-operative and other Societies. Without such capacity, construction in and against (but also beyond) one whole society – mode of production – towards another is inconceivable. Class projects are articulated against other social groups or classes, and in England bourgeois class formation/struggle took place in a long social movement, its own great arch, constructed in and against a manifestly archaic, predecessor regime.

The particular forms of state, here, meant that it could seem – and to an extent actually be – quite local, with political representation by place as well as by social layer: local justice, the magistracy and the jury, for example, being voluntary. There was centralisation and coherence, but without some of the things (relations) which went with it in other places. A strong standing army was missing. So was a royal absolutism possessing, at least for any length of time, a taxation base independent of Parliament. So was a ruling bureaucracy 'under which the instruments of public power became exercisable in a uniform way'.[361] It was the concentration of sovereignty *and* its dispersal through real, located, agents – in a material unity of opposites – which made it effective and made it cohere. A degree of self-administration in the counties was a medium for effective royal power even in feudal England, before the much-vaunted JPs of the early-modern epoch.[362] One of J.H. Plumb's themes in his influential 1966 Ford Lectures was, precisely, the realisation (rather than the abolition) of contradictions between accumulations of local power and central authority. Either could have broken apart from the other or never formed a part of the same field-of-force. This would have made for a very different subsequent English (and thus British and thus world) modern history.[363]

Clusters of initiative, independence, enterprise ('capital') found room to accumulate but also found, quite literally, canals to join them. England already formed 'something like a single internal market' by the late seventeenth century.[364] Like all markets, this implied coherence, but also diversity: activity could be diffuse because it was also integrated. Clusters of activity grew in the Country away from but related to the Court, forming 'Civil Society' separable from but defined in relation to a State. 'Civil society as such develops only with the bourgeoisie': *bürgerliche Gesellschaft* stands for both the bourgeoisie *qua* class and civil *qua* society. But precisely because it (civil society) 'transcends the state and nation' and 'embraces the whole material intercourse of individuals within a definite state of the development of productive forces',[365] it is a concourse for change. 'Private spheres' winning 'an independent existence' and, from a relatively autonomous space constructing novel (ellipse-shaped) forms of private–public relation(ships), cut a fundamental, progressive passage through human history:

> The political constitution is brought into being only where the private spheres have won an independent existence. Where trade and landed property are not free and have not yet become independent, the political constitution too does not yet exist. [366]

'Independence' may be understood materially. It may thus be understood as having to do with things like means for the production of association and political constitution, ways of making new things and relations, including associational forms for enjoyment, leisure, education, distribution, and exchange. Understood in this way, the potential of 'independence' for giving meaning to 'private labour' as well as for more manifest 'private capital' becomes clearer – more available to the many as well as the few. As Michael Walzer traced in *The Revolution of the Saints* (1965), it was indeed a revolutionary step to construct and associate in the interstices of one social formation in such a way as to necessitate, to enable, and even to plan another formation, in and leading beyond capitalism.

The contradictions become difficult to describe clearly because, as capitalism develops, the lines of future-possible victory for *any* emergent social formation run closer and closer to the lines of defeat by the dominant host. What constitutes success and what seems like failure, or rather *whose* is the success and whose the failure at any one moment, gets harder and harder to distinguish. As rival modes of production (ways of making things and more, or less, social relations) develop, victory and defeat take place more and more through the same instruments and in the same spaces; for example, through the spaces and instruments in and around 'the State', 'based on the contradiction between *public* and *private* life, on the contradiction between *general interests* and *private interests*'.[367] State regulation of the hours of labour in nineteenth-century England, for example (Factory Acts were the subject of the longest chapter in Marx's *Capital* volume I), was at one and the same time helpful to large-scale industry *and* a germ of future-possible socialisation of capital on labour's terms. A reform which was functional for large-scale capitals was also exciting to Marx as the first clear victory of the political economy of labour over that of capital. 'What a great change from that time!' The magic formula 'after the revolution', as used by socialists, wishfully thinks and anticipates that all such contradictions will wither away for socialists. 'The English factory workers were the champions not only of the English working class, but of the modern working class in general, just as their theorists were the first to throw down the gauntlet to the theory of the capitalist.' 'Since the contest takes place in the arena of modern industry, it is fought out first of all in the homeland of that industry – England.'[368]

By the mid-nineteenth century in England, historical materialism could be forged, from facts as well as epistemological breaks, from emergent relations as well as theoretical imaginations. It could be forged among the mills of industrial capitalism in the 'shock city' of a major moment in capitalist development: Manchester. And it could be forged with and *about* something, some actually-existing as well as future-possible relations. Not only about how capitalism worked as viewed from outside or from above – explanations of its mechanisms with 'here cause, there effect' – but also about how, materially, it could/would change, be transformed from within, through lots of (working) people's own consciousness and practices.

Engels' exasperation at the peculiarities of the English, expressed during the 1890s, has already been quoted. Fifty years before that, in the period immediately following his first visit late in 1842, those same peculiarities had excited Engels and educated him greatly, and through him Marx. Engels was much clearer about England in the mid-1840s than he became by the 1890s. In 1977, in an essay on 'Engels and the Genesis of Marxism', Gareth Stedman Jones traced Engels' openness to and transmission of crucial raw materials for the theorising of historical materialism between 1842 and 1845-6.[369] From Manchester, Engels learned of the possible primacy of real social (class) movements rather than abstract 'principles' in the making of a new epoch. He learned of the strength of 'interests' over against ideals/ideologies, and he learned just how far actually existing changes in industry were *already going on* in England:

> The importance of Engels' contribution derived less from this moment of theoretical originality than from his ability to transmit elements of thinking and practice developed within the working class movement itself in a form in which it could be an intrinsic part of the architecture of the new theory.

How much which is integral to socialist construction was already happening, in England, long before Modern Socialism, in and against capitalism!

Less abstractly
As an early British Socialist said, 'the use of abstract, as of general terms, without explanation or limitation, and of similar mystifying, is one of the means employed to delude labourers and hide from them their interest'.[370] It might be helpful to be a little less general.

Listen, first, to a very un-deluded mid-eighteenth-century dock worker. *Lloyd's Evening Post* for 18–21 July 1760 reported the following *Dialogue between an Artificer in a dockyard and those who required his vote in the next election for Kent*:

> *Officer:* We are come, expecting your vote for Sir William, in the room of Mr. W..., made a Lord... The Government espouses Sir William, and you are a Freeholder.
> *Artificer:* I am so, but must think myself at liberty to vote as I please.
> *Officer:* As you please! Very fancy, truly; don't the Government employ and pay you?
> *Artificer:* Yes, and I honour the Government, know my

business, and earn my pay with diligence and honesty.
Officer: But are you not under their power, and obliged to do as they please?
Artificer: Yes, as an Artificer, but not as a Freeholder ... I am, as an Englishman, at liberty to chuse my representative.
Officer: And the Government to turn you out of your bread.
Artificer: Not so indeed. I do my duty as they expect, and this is a case where they can have no just reason for resentment ...
Officer: We did not expect this obstinacy; and to prevent its spreading, we will report it, so you have warning.
Artificer: I will be as early as I can in reporting it myself, and am glad, Gentlemen, this is all the ill report you can make of me.[371]

Our nameless Artificer worked in the national (royal) dockyards. Before the factory system these were the largest units of industrial organisation, indeed 'larger than anything seen in Europe since the fall of Rome'.[372] As often with such exceptionally large capitals, they were nationalised. Working in such a place, the Artificer had relative job security. Shipwrights around him had begun to associate, for themselves. A society or union had started, not as a trade union in the modern sense (though a union of tradesmen) but as a co-operative society.[373] Production on their own account had commenced, with a bakery at Chatham, a butcher's shop in Deptford, and a cornmill in Woolwich. The Red Flag had been hoisted near the mill. Attempts were made by antagonists of the shipwrights to drive such associations out by law. These failed. Then one Sunday night the mill was mysteriously burned down.

What the Artificer was doing in the reported dialogue was to insist 'as an Englishman' that the historic bourgeois achievement of making the economic relatively autonomous from the 'political', and in that sense 'free', could work towards his independence – and that of his fellow 'freeholders' – rather than his subordination. The historic achievement, as we can see it now, was still work very much in progress in 1760. It was not a finished result. But our Artificer was taking 'freedom' seriously. It would be a long time – a whole epoch in fact – before, if ever, the economic and the political could be reunited in the interests of everyone equally. Meanwhile, the Artificer implied, 'me too' or 'us too', as far as public–private relations were concerned. To put it another way, he was insisting on some autonomy for himself in a public sphere. Furthermore, 'as an Englishman' and because of England's history, he was confident that his liberty to choose was legitimate: 'I will be as early as I can in reporting it myself.' Being in a waged sense a state servant did not, he thought, imply that 'the Government' owned him. He and his co-workers had private spaces to associate on their own account, to make their own Societies. And their particular associational forms, as the lawsuits and arson showed, were, to put it mildly, not identical to the capitalist ones around. Were they to be extended, they might even reconstitute the existing 'public' altogether. But they were, our English Artificer thought, legitimate.

A generation later, in 1796, another artificer – a Shoreditch silversmith called John Baxter – published an 830-page *New and Impartial History of England*. Those were dangerous times for Radicals, members of Corresponding Societies like Baxter: they were days of vigorous, vicious reaction. Baxter himself became a fellow prisoner with Thomas Hardy during the treason trials of the time. Baxter's book was a kind of *samizdat* claiming specifically English rights to resistance or subversion, rights which reached back to the Saxons. From a shared store of language, myth, and precedent he reached back in time in order to make going forward legitimate. That there was a shared store is the point. 'Baxter's "Saxons"', E.P.

Thompson suggested, 'were Jacobins and sans culottes to a man. "Pristine purity" and "our own ancestors" became, for many such Jacobins, almost any constitutional innovation for which a Saxon precedent could be vamped up.'[374] The *New and Impartial History* worked with the idea of an original English Constitution subverted by foreign conquest, partly restored at various times, including 1688, but with much 'restoration', which could amount to revolution in the eyes of its enemies, still to be done.

Plebeian radicalism, fecund as it was in ideas and associational forms, claimed Englishness, English history, the English constitution, the nation, and (a key word) 'patriotism' for itself and its class, over against usurping, parasitic Governments. 'The People' (another key formulation) claimed to have English history and the English constitution on their side. One climax in this history was the Chartist Convention of 1839. The idea of a constitutional Convention was one among a wide array of means of popular political production available in England. They included the Address, the County Meeting, the Petition, as well as the unstamped press, the election platform, and, on occasion, the pulpit. Of them all, forms of association and 'combination' have probably been the most strongly contested, through to today. The 1839 Chartist Convention was assembled to present one of the old Constitutional devices, the Petition, but in a modern, mass, form, to Parliament, on behalf of political reform. The idea among some Chartists was to meet Parliament's anticipated rejection of their Petition by proceeding to measures ulterior to merely political reform. They were to move on to the fundamental business of a Convention, namely constitution making. Ulterior Measures were to be adopted. Material support was to be withdrawn from the existing system, to weaken it and to enable working-class independence.[375]

An Englishman did not have to be a Socialist or a Chartist to be fanatical about the details of self-government. In the years after 1845 Joshua Toulmin Smith (1816–1869), for instance, took up a sustained and scholarly struggle against utilitarian, Chadwickian 'improvement' and centralisation. He took care to distance himself from the Six Points of the Charter. But he was a dedicated opponent of what he saw as an emergent system of 'Functionarism and Bureaucratic control'. The main enemy, as Toulmin saw it, was a collectivism which 'would in fact put the whole earth in commission and deliver over the whole human race saved from the flood to "Inspectors" and "Assistant Commissioners"'. His 'improving' enemies were uncomfortably like some state systems constructed by Modern Socialists.[376]

To see Toulmin Smith's observations as 'early' would be to adopt a familiar way of marginalising them. It would be to suggest that, for serious oppositional purposes, they had to be superseded, and that a definitive 'break' had to be made with this pre-scientific, English stuff, a break often seen as epistemological and awaiting Marxism as a new science, an -ism foretelling the abolition of historical contradiction once and for all, rather than re-presenting or *realising* plural, historical contradictions.

Marx himself went on working for the rest of his life with the grain of residual as well as emergent facts and movements in English capitalism, as well as in capitalism as *system*. Not only but also, his work had, perforce, to brush *against* the grain of other, dominant facts and movements. But there was plenty to work with. 'Only in England', Engels argued, during the 1840s, 'have individuals as such, without consciously standing for universal principles, furthered national development and brought it near to its conclusion. Only here have the masses acted as masses, for the sake of their interests as individuals; only here have principles been turned into interests before they are able to influence history.' 'The democracy towards which England is moving is a *social* democracy':

> The English, a nation that is a mixture of German and French elements who therefore embody both sides of the antithesis and are for that reason more universal than either of the two factors (German philosophy, French politics) taken separately, were for that reason drawn into a more universal, a social revolution.[377]

In the developing work of Marx and Engels throughout the next three decades there was a powerful sense of how materially possible it was becoming to alter relations, to endow them with *social* possibilities in the sense of a sequence developing from a moral economy, to a political economy, to a social economy. In *Capital* volume 1(1867) the emergence of large-scale industry is traced and analysed, in a sequence running from simple co-operation, through to handicraft, manufacture, and thence to machine production. Large-scale industry is seen as a fully or adequately capitalist form of modern production, in which labour is newly divided from the means of production which now include science or knowledge. In that sense labour becomes really, or materially, subordinate to capital. In the new relations of production,

> The co-operation of wage-labourers is entirely brought about by the capital that employs them. Their unification into one single productive body, and the establishment of a connection between their individual functions, lies outside their competence. These things are not their own act, but the act of the capital that brings them together and maintains

them in that situation. Hence the interconnection between their various labours confronts them, in the realm of ideas, as a plan drawn up by the capitalist, and in practice, as his authority, as the powerful will of a being outside them, who subjects their activity to his purpose.[378]

In and against such developments, however, there was also the material promise of labour's ultimate 'education' or emancipation.[379] In *Capital* volume I, based as it was on his observation of developments in England, Marx described the

> protracted and more or less concealed civil war between the capitalist class and the working class. Since the contest takes place in the arena of modern industry, it is fought out first of all in the homeland of that industry – England. The English factory workers were the champions, not only of the English working class, but of the modern working class in general, just as their theorists were the first to throw down the gauntlet to the theory of the capitalists.[380]

Factory legislation was functional to capital, giving advantage to large capitals in their quest for relative surplus value. It did no harm to productivity, or to the quest for relative surplus value. But in its later forms it was also more than a nominal concession won by labour. In 1864, indeed, Marx referred to the Ten Hours Bill as 'the first time that in broad daylight the political economy of the middle class succumbed to the political economy of the working class'. 'An all-powerful social barrier by which they can be prevented from selling themselves and their families into slavery and death by voluntary contract with capital' had been erected. It may have been a 'modest Magna Carta', but 'What a great change from that time!'[381] How excited was Marx with the potential of a class in the act of coming together! As we saw earlier with the unions:

> Unconsciously to themselves the trade unions were forming *centres of organisation* [Marx's italics] of the working class, as the medieval municipalities and communes did for the middle class. If the trade unions are required for the guerrilla fights between capital and labour, they are still more important as organized agencies for superseding the very system of wage labour and capital rule.[382]

Writing in 1864, Marx was also excited by the possibilities of the co-operative movement. He thought that the seeds of this movement had been sown in England by Robert Owen. The movement – co-operative forms of production, distribution, and exchange – would get nowhere if 'kept within the narrow circle of the casual efforts of private workmen'. It needed to aggregate, becoming national as well as political. For Marx this never meant an eclipse of the private and economic by the public and the political. The revolutionary project is to hold the two together, to reconstruct them both. The third of the Provisional Rules of the International, drafted by Marx, read: 'that the economical emancipation of the working-class is therefore the great end to which every political movement ought to be subordinate as a means'. The 'value of these great social experiments cannot be overrated':

> By deed, instead of by argument, they have shown that production on a large scale, and in accord with the behests of modern science, may be carried on without the existence of a class of masters employing a class of hands; that to bear fruit, the means of labour need not be monopolised as a means of dominion over, and of extortion against the labouring man

himself; and that, like slave labour, like serf labour, hired labour is but a transitory form, destined to disappear before associated labour plying its toil with a willing hand, a ready mind, and a joyous heart.[383]

In a footnote to *Capital* volume I, Marx played with the 'philistine English periodical, the Spectator' in its reaction to 'the Rochdale co-operative experiments'. 'They showed that associations of workmen could manage shops, mills, and almost all forms of industry with success, and they immediately improved the condition of the men but they did not leave a clear place for masters. Quelle horreur!'[384] In *Capital* volume III, Marx pointed forward to how 'a new mode of production naturally grows out of an old one'. Socialisation of capital on capital's terms, as in forms of joint stock enterprise and associations for credit, had pointed to the possibility of transitional forms of socialisation on labour's terms. These could be 'transitional forms from the capitalist mode of production to the associated one'.[385]

Marx knew of the formidable class resistances there already were, and would be in the future, to seeing such contradictory forces and relations of production in and beyond capitalism *as* contradictions: Thompson's 'moments of co-existent opposed possibilities'. 'The vulgus is unable to conceive the forms developed in the lap of capitalist character.'[386] Particularly when it was working people acting for themselves, all kinds of denials happened:

> It is a strange fact. In spite of all the tall talk and all the immense literature for the last sixty years, about the emancipation of labour, no sooner do the working men anywhere take the subject into their own hands with a will, than up rises at once all the apologetic phraseology of the mouthpieces of present

society with its two poles of capital and wage slavery...as if capitalist society was still in its purest state of virgin innocence, with its antagonism still undeveloped, with its delusions still unexploded, with its prostitute realities not yet laid bare.[387]

How much yeast there was, for Marx, in that dough!

Working people in England took a wide range of subjects into their own hands during the second half of the nineteenth century, and on a considerable scale. 'Union' had long been a keyword for labour, perhaps as a response to advocates of the 'division' of labour from Adam Smith and Andrew Ure onwards. *Trades* Unions grew in episodic waves during the nineteenth century, reaching majority status among employed working people after World War I. It was not until after about 1850 that the word 'union', attached to working-class forms and activities, became as firmly attached as it now is to *trades* union forms and activities.[388] Other forms of union or association were equally salient. At first under middle-class, financial, and 'vice-presidential' patronage – 'realising' rather than abolishing all the tensions and contradictions which went with that – large-scale Unions (like the Co-operative Union and the Club and Institute Union) found ways of casting off the patronage. 'Independence' was the goal. One of the ways of articulating class 'freedom', an associational route to independence was to go *national* through affiliated and federal forms. Another way was to collect small, affordable sums from very large numbers of people, spreading the risk in order to construct *continuous* associations, rather than intermittent or merely local forms. Advocates of co-operative association also pressed for political change through Industrial and Provident Society legislation, at the level of the State. It is in productive activity that we should look for working-class culture in nineteenth-century England, rather than in more traditional cultural artefacts. 'Going into

Union', as in the Congregational Union of England and Wales, the Baptist Union, and the Union of Free Churches, was a way of federating fiercely independent, earlier sectarian forms. But so too were the Trades Union *Congress*, the Working Men's Club and Institute Union, and the Co-operative Union. The largest Friendly Society federations opted for the language of 'Ancient Orders', for example of Foresters, or 'Unities', as in the Manchester Unity of Oddfellows.

Some contemporaries were mightily impressed, almost against themselves. A visiting Austrian, J.M. Baernreither, studied the culture in some detail. He thought it constituted a 'revolution'. 'It would be an entire error', he argued, 'to suppose that the English workman does not extend his thought to the distant future, or picture to himself one very different from today; but in his acts and conduct he reckons with present facts, and he employs the freedom of movement which he enjoys without limit in his associations, to obtain one thing after another.' Baernreither called it 'the social self-government of the working classes in England'. 'We must not forget that all these associations have become the governing centre for the various branches of social administration which they manage, and that the influence they exercise on the relations of wages, the system of insurance, the food-supply, and the intellectual training and education of the working class collectively, extends far beyond the association itself, and benefits also those who are outside it.'

> England is at present the theatre of a gigantic development of associated life, which gives to her labour, her education, her social intercourse, nay, to the entire development of her culture, a pronounced direction, a decisive stamp. The tendency towards the union of forces and the working of this union are now-a-days more powerful in England than ever, and more

powerful than anywhere else. The free union of individuals for the attainment of a common object is the great psychological fact in the life of this people, its great characteristic feature. This union of individual forces has operated even there, where adverse relations have sought to restrain it; but now, freed from all fetters, and yet at the same time under discipline, it has become a mighty moving wheel of social development in general, and especially in the elevation of the working classes. Since the repeal of the laws prohibiting Combinations (1824), which has been the turning-point in the history of the English working class, the working-men's associations have gained immensely in importance; they have become more organized, more enlightened, more firmly established. The power of union, the capacity of submitting to the lead of others, the pertinacity and energy which they display in the pursuit of fixed aims, are amazing. In the course of the last decade these associations have become more and more differentiated, according to their various objects, and are now well-defined, economic, and legal institutions. The combination of the earlier, more scattered and disconnected groups into great centralized associations has extraordinarily increased their power.[389]

Baernreither's ideal English workman went from workshop to Foresters' Hall, from Union to Public meeting, using to the full all the 'private' spaces in civil society to move towards a new society, utterly different, he thought, from the exploitative order of the early Industrial Revolution. His emphasis remained on *men* throughout. Like most men of his time he was not much concerned with unreconstructed domestic relations. Women were mostly to be confined to private and 'unskilled' spheres. J.M. Ludlow, introducing the 1893 edition of Baernreither's book, thought that it was a matter of the public sphere catching up with 'a new class of men':

> The progress made in the methods of production of the present day, which depends on the ever-increasing application of mechanical power, has brought the working classes everywhere into a wholly new position towards society ... Concurrently with this progress should have gone a complete transformation of the relations of this class to society in point of private and public rights; but while the modern modes of production created, so to speak, a new class of men ... the legislation and the public institutions...remained far behind.

Baernreither saw it as a change from working-men's associations being 'narrow-minded representations of self-interest', to them acquiring 'a public character'.[390] Private labour was claiming for itself, collectively, equivalent rights and associational forms – adapted because multiplied – as private capital. The adaptations were necessary and profound. The similarities were not seen as pale imitations but as full-bodied replacements. This was a culture of detail and of connection. Connections were made between spheres of activity kept separate elsewhere, such as education and material consumption and production, or sociality and insurance, or entertainment and collective self-help. The details of how ancillary activities should be run so as not to conflict with central aims were thought out, and accessible forms of democratic control were worked for. There was thinking, for instance, on details like *where* voting should take place in quarterly elections, whether they should be in branch stores or central stores? Would de-centralisation mean loss of coherent interest? There was thinking on whether canvassing was democratic; on what forms choirs should take in Co-operative Societies; on whether subscriptions should only be paid by members being physically present at a branch or other meeting; and on whether 'treating' at the bar in a CIU Club amounted to patronage of one member by another. A special correspondent writing for *The Englishman* in 1910 was impressed by 'The Truth about the Working Men's Clubs'. He claimed that the clubs, more than any other organisations in London, tended to develop 'that class confidence without which the class consciousness of the Socialist is useless ... Their success is a signal proof of the capacity to administer and to organise inherent in the working classes.'[391] Some of the deep sources of 'Englishness' already described were also tapped into by these associations. Co-operative Societies traced their kinds of direct democracy back to medieval guilds, or further back to the Saxons. Friendly Societies used a lot of medieval, Robin Hood type of imagery.

By the end of the century, J.M. Ludlow was worried. What he understood as Socialism seemed not to be dominant any longer in the culture. 'In these days,' he wrote during the 1890s,

> when the term 'Socialism' is sought to be narrowed in the using to this or that particular system, and the patent meaning of the word, and its history in this country as well as elsewhere, are so grossly overlooked that 'Co-operation' and 'Socialism' are actually treated as antagonistic, both by men who call themselves Socialists and by men who call themselves Co-operators, one cannot too strenuously insist upon the cardinal value of Mr. Maurice's declaration (that) 'the watchword of the Socialist is Co-operation; the watchword of the anti-socialist is competition'. Anyone who recognised the principle of Co-operation as a stronger and truer principle than that of competition has a right to the honour, or the disgrace of being called a Socialist.[392]

Ludlow ran his finger along a major fracture in English culture, going through 'socialism' and, in effect, breaking it apart. There have been many competing versions of the socialist project. New and transformed versions of the public/ private relationship were at stake in this project, new forms of 'state', new versions of what constitutes civil society, held together in living, active tension. These new versions would have had to be as different from their predecessors as capitalist versions of a 'state', civil society, the public and the private, and so on were from their feudal and pre-feudal predecesssors. They would still have had to negotiate deep contradictions, no doubt, but in different spaces, within different fields of force. With all the English inheritance of State and civil society already described, however, there *was* a powerful working-class associational culture running through much of nineteenth- and twentieth-century English society. It was probably at its strongest between the 1870s and the 1930s.

At various points in this essay I have referred to this as 'private labour' by contrast with the more familiar phrase 'private capital'. Private labour may be seen as a preparation, a major resource, no, a *precondition* for the construction of any society as much of and for working people as capitalism was of and for its characteristic class of owners and principal beneficiaries. Although it was especially strong – as well as early – in England, this culture of association-for-labour did not, for the most part, see itself as 'socialist'. It tended towards anti-Statism.[393] This was in reaction to the fact that those who *did* call themselves 'socialist' were intent on 'capturing' the State and 'winning power', rather than transforming such things (relations). Socialists tended, in that sense, to be Statist. Or they had projects of supervision and transformation, but in the interests of a social group other than the working class. This group has been referred to already as the Professional and Managerial Class, and its project as Collectivism.

In the Associational culture of autonomy, the key values were collective self-help, independence, an open-ended idea of progress, and co-operation. The effort was to do without Masters as much as possible: if members were to be Servants, it had to be in a grander cause than existed below stairs. Before a Labour Party existed, most 'associationists' would probably have voted Liberal, if they could vote at all. A quintessential figure like J.T.W. Mitchell (1828–95) – 'the most remarkable personality that the British Co-operative Movement has thrown up' (Beatrice Webb) – would certainly have done so. At the end of his life Mitchell stood in local government elections as a Radical Liberal in Rochdale. But to admit him and his project – he was Chairman of the CWS between 1874 and 1895, and the main actor in its project – into 'liberalism' is to extend dominant understandings of the meanings of that term. Holyoake called co-operative liberalism 'deliberate', rather than 'stationary'. The Co-operative Wholesale Society vision was nothing less than to take over all production. At the 1887 Co-operative Congress Mitchell saw:

> There was no higher form of co-operative production upon the face of the earth than the Wholesale Society manifested in its co-operative works ... He would start productive works, when they would pay, in every centre in the United Kingdom; and would never be satisfied until the Wholesale manufactured everything that its members wore ... If co-operation was to be permanently successful we should have to finally settle this question – To whom does profit and the increment of value belong? He held that as it was created by the industrious classes it belonged to them ... He advised co-operators never to be satisfied until they got control of the entire producing, banking, shipping and every other interest in the country. The Wholesale had £100,000 in consols, and in course of time co-operators might possess the whole of

the National Debt of this country. If co-operators saved their money they might in time possess the railways and canals, besides finding employment for themselves.[394]

By supplying all the needs of affiliated, autonomous, member stores, the Wholesale would, in the end, get into producing, distributing, and exchanging everything. The project was to unite capital and labour in the same body. At the Royal Commission on Labour in the early 1890s, one can sense the amazement of a socialist like Tom Mann at Mitchell's cool ambition. And well into the twentieth century the CWS still had a position from which to offer solid critiques of the main directions that Political Labour was taking. After a Labour Party Conference in Manchester in 1917, the CWS magazine *The Producer* ('with which is incorporated The Consumer') editorialised in the remarkable way that I have already cited in 'The Three Socialisms':

> With all its teaching and agitation, its preaching and writing, its local and Parliamentary representation, the Labour Party does not yet seem to have realised that for the economic betterment of the common people collectively-owned fields, factories and workshops are better than speeches and resolutions; they could, in fact, be made more effective in the economic welfare of the workers than almost any kind of legislation. When we are treading the paths of national legislation we are upon very uncertain ground, that is apt to give way at any moment. But when we acquire fields and grow wheat, build factories and manufacture goods, erect warehouses and distribute the contents one to another, we know we are getting on solid ground.
>
> The Labour Party does not proceed in this way. It calls for higher wages, and leaves those who supply the commodities

of life to exploit the higher earnings by increased cost of living ... What is and always had been the failure of the Labour Party from a business point of view? It is that they have asked other people to do things for them rather than do things for themselves ... And when all has been said in favour of a high legal rate of pay, what does the term suggest? It suggests that the workers are still dependent upon other people for wages, as they are for the price of the means of life. They are between two oppressive stools – one to keep down wages, one to inflate prices. How can they disentangle themselves from the position? We presume some would say by State action; perhaps by forcing the Government to own and control industry and the distribution of food. But how full of doubt, uncertainty, and perhaps corruption such a course would be. Would it not be better, and as quickly done in the long run, for the people to get hold of the machinery of production by co-operative means?

Once that process was anything like complete the workers could then determine by collective action their own rate of pay, their own price of food, clothing and shelter. And co-operators would then be so numerous that they could walk into the Houses of Parliament and take over the reins of government without any further palaver. This is not a dream. It is simply a business problem.[395]

Early in the twentieth century the Co-operative Wholesale Society was 'the most varied if not the largest business enterprise in the world'. It was the most fully developed of the visions by and on behalf of private labour in Britain at this time. And it happened away from the State, and away from the social history of dominant meanings of socialism and communism in Britain.

Whether they intended it or not, English Associations of Working Men were of considerable interest to the State. That there had to be a Royal Commision on 'Labour' in the early 1890s is indicative of that interest. But it stretched further back than that. From the 1850s through to the 1910s there was a great deal of legislative preoccupation with working-class association. What were its state-enforced liabilities and limits to be?

From a revolutionary Left point of view, large-scale, liberal-minded, 'non-Political' working-class associations have been patronised – particularly by writers with an obsession with 'positions' in a heady, theoretical sense rather than positions in a social, relational sense. It has been said that they were 'corporate' rather than 'hegemonic' in their ambition, having no ambition for general or state power, living in closed, class-bound worlds. But whether they intended to or not, working people in this associational culture *did* raise the nature of wider social and productive relations, simply by means of their presence and practice.

The problem for 'the state' was how, and on what terms, to admit working-class association or combination. That capitalists could and must combine was axiomatic. But workers? As Hore Belisha MP said in 1933 when debating the tax position of co-operative societies, 'there must be some limit to the principle of mutuality'.[396] From the 1850s onwards, Industrial and Provident Society legislation was concerned with the terms upon which large-scale working-class association could be licensed. This had roots going back to Combination Acts and Friendly Society Acts of the 1790s, and reaches forward to the Labour and Conservative obsession with Trade Union legislation from the 1960s onwards. How much of what private capital legitimately did or had could private labour do or have? At what point would regulation and licensing have to give way to suppression? *When* – if at all – could private labour's *powers* to associate in a range of different ways be turned safely into legal *rights*? To what extent should the liability of labour's associations be limited in the way that capital's Companies had been since 1862? Should labour's associations have the right to make exclusive agreements, or was/is that to be judged as trade interference and an illegal limitation on the 'freedom of contract' of their competitors? How level should the playing field be when labour takes on capital? Do workers have the right to assemble freely, in any numbers and form of association – parliament, congress, convention, syndicate, general/annual assembly – to take decisions about their own means of production, distribution, education and government? How come picketing is hedged around with statutory interpretation? Why were Co-operatives for a time prevented from owning and trading in land, and from spending their trading surplus on education? What should be the tax position of Co-operative Societies, or the licensing position of Working Men's Clubs? After all, as Hore Belisha's speech went on, 'if the whole country were covered by Co-operative Stores the Revenue would receive no income tax at all'. To what extent should workers' associations be able to tender for, or even administer, universal public services such as National Insurance in 1911: on the same terms as private industrial insurance companies like the Prudential? What about autonomous working-class education: could that be allowed? Was the Workers' Educational Association a safe enough antidote to Marxist organisations like the Plebs League? The history of changing answers to these questions from a *trade* union point of view became well known as a result of the renewed crisis of trade unionism and the State from the mid-1960s onwards – a crisis which is not yet entirely over.

That there is also a parallel story from the point of view of English associations of working people more generally is less well known. There are fascinating episodes still to be unravelled from a class, rather than from a 'national', point of view. From the point of view of Working Men's Clubs, there were conflicts over Licensing legislation in the early 1900s. From the Friendly Societies' point of view a great struggle took place between them, private capital, and the State, in 1911.[397] W.H. Lever took Co-operative Societies to court during the second decade of the twentieth century in an attempt to force them to stock Sunlight Soap, rather than to trade exclusively in CWS-manufactured brands. The tax position of Co-operative Societies and their members was attacked, as they saw it, by Ramsay MacDonald and Neville Chamberlain in the Finance Act of 1933, and in spite of a petition with three million signatories.

The broad chronology is approximately the same for every major branch of working-class association. During the 1870s and 1880s working-class associations forced the polity – Conservative as well as Liberal – to move over. What were later seen as 'privileged' positions in law were won (or 'granted'), as rewards for 'respectability' and 'self help' among the 'aristocracy of labour'. There was then a legal counter-attack on trade unions during the 1890s.[398] The Taff Vale judgement, making Unions legally and financially responsible for losses arising from strike action, was only partly reversed by the Liberal government in the Trade Disputes Act of 1906. A settlement was achieved which was enduring enough for the Thatcher government to need, as they saw it, to get back behind that settlement during the 1980s, in the interests of 'the competitiveness of the British economy' and to resolve the question 'Who rules Britain?'. Trade unions had been found to have 'too much power'. In the intervals during which the Labour Party was in power during the twentieth century, Labour governments failed to put up an umbrella under which labour's associations could flourish and federate sufficiently to challenge the State on their own terms. When in office, the answer that Political Labour gave to the question 'Who rules Britain?' was 'We do'. We either already conjugate and constitute the State right now, since 'the election', or we will do so when voted into power at the next one. Leave it to us, give us your votes, and we will do it for you ...

The subjects and objects addressed by Marx, which are at least as interesting as Marxism as a finished science, have been alluded to more than once in this essay. They are things (relations) like class, and class struggle; working-class movement, combination, and association; large-scale industry and the differences between it and earlier 'manufacture'; exploitation and its varying state and national forms and locations; and regulation, power, ideology, and hegemony. These are the subjects about which Marx and Marxists have had much to say. What is striking about England, however, is how much of this agenda for thinking and acting went through L(l)iberalism rather than through Socialism/ Marxism. Liberalism was a very big carrier of nineteenth-century political, economic, and would-be social discourse. During the late nineteenth and early twentieth centuries it too – 'New Liberalism' – needed to be expansive and elastic enough to move over a bit, to accommodate what was going on around it. It was J.L. and Barbara Hammond, for instance, who, among all other historians between the first half of the twentieth century and our own time, came nearest to E.P. Thompson's view of early-nineteenth-century history, with their account of that period as civil or class war. Another Liberal, L.T. Hobhouse, came near to theorising what Gramsci came to describe as 'hegemony', for example in his work on the stratification within the working class in reaction to the crisis of the Boer War. Hobhouse was fascinated by the theories and practices – in fact the hegemonic culture – that kept organised labour subordinate during the late nineteenth and early twentieth centuries. And it was J.A. Hobson, another Liberal, who not only took up the chronology of large-scale industry in his book *The Evolution of Modern Capitalism* (1894), but who also came close to Lenin's later analysis, in his work on *Imperialism* published in 1902. Even Gladstonian Liberals were not afraid to face the central difficulties inherent in political 'representation'. They knew the problems posed by any one person, still less a class of persons, claiming to 'represent' another. In these respects they were nearer to the base camp from which a revolutionary political modernism could have broken through than Parliamentary Labour Politics or Social Democracy was during the twentieth century. English Associations of Working Men faced these issues too, but in practice. With their careful financial arrangements; their thought-through practice concerning the relations between centre and localities in their own associations; their quarterly units for elections; their self-conscious Congresses with inventions like the block vote; and their tendency to prefer direct democracy practices such as mandation and delegation, they addressed the difficult issues of class and political representation. How much yeast was in that dough! By contrast, Keir Hardie's view was that, in order to succeed, Political Labour 'must conform as nearly as possible to the political institutions already in existence with which the public mind is familiar'.

News from Somewere
With so much behind them, one might expect at least some of the socialisms which emerged in England at the end of the nineteenth century to be extraordinary. Among a number of possible examples I will choose two: Thomas Kirkup and William Morris.

Thomas Kirkup (1844–1912)
Thomas Kirkup was a Northumberland-born shepherd boy. Through the pupil–teacher system and Edinburgh University, he became an author and publisher's adviser. He is unknown

today. In his time, however, he was a much published, reprinted, and well-received student of socialism. And among the three works which Mao Zedong said 'especially deeply carved my mind' as he moved into Marxist theory and practice during 1919-20, Kirkup's *History of Socialism* was one.[399]

Re-reading Kirkup today, his late entry into a main artery of twentieth-century 'communalist' socialism is not surprising.[400] He had, to begin with, a strong sense of the epochal (i.e. revolutionary but not necessarily 'sanguinary') nature of the project. He combined this with a commitment to working people like himself, in whose interests and through whose activity the socialist project, as he understood it, was to be undertaken. He found the mental-manual division of labour oppressive. In his version of the socialist project, it was no failure to 'have done efficient work as a navvy or hodman'. He knew about the extent of the change he was advocating:

> While its basis is economic, socialism implies and carries with it a change in the political, ethical, technical and artistic arrangements and institutions of society, which would constitute a revolution greater than has ever taken place in human history, greater than the transition from the ancient to the medieval world, or from the latter to the existing order of society.

While the 'most thoroughly democratic organisation of society' was the 'political complement' of such transformation, ethics and culture were necessarily involved – culture, for Kirkup, being written into subsistence in an unusually material way. A central aim of socialism was to 'terminate the divorce of the workers from the natural sources of subsistence and culture'. He used the language of association. 'It must be the aim of the socialist movement also to terminate this incessant divorce between labour and intelligence, by providing within the groups of associated workers due scope for the best talent.' There was a personal edge to some of his cool, class-informed prose. 'In the history and condition of the working people it is a pathetic fact that their sons who have been gifted with exceptional capacity generally go over to the richer classes. Their services are thus lost to the class from which they sprang.'

Fellow travellers needed reminding, he thought, that socialism claims 'to represent the aspirations after a better life of the toiling and suffering millions of the human race'.[401] What he called 'abstract collectivism' might eclipse that. Rural change mattered to Kirkup, and abstract collectivism was making it 'difficult for [Marx's] followers to draw up a reasonable agrarian policy suitable to the peasantry'. It was also preventing the realisation that *struggle* was the instrument, for now, as always, 'progress must be attained through struggle, and perfection through suffering'.[402] Working people's aspirations were not necessarily neatly programmatic.

> Probably the most striking feature in recent history may be found in the symptoms, that so frequently appear, of a latent and undefined socialism, which only needs a fitting occasion to call it forth, and which forms a serious but incalculable quantity in the social forces of the time.

Kirkup was interested in this 'quantity' not only in England but also, already in 1892, in Russia:

> We cannot too often emphasise the fact that it is not an abstract system but a thing in movement. It is not wedded to any stereotyped set of formulae whether of Marx or any other, but must be rooted in reality and while moulding facts it must adapt itself to them.

Anything 'absolute' was to be suspected, for example the enduring problem for socialists as for others, of achieving optimal relations between centres and localities. 'No absolute rules can be laid down for the relations of the two to each other; these must be determined by considerations of time and circumstances.' 'Texts and systems' could not deal with such matters, nor could 'absolute principles': only history and practice. 'It would be a serious mistake to identify socialism with any of its forms, past or present. They are only passing phases in a movement which will endure.'

Two tendencies, Kirkup argued, could be extracted from the living history of the socialist movement. One was broadly statist, the other broadly communal or voluntary.[403] The latter was deeply rooted in local possibility – though getting less so, he thought, as he watched wider social developments. 'The cardinal thing in socialism is the living and active principle of association.' 'Socialism ... simply means that the normal social organisation of the future will and should be an associated or co-operative one.'

> Through the fog of controversy we should clearly see that the fundamental principle of socialism is marked by extreme simplicity. The keynote of socialism is the principle of association. Only by associating for the ownership and control of land and capital can the people protect themselves against the evils of competition and monopoly. Only by association can they control and utilise the large industry for the general good. It means that industry should be carried on by free associated workers utilising a joint capital with a view to an equitable system of distribution. And in the political organisation of society it has for complement a like ideal, namely, that the old methods of force, subject and exploitation should give place to the principle of free association. Through the application

and development of the principle of free association it seeks to transform State, municipality, and industry in all their departments.[404]

'Rationally interpreted', socialism was 'simply a movement for unifying labour and capital through the principle of association.' Most co-operators in the dynamic, shop-keeping phase of the co-operative movement during the second half of the nineteenth century would have agreed with such a proposition, while not usually often labelling theirs as a socialist cause. 'By reasonable socialism, the state should be regarded as the association of people on a large scale', the municipality or commune as the association for local purposes.

When arguing about the state, Kirkup knew he had allies in England. Perhaps too easily, he contrasted such allies with Prussians. But he also knew that he had English antagonists. There were local socialists who were 'too much influenced by the Prussian type of government and theory of the State' – too keen on hierarchy, management from above, and centralisation as an absolute.

> Such a view may suit people that are used to a centralising autocracy and bureaucracy associated with militarism, but is entirely opposed to English ideas ... and industrial and economic system which would remind us at every step of the Prussian army, the Prussian police and Prussian officialism, is not attractive to those who have breathed a freer air.

'It is ... most misleading to speak as if socialism must proceed from the State as we know it.'[405] The voices around Kirkup who did speak in that way were getting louder. After all, as one of them said, 'it is easier to get control over existing machinery than to make machinery for yourself'. Kirkup's worry about this became more evident in the final (1909) edition of the *History* to be issued in his life-time. He had seen England as a resource against collectivism. But he became fearful of the depletion of that resource. 'The direct action of the State' had been a feature in English social development, encouraging the notion that 'everything will be done by it'. Grotesque and absurd (his words) though that belief was, it had become more influential among critics of socialism but 'apparently also by some of its adherents'. Fabians were the most obvious examples.

> The State has very great power, but it has no magical power. And it is a grave mistake to regard it too much as the pivot of social evolution. We can trace its rise and progress in history and its record has not been a good one ... it has too long and too much been an organ for the exploiting of the mass of the people by the ruling minority.

This mistake was being made more and more within 'recent English socialism'. The bureaucrat had been identified too closely with socialism. 'In its propaganda the Fabian Society has too often interpreted socialism in terms of the State and the municipality ... In this and in other points the language of the Fabian Basis is too suggestive of the rigid and abstract collectivism set forth in the prevalent socialism.'[406]

William Morris (1834–1896)

Morris was one of the most original socialists of the Second International period.[407] He went far enough forward in epochal as well as in 'English' terms for it to be difficult, even now, for anyone on the Left to have caught up with him. And yet he was more evidently rooted in an English radical tradition than a thinker such as Kirkup. 'Our poet starts from a tangible reality and deduces its future from its past and present. His utopia posseses history and geography.'[408]

Morris oscillated between great hopes and big fears for any *located* socialism worthy of the name. His location happened to be the banks of the River Thames. His preferred name for the project was Communism. Sometimes he thought that all he longed for could and would happen, uniquely, in England At other times he knew how much there was to stop it, and how much compromise would have to be endured.

In 1887 Morris produced the first of two sustained theorisations or visions of the transition to socialism. In it he contrasted the Policy of Parliamentary Action with what he called the Policy of Abstention.[409] The latter meant the construction of a great 'Labour Combination' powerful enough to replace the capital *P* of Politics. Such a construction would, Morris thought, require productive capacity, a material life of its own:

> Its aim would be to act directly, whatever was done in it would be done by the people themselves; there would consequently be no possibility of compromise, of the association becoming anything else than it was intended to be; nothing could take its place: before all its members would be but one alternative to complete success, complete failure.

The Labour Combination would also constitute a 'Labour Parliament'. As it grew and as the crisis of monopoly capitalism deepened, people would ally with its decrees rather than with those of the 'Westminster Committee'. It would have to undertake 'the maintenance of its people' as well as resistance to erstwhile constitutional, because already constituted, authority. 'No mere aggregation of discontent', it would be 'the representative of the society of production, the direct opposite to the society of exploitation which will be represented by the constitutional government'. The 'vast labour organisation', the Combined Workers or Federation, would set about the active transformation of the 'raw material and instruments of labour' into common property:

> Let them settle e.g. what wages are to be paid by their temporary managers, what number of hours it may be expedient to work: let them arrange for the filling of the military chest, the care of the sick, the unemployed, the dismissed: let them learn also how to administer their own affairs. Time and also power fails me to give any scheme for how all this could be done; but granting the formation of such a body I cannot help thinking that for the last two purposes they might make use of the so-called plan of co-operation.

Morris gave a fuller account of how all this would happen in 1890 in an extraordinary chapter of *News from Nowhere* called 'How the Change Came'. In this chapter events were *placed* – in the manner of a tapestry – in a very precise English scene. The story of an English revolution was told in unusual detail.[410] 'Whatever may be said of the possibility of such construction in other countries, in Britain it is possible', Morris thought, because, even though there were places where the suffrage was more extended, nowhere else had 'the habit of democracy' gained such sway across the whole culture.[411] Morris connected such a habit to 'the ancient constitution of the land' and even to the forgotten tradition of direct assemblies among Germanic peoples. These nourished 'an Englishman's wholesome horror of government interference and centralisation'.[412]

For Morris, states in general and 'the state' in particular were major preoccupations. Like all forces dividing labour, the centralised state tried to 'administer the affairs of the people living a long way off, whose conditions and surroundings they cannot thoroughly understand'. 'It is always and everywhere good that people should do their own business, and in order that they may do it well, every citizen should have some share of it, and take on his shoulders some part of the responsibility.' But as 'society organised for the production and distribution of wealth' – an unusually succinct definition – the State could not simply disappear:

> The great federal organisation power, whatever form it took, would have the function of the administration of production in its wider sense. It would have to see to, for instance, the collection and distribution of all information as to the wants of the population and the possibilities of supplying them, leaving all details to subordinate bodies, local or industrial.'[413]

Morris feared that theories of reform which already had a stronghold where he lived and worked, and which were based on the enlargement and extension of the existing State, would come to dominate and define Socialism. He knew how necessary for capitalism's survival such theories were, how likely their multiplication would be, and so how available they were in England as a mould for counterfeiting, as he saw it, socialism. He knew that such theories might easily eclipse all other meanings of socialism and suppress the real, mass, beneficiaries of socialism (communism), in the interests of a newish class, or layer, of persons whom he did not much like. 'I should like our friend to understand', he wrote to a correspondent in *Commonweal* in July 1885,

> whither the whole system of palliation tends – namely, towards the creation of a new middle class to act as a buffer

between the proletariat and their direct and obvious masters; the only hope of the bourgeois for retarding the advance of Socialism lies in this device.

He knew that some socialists around him did not even intend to transform the relations of production of modern industry from a working-class point of view. They had quite other fish to fry. Of this kind of socialism Morris wrote:

> It has two faces to it. One of which says to the working man 'This is Socialism or the beginning of it' (which it is not) and the other says to the capitalist, 'This is sham Socialism; if you can get the workers, or part of them, to accept this, it will create a new lower middle-class, a buffer to push in between Privilege and Socialism.'[414]

Some 'revolutionists' around Morris thought they could use 'the old bureaucratic states' like the English one, 'rather than have any disruption of them prior to the realisation of the new social system'. That element in the useable past, as already indicated, was very available in England. There was a lot of State here, as it were, to take for granted. But it constituted a deplorable separation, for Morris, of means from ends, processes from results. He could see that it also had an inevitability about it in England. He realised that there would probably have to be a 'transitional stage of progress'. 'Before the habit of working for the whole was formed some compulsion would have to be exercised. That compulsion would be found in the very remains of competition which would render the state imperfect.'[415]

Concessions *would* be wrung from the masters. But *agency* or *process* or struggle – who did what and how – was fundamental to Morris. Anything given by private capital or by its State and related agencies like Parliament – even though asked for by Labour – would not, he hoped, be internalised by labour and regarded as part of its own, class project, even though improvements in the life of labour would undoubtedly result. 'We should be clear that they are not *our* measures.' Legislation could help the conditions of work and leisure, and could not be refused. But it should not be mistaken for real socialism. Improvements produced through agencies other than labour's own will and association would be 'damaging to the cause if put forward by socialists as part of socialism'. Property was going to have to pay a ransom. He knew that. So did many other politicians, businessmen, and fit and proper persons around him who scrambled for the socialist label at this time. The trouble was that the ransom was going to be called Socialism by friend and foe alike:

> The great mass of what most non-socialists at least consider at present to be socialism, seems to me nothing more than a *machinery* of socialism, which I think it probable that socialism *must* use in its militant condition; and which I think it *may* use for some time after it is practically established; but it does not seem to me to be of its essence.

A version of the future which Morris contested strongly and which had already invaded (and still occupies) a great deal of 'socialist' space was the hierarchical, technological romanticism which suggested that, as machinery developed, it would entirely supersede handwork. Automation would be welcomed as delivering what could only be delivered in a sustainable way by associated human agency. 'While the ordinary daily work of the world would be done entirely by automatic machinery, the energies of the more intelligent part of mankind would be set free to follow the higher forms of the arts, as well as science and the study of history.' '"It was strange," commented Henry Morsom, an imagined citizen of Nowhere, "was it not, that they should thus ignore that aspiration after complete equality which we now recognise as the bond of all happy human society."' Work-pleasure as 'art' and art as 'work-pleasure' was the only viable force which could make (produce) communism in an enduring way. It was as though creativity (the making of art as work pleasure and the making of work pleasure as art) was the precondition of socialism as well as its result. It was on the relations of production that hierarchy was currently based within capitalism, and could so easily be reasserted within socialism. This was the point at which Morris made one of his most important distinctions: that between Socialism and Communism. If Socialism was defined as a 'mere system of property holding', if its task was simply to take over an already existing, well-developed economic, political, and administrative cultural machine or state, developing it in 'rational', straight lines, then it seemed to Morris to constitute a minor and temporary improvement on capitalism. In some of Morris's moods, barbarism seemed preferable. Working very much within an English context, however, he could see a communism which went way beyond rational statism. At the same time he feared a depressive, arrested set of developments which might be profoundly confusing to working people. He could see its beneficiaries all around him, wearing socialist livery and being taken too seriously. Apologists for statism and collectivism were strong enough presences for Morris to understand them theoretically and construct against them culturally and politically ('up at the Branch') with an intensity rare in the subsequent history of the search for less statist, less expert, alternative socialisms.

Statism and collectivism would each leave production as a surviving material basis for hierarchy. Under them it would be at best 'from each according to his abilities, to each according to his work', rather than the communist precept of 'from each according to his abilities, to each according to his needs'. Here Morris was drawing on a distinction familiar within the Co-operative tradition, present for example in the early-nineteenth-century work of William Thompson. How could you relate rewards received to work done, when 'the production of wares and the service of the community must always be a matter of co-operation?' It is not possible

> really to proportion the reward to labour, and ... if you were able to do so you would still have to redress by charity the wrongs of the weak against the strong, you would still not be able to avoid a poor-law: the due exercise of one's energies for the common good and capacity for personal use we say form the only claims on the possession of wealth, and this right of property, the only safeguard against the creation of fresh privilege, which would have to be abolished like the old privilege.[416]

'Fresh privilege' different from private capitalism but arising out of its transformation was always a distinct possibility for Morris. And privileges could easily become habits, ways of acting, new interest groups or even new classes. Morris was interested in those 'who occupy a middle position between the producers and the non-producers'. By these he meant 'artists and literary men, doctors, school-masters etc.'.

> They are doing useful service, and ought to be doing it for the community at large, but practically they are only working for a class, and in their present position are little better than hangers-on of the non-producing class, from whom they receive a share of their privilege, together with a kind of contemptuous recognition of their position as gentlemen – heaven save the mark.[417]

Morris anticipated

> the danger of the community falling into bureaucracy, the multiplication of boards and offices, and all the paraphernalia of official authority, which is, after all, a burden, even when it is exercised by the delegation of the whole people and in accordance with their wishes.[418]

There were whole categories of occupation 'which would have no place in a reasonable condition of society as e.g. lawyers, judges, jailers and soldiers of the highest grades, and most Government officials.'[419] 'Directors of labour' and 'men of genius' had to be watched. Masterdom based on property in knowledge was as much masterdom as that based in any other kind of property. 'A decent life, a share in the common life of all is the only "reward" that any man can honestly take for his work, whatever it is; if he asks for more, that means that he intends to play the master over somebody.'[420]

There was an inheritance to which Morris urged resistance throughout his communist life. This was the view that 'revolutionists' could use the old bureaucratic states 'rather than [have] any disruption of them prior to the realisation of the new social system'. He suggested that 'while the national systems cannot at present be directly attacked with success as to their more fundamental elements', a process of 'starving out' or 'sapping' should go on. More and more responsibility could be taken by local associations as the carriers of transition, and by working-class unions as the limbs of a future socialist commonwealth. By means of multiple, federal links these should already be dealing with 'the details of change'.[421] During the period in which archaic, political nations were weakening into dissolution,

> The form which the decentralisation or Federation will take is bound to be a matter of experiment and growth; what unit of administration is to be, what the groups of Federation are to be, whether or not there will be cross-Federation, as, e.g. Craftsguilds and Co-operative Societies going side by side with the geographical division of wards, communes and the like, all this is a matter for speculation and I don't pretend to prophesy about it.[422]

Aspiration – the instinct for socialism – plus active, experimental federation from below were, for Morris, the 'only means' for 'bringing about the beginning of the Socialistic system'. These were the enduring contents of revolution, whatever its day-to-day episodes might be. About the latter he was unusually specific in the chapter on 'how the change came', cited already from *News from Nowhere*. However the struggle went, 'there must be a great party, a great organisation outside parliament actively engaged in reconstructing society and learning administration'.[423] Morris knew of the ubiquity of capitalism, evident on the banks of the Thames as well as in factories, in the looks on people's faces as well as in wage payments. But in spite of this, perhaps because of it, capitalism could best be replaced while it was still there, not only on the morrow of the revolution. There had to be 'the token', at least, 'of the gradual formation of a new order of things underneath the decaying order.'[424] 'Capacity for administration' would have to grow, even through associations as frail as the Hammersmith Socialist Society, 'so that when the present system is overthrown, they might be able to carry on the business of the community without waste or disaster.'[425] Whether any of this could happen through Socialism as a transition to Communism, or whether Socialism might function to vaccinate against working people's desire for a just society, was an urgent question which haunted Morris. He cannot be fitted easily into any evolutionary 'stages of history' Marxism in which climaxes – revolutionary transitions or makings – can (must) only happen at the uniquely appropriate, historically appointed moment. Such Marxisms have been deployed to ratify the inequities of actually existing socialist states. Their mistakes and crimes can be excused if seen as necessary, inevitable, first-stage – because it had happened 'too early' – socialism.

In some sense, Morris did not need Marxism, still less specific texts by Engels, to make critical – and *moral*– distinctions where he lived and worked This is the burden of E.P. Thompson's 'Postscript: 1976' to the revised edition of his *William Morris, Romantic to Revolutionary*, first published in 1955. Some of what Morris thought about socialism was evident, to him, way back in the 'Englishness' – to use a shorthand – of the inheritance available to him. And some of what he meant is evident in his own poetic, artistic production even before he crossed what he, and Edward Thompson, called his 'river of fire', that is to say his *conversion*, for that is what it was, from Ruskinian to Marxian socialist theory and practice. And he did not need Marxism as science, in any way separable from his own analysis and experience, to see that, with his English inheritance, what *he* meant by Socialism *would* happen, but also that what he meant by Communism *could* happen. Both were inscribed in preceding facts about England, and consequent ideas of Englishness.

> I know there are some to whom this possibility of the getting rid of class degradation may come, not as a hope, but as a fear. These may comfort themselves by thinking that this Socialist matter is a hollow scare, in England at least; that the proletariat have no hope, and therefore will lie quiet in this country, where the rapid and nearly complete development

of commercialisation has crushed the power of combination out of the lower classes ... It may be that in England the mass of the working classes has no hope; that it will not be hard to keep them down for a while, possibly a long while. The hope that this may be so I will say plainly is a dastard's hope, for it is founded on the chance of their degradation. I say such an expectation is that of slave-holders or the hangers-on of slave-holders. I believe, however, that hope is growing among the working classes even in England; at any rate you may be sure of one thing, that there is at least discontent. Can any of us doubt that, since there is unjust suffering?[426]

So, what went wrong?
While 'unjust suffering' and 'discontent' are as manifest as ever in 2018, 'hope' for socialism as its terminus is less evident in England than in Morris's day. He was in a hurry, while also knowing that in England there would be no rush. He thought that 'making socialists' was probably the best, if not the only, way forward. By the time that 'Guest' had arrived there, the socialist society evoked in News from Nowhere had been developing for one hundred and fifty years. 'Guest' was Morris's imagined visitor to Nowhere and the main interlocutor of its inhabitants for readers of News. The revolutionary crisis described in the vision ('a vision not a dream') in Nowhere was anticipated by Morris – writing in the excited years of the late-1880s – coming to a head some time in the 1950s. During the second decade of the twenty-first century, it is hard to see ourselves with much conviction as being anywhere on that route. Defence against deep, anti-democratic reaction – or the centralised socialist regime described in Edward Bellamy's Looking Backward (1888) – is now a more pressing task. It would be hard even to propose – as Morris did in 'Where Are We Now?', published in Commonweal in November 1890 – that

'the hope of the partial, and so to say, vulgarised realisation of socialism is now pressing on us'. Defeat, or 'the loss of the future', is now fully acknowledged among socialists.[427]

So, what went wrong? I have asked the same question in all three parts of this book, searching for an adequate answer. The main answers to the question obviously lie way beyond England and socialism, as well as way beyond my own synoptic or narrative capacity. It would be absurd to moralise the disastrously destructive, violent themes of twentieth-century world history into some 'fault' among socialists in general, let alone among socialisms here in England. In so far as socialists *have* been party to – or even abetted – what went wrong, all that can reasonably be done, perhaps, is to own up. 'No enemies to the left' is not a helpful slogan now for anyone interested in the project described by Marx as 'the associated mode' or lived by Morris 'in essence and in spirit, even now when we cannot be socialists economically'.

In the case of the projects of Kirkup and Morris outlined above, they clearly had active and direct antagonists who saw themselves as socialists too. The marginalisation of Morris has not always been easy to see, because so much of it has consisted of attempts to incorporate him comfortably into subsequently dominant projects very different from his own. The resistance to Morris's (and Thompson's) socialism/communism (the well-spring of their life work) has been well described in Thompson's 1976 *Postcript* to the revised edition of his *William Morris Romantic to Revolutionary* (1955). From the Left, Communists who seek to justify actually existing socialist regimes as staging posts towards real communism; social democrats who substitute bits of brotherhood, plus arts and crafts, or English genius for epochal change; Trotskyites looking for a hard-Marxist critique of 'reformism': they have all tried to hitch him to their waggon. Morris was engaged in active critique of many such positions for most of his communist life. He never pulled his punches about Fabianism or Statism or even unconstructive Anarchism. Towards the end of his life he knew he was not winning. 'The world is going your way at present Webb,' he told Sidney Webb in 1895, 'but it is not the right way in the end.'[428] Morris's project was clearly among those 'primitive' ones which Sidney Webb tried to tidy up in his pamphlet on *Socialism in England* in 1893:

> If our aim is the transformation of England into a Social Democracy we must frankly accept the changes brought about by the Industrial Revolution, the factory system, the massing of populations into great cities, the elaborate differentiation and complication of modern civilisation, the subordination of the worker to the citizen, and of the individual to the community. We must rid ourselves resolutely of all those schemes and projects of bygone socialisms which have now passed out of date.

There was a lot of self-consciously 'modern', sweeping-clean, anti-sentimental and sometimes quite viciously anti-working class, anti-democratic, and would-be 'scientific' sentiment in and around Fabian and other socialisms during the late nineteenth and early twentieth centuries. Much of it has been quoted in the Three Socialisms chapter in this book.

In Kirkup's case, the treatment was direct. A fifth edition of his *History of Socialism*, and the only one available to students in many libraries, was brought out in 1913. Its editor was Edward R. Pease, secretary of the Fabian Society for twenty-five years and author of an early *History* of the Society in 1916. Margaret Cole dubbed him 'the quintessential Fabian'. In 1913 Pease was convinced that historians in the future will recognise, as indeed they are beginning to realise already, that the succession to Karl Marx in the leadership of Socialist thought belongs to Sidney Webb. Marx perceived that industry must be the business of the State, but he did not foresee how this could come about. This has been the work of the English School of Socialism, which has for long prevailed here.[429]

This, as we have seen, had been Kirkup's precise worry in his own 1909 edition, as well as earlier editions. In the 1913 edition, 'revised and largely rewritten', Pease simply left out Kirkup's worries about Fabianism and the State.[430] In a little-noticed bit of 'permeation', Pease substituted a panegyric of his heroes and their Society. What had been seen by Kirkup as *problem* was frankly written up as opportunity. I have cited this passage but need to do so again in this precise context:

> To the ordinary citizen, and especially to the workman, the Government is a thing apart, a great machine of which he knows little and over which he has no control, except as an elector, and then only, so to speak, by force. The Fabians were many of them in Government service as first division clerks ... To Government clerks at Whitehall, even the juniors, Government is a delicate machine whose working they have to control ... To men in such service many ways of influencing political action are apparent which the outside cannot realise. The country is not so much governed by the votes of the electors, as by the ideas put into the heads of official persons whether parliamentary chiefs or permanent civil servants. What is true of government is equally true of outside organisations. The policy of a political association is determined within limits, by the man who drafts its resolutions and reports. Know more than other people, know what you

want, and you can make other people carry out your ideas. It is easier to get control over existing machinery than to make machinery for yourself.[431]

It was evidently also easier to get control over existing books than to make them yourself!

There was much more of such repression around in this period than labour historians have yet uncovered, with Fabians fighting against 'bygone socialism' and its carriers with a vigour which recalls New Labour's battle against what they called Old Labour. A rank and file Fabian, who called his son Bernard Sidney after his two heroes, and who was thought by H.G. Wells to be a good specimen of 'English mentality in the period 1906–14', found his niche in 1910 as manager of the Leeds Labour Exchange. In a letter before he got to Leeds he wrote:

> I care more for the State than I care for or have ever cared for myself, or for any other human being ... I have lost all my dogmas except a passionate faith in the development of a collectivist spirit in relation to property and breeding.

After he got to Leeds he told a correspondent:

> I am enjoying life hugely now ... I am getting a passion for studying this place. I have had a unique life in my chances of seeing different classes of society – really getting to know them. I am pushing on this experience in that direction as much as I can. I have even joined the Leeds Club – the exclusive snobbish club of the place – for the purpose of observing the habits of employers more closely. The only way to be sure of defeating a man is to be able to beat him at his own game. We have got to be better capitalists than the capitalists are.

When we – that is the administrative classes – have more will, more relentlessness, more austerity, more organizing ability, more class consciousness than they have, we shall crumple them in our hands. And by God! you and I may live to see the beginning of the end.

I am more of a puritan than ever. Austerity is what is needed. These miserable employers are poor creatures in many ways. They eat too much; they drink too much; they want their women too much. By God! I will out Bacchus any man when I choose. But it shall be of my free choice – not of a limp necessity. From day to day my dream shall be of a new model army, of vigilant administration supplanting property by organisation, inch by inch, steadily and slowly – with a jovial carouse to loosen the muscles now again. And to hell with the snufflers and the pimps alike. They shall go in pairs, one of each to a hurdle after the precedent set by Henry VIII.[432]

Collectivism has been characterised at length in this book. It was a kind of socialism which often characterised itself as 'English', at a time when Englishness tended to stand for 'reform' rather than for the revolution which General William Booth, founder of the Salvation Army, in his book *In Darkest England and the Way Out* (1890), anticipated as a' general overturn'. Admittedly in time of war, a driven, authoritarian tone was quite evident even in un-strident Sidney Webb's recommendation of the 'Universal Submission' he would 'decree', 'if I were in power'.[433] Belfort Bax's location of expert, policy-driven reform among a new class rather than among workers was clear: 'Fabianism is the special movement of the Government official just as militarism is of the soldier and clericalism of the priest.'[434]

This sociology is, perhaps, made intelligible by some of the facts about England and, consequent ideas of Englishness already rehearsed. There was, as we have seen, a long inheritance of state service and State Servants 'as opposed to private interests'. The 'age of improvement' during the first half of the nineteenth century produced, and was produced by, a remarkable group of State Servants whose project was cousin to that of Fabian collectivism.[435] Even a classic text of large-scale industry like Andrew Ure's *The Philosophy of Manufactures* (1835) made promises akin to those of a collectivist brave new world: beneficent but stern supervision, steady wages, clean homes, light work, little responsibility, science as *our* expertise working *for* you rather than *your* learned experience working together. Believe us, we are good for you, don't try to understand more than is necessary, profit from your place within divisions of labour which entirely suit your moral worth and productive potential. Within this tradition of an expert, public sphere, 'civil' officials made sense, a would-be common sense. Public people, women as well as men, learn to assume an identity between their own interest and the general good. And in England there was a prodigious body of social knowledge, an emergent new science of sociology in state bluebooks and official publications within which new scientists could trace their sources and find their home. Industrial wealth and attendant social position was old enough in England, well into its second and third generations, for its sons and daughter to have the material and the means to reject it, worry about it, and use it for more-than-economic social/ political ends. Beatrice Webb's account of her family home and her search for a role outside it in *My Apprenticeship* is the best example here.

'Collectivism' at its apogee of self-consciousness in early-twentieth-century England was firmly attached to the Nation as 'a body of people kept together for purposes of rivalry with other similar bodies'. There was a group called 'the Coefficients' in Edwardian England, the scandal of whose views from the point of view of any connection with a political Left is not yet widely acknowledged. They were elitist, imperialist, racist, eugenicist – just about as far from associationism as they could possibly be – and, as representatives of 'English Social-Imperial Thought' as Bernard Semmel called it, they included 'collectivist' socialists.[436] Even after World War I the Webbs were still committed to 'world struggle' and 'scientific truth'.[437] It was against such 'practical men' of the World Market that William Morris spent his spirit.

Collectivists had the confidence of a social group (a 'new class') with a definite place in production. They were, as already indicated, writers, first-division clerks in the civil service, administrators, supervisors, experts – people who could 'put it all together', have an 'overview', supervise the relations of production characteristic of large-scale industry. So far from being a problem to them, those arrangements were their opportunity. They were nearer to management than to labour, nearer to the cutting edge of large-scale capitalism than to that of associated labour. In the Webbs' Socialist Commonwealth, managers must manage, 'it is a matter of a psychology'. Democracy had its limitations: definite, economic, scientific and everything else:

> No industrial enterprise ... has yet made its administration successful on the lines of letting the employees elect or dismiss the executive officers whose directions these particular groups of employees have to obey ... It is, in fact, a matter of psychology. The relationship set up between a manager who has to give orders all day to his staff, and the members of his staff who, sitting as a committee of management, criticise his action in the evening, with the power of dismissing him if he fails to conform to their wishes, has been found by experience to be an impossible one.[438]

Who was in a position to resist such a confident 'in fact', such a plain 'matter of psychology'?

What, for shorthand purposes, I have labelled 'statism' has been much less precise in its articulation than collectivism. 'It is sometimes charged against the ILP', wrote Keir Hardie in 1908, 'that it has never formulated its theory of socialism. That is true, and therein lies its strength.'[439]

With 'statism' we are dealing with a set of dominant assumptions and practices, highly characteristic of twentieth-century English Labour Politics, rather than a confident 'theory' as such. We, its observers and chroniclers, have to do the theoretical work, as it were, as opposed to having it all exposed for us in volumes like those of the Webbs. All I can do here is to revisit some of those assumptions and practices, and illustrate them enough to indicate just how antagonistic they have been to the project of associated labour.

What emerged in twentieth-century England, and became dominant against all other socialisms, was a strong, would-be monopolistic 'Labour' politics, capable from time to time of winning elections, aspiring to be 'the natural party of government', and near enough to the levers of power for long enough to think in terms of 'winning' it, perhaps for ever. Such thoughts in turn determined what statists thought power consists of, was and is – in advanced capitalisms. Many of the impulses behind class and association outlined in this book became annexed to power Politics and were thereby deformed by it.

The beginnings of an answer to how and why this happened are implicit in four characteristics of Statism. First, it was strongly evolutionary. Working with the grain, as they thought, of tendencies already operating in their societies, Statists thought that they had time on their side: their project, indeed, was only a matter of time. Individual humans grew up, from babies to adults: so too societies evolved, through lower to higher stages. And the adult stage of human society (socialism) was to be made available, soon, through the long centuries of English (British) evolution. Others might have to wait longer, but here, and maybe quite soon, Socialism of their kind was available. Ramsay MacDonald was the best at articulating this view before 1914.

Secondly, Statism tended to anthropomorphise the State. There was an available inheritance, a known history of groups and classes of persons succeeding each other over many centuries. So it could be taken for granted that we the workers, or we Labour's Leaders on behalf of the workers, could simply become it, occupy its benches and corridors. In 1912 the ILP paper the *Labour Leader* wanted to distance itself from Fred Jowett's pressure for socialist changes in Parliamentary forms:

> We feel, for our part, whilst recognising the disinterested advocacy of Mr. Jowett, that changes in Parliamentary procedure are not the supremely important matter for our movement ... As Mr. Snowden said, *our central grievance is that we ourselves are not the Cabinet.* With the rise of Labour to power *many* of the Parliamentary difficulties would tend to adjust themselves.[440]

If that was the central grievance, after comfortable election victories like those of 1945, 1966, and 1997, it had clearly been met. Union leaders, 'our people', should be pleased that they would now be negotiating with friends. At the Annual Conference of Trades Councils in 1945 H.W.Harrison said: 'We are no longer petitioning for a place in the counsels of the State, we are the State.'[441]

This was the idea of the personalised State which George II talked about with Chancellor Hardwick. Instead of a person or persons, the State was sometimes seen as a ship, as in Ramsay MacDonald's *A Policy for the Labour Party* (1920), where he set out some reform legislation 'to launch the ship of State well manned and well equipped on its future voyages'.

Thirdly, Statism worked within the confusion already mentioned between Parliament in its established, representational forms, and 'the State'. The apparatus or machinery of State was so present and venerated that Statists could seldom see it from an outsider's point of view. So they reduced the real problem of representation, or how one person, still less a whole class of persons, could 'represent' another, to the fact of more or less regular elections. The best they could do was to put on its robes, kiss its hands, conform to its white and black bow-tie codes, put away anything which resembled workwear on state occasions (like Michael Foot's donkey jacket on Remembrance Sunday) and rejoice, as Harold Wilson did when he first got to Downing Street in 1964, that things there seemed to work for Labour in the same way that they did for any other Party in power. A contemporary observer described Wilson as displaying 'a profound reverence for the orders and mysteries of the civil service'. His Personal and Political Secretary deplored 'the fact that he does have such an admiration for and such a working knowledge of "the System" that he tends to lean over backwards in his relationship to it'.[442] Levers (of power) were to hand, even if what was supposed to happen when they were pushed or pulled, especially as regards 'the economy', didn't always seem to.

Accepting an old, evolving, and available State means that statists tend to go along with the confinement of Politics to licensed, official forms thereof. With Statism, a group without a direct base in material production, and therefore not a class, seeks to exercise control over circulation rather than production. They accept the great bourgeois achievement of the separation of politics from economics: this division of labour remains in place. But then they find that reaching out from the top of politics to control the economics, through projects of planning, nationalisation, and 'socialisation' (Sidney Webb's preferred phrase) does not necessarily bring it to heel. On the one hand Statists have their own movement or party. This is necessary to get them near State power – and important to many of them as a livelihood – and on the other hand there is The State. 'It', the state, may be seen as needing strengthening or modernising. Its servants may need replacing by less biased ones. But 'it' is never seen as available for reconstruction through working people's associated (already emergent), 'voluntary' efforts. There are missing links between movement and state, private (civil) action and public (political) action, between economics and politics. Across these gaps ugly, authoritarian styles of politics (Caesarisms) from time to time make great leaps. They can enter from Right or from Left. Statism's tragedy is that it often seems to have been in power, in a previous time in Government, however unwittingly, preparing the stage for its own crises.

Statism is, finally, a very public brand of socialism. Working within the inherited English framework of a strong public realm, it dreams that it can itself oppose, even replace – by means of public ownership and welfare legislation – 'private' capitalism altogether. It neglects contradictions, struggle, and growth points within the private sphere. It neglects private labour. I have argued that the spaces for private labour were especially open in England. With the early cutting of 'private' passages by the middle class, and with the subsequent occupation of large areas of 'civil society' by ambitious working-class associations, it is difficult to understand the neglect of all this by Political Labour and Statist Socialism during the twentieth century.

Fertile fields have been left uncultivated, including the *forms* of production, the *forms* and content of education, sport, 'culture' itself, the means of communication, even the family have been left unproblematised from a class point of view. Brave New Left, feminist, and community movements have had to try to do the work themselves. Statists in power even act as if 'industrial relations' must be kept free from politics. The result is that Labour has been ambushed by developments in those spheres as they became more and more characteristically capitalist.

Why is this? Is it because of the seeming imminence of socialism in this country, particularly when seen from the vantage point of the late nineteenth, early twentieth century? Is it because Britain has seemed at times so specially available for socialism – 'warrened with democratic processes, Committees, voluntary organisations, councils, electoral procedures?' – that England and its fellow nations are *over*-ripe for socialism? This was E.P.Thompson's proposition in 'At the Point of Decay', an essay written in 1959–60 which speaks as powerfully to the Britain of sixty years later.[443] Thompson used the metaphor of an unpruned apple tree to describe this country from a socialist point of view.

> 'Last-stage' capitalism is not a healthy growth; rather, it is like a cramped apple tree, starved of sun and air, which has begun to shoot at the top. And the immanent community of socialism, which is expressed in the powerful institutions of the Labour Movement and in a hundred forms of democratic association and control, is like a man whose psychic and physical energies are exhausted because they are exerted in a struggle *against* himself, in an effort to bring the demons of rebellion within him under control. Throughout the movement there are inhibitions, checks,

taboos, constitutional impediments, designed to prevent the democratic organisations of the people from fulfilling active democratic functions; restraining or turning back upon themselves energies which might otherwise flow rebelliously outwards into public life. *The impulse is divided from the function* [my emphasis] ... People have, increasingly, looked to *private* solutions to *public* evils.[444]

Among socialists in the Labour Party has there been a succession of hoped-for dashes for the finishing line, as it were: understandable attempts to go for the tape all at once, by means of Political monopoly and Party discipline? It is hard to explain. Worse than neglect, there has been positive resistance, even antagonism to other, perhaps slower, ways forward. It is as though all the yeast has been deliberately thrown away. Autonomous construction and independent struggles by trade unions have been seen as problems rather than opportunities by Political Labour. Friendly Societies have been nationalised (in their functions) and then abandoned as discrete social circles or struggling insurance businesses, rather than seen as cells for future class construction. The same is true of the Co-operative Movement. For example, it was Ramsay MacDonald who was Prime Minister when an assault was launched on the Movement in 1933, in an attempt to alter the tax status of the Co-operative dividend. And it was Social Democrats like Hugh Gaitskell and Anthony Crosland who urged 'The Co-op' to 'modernise' as another consumer business in the Independent Commission Report of 1955.[445] The 'voluntary' has been de-politicised, left as a 'sector', or abandoned to the Right, rather than being nurtured by the Left. The same is now happening to charities, contracted and funded to deliver outcomes specified by government. And dynamic young associates and fellow travellers of the

Labour Party itself – members, activists, and recruits to its constituency parties from movements like Momentum – are seen as problems for Labour to 'deal with' almost as urgently as capitalism itself. Why?[446]

Endnotes and References

NOTES AND REFERENCES FOR PART I

1. Hans Magnus Enzensberger, *New Selected Poems, Translated by David Constantine* (Hexham: Bloodaxe Books, 2015), p.104. For an explicitly political plea for 'openness' in exactly this sense, see Naomi Klein, *No Is Not Enough* (Canada & Great Britain: Random House & Allen Lane, 2017), p.243.
2. In *The Fall of Public Man* (Cambridge: Cambridge University Press, 1977), p.253.
3. Mark Bevir, *The Making of British Socialism* (Princeton: Princeton University Press, 2011), pp. 11-13, 23-27, 40-42, deploys the notion of a 'tradition' in intellectual history, as applied to distinct strands in the history of socialism in late-nineteenth-century Britain, one of which is the 'ethical' socialism of my 'New Life' essay in this book. See also Carl Boggs, *The Socialist Tradition from Crisis to Decline* (London and New York: Routledge, 1995). In *Victorian Agitator: G.J. Holyoake (1817–1906). Co-operation as 'This New Order of Life'* (Brighton: Edward Everett Root, 2017), I use 'tradition' in a sense derived from Alasdair MacIntyre, who uses it to distinguish philosophical/ ethical/religious 'traditions' one from another. Gregory Claeys' *Citizens and Saints: Politics and Antipolitics in Early British Socialism* (Cambridge: Cambridge University Press, 1989) is an outstanding modern contribution to the history of socialism as idea and as practice in Britain. Claeys and Bevir make full use of the committed periodical literature without which socialists and their movements cannot be understood. They also follow wide cross-cultural links and construct inclusive intellectual/ideological ecologies, offering comprehensive bibliographical guides to modern scholarship in related fields. Their work owes much to the prolific 'Cambridge school' – and later the Sussex school – of intellectual history, led by John Dunn, J.G.A. Pocock, Quentin Skinner, Donald Winch, John Burrows, and Stefan Collini. For this school of history focused on socialism, see John Dunn, *The Politics of Socialism: An Essay in Political Theory* (Cambridge: Cambridge University Press, 1984), on pp.xvi–xvii of which Dunn states that 'the classic questions of socialist theory concern the form of the state and the organization of the economy', and 'what really matters about socialism in the long run is whether it can be made

into an adequate political theory, and whether it possesses the intrinsic intellectual and moral resources to guide political action for the better'. And for an earlier, wide-ranging pedigree and bibliography, see George Lichtheim, *The Origins of Socialism* (New York: Praeger, 1969).

4. Protestantism, Nonconformity, and the 'Free Churches' have once again become of interest to historians in this context. See P. Ackers and Alistair Reid (eds.), *Alternatives to State Socialism in Britain: Other Worlds of Labour in the 20th Century* (London: Palgrave, 2016) and Peter Catterall, *Labour and the Free Churches, 1918–1939* (London: Bloomsbury, 2016). A foundation for work in this field remains Michael Walzer, *The Revolution of the Saints: a Study in the Origins of Radical Politics* (Boston: Harvard University Press, 1965). For the language of 'association' and its contested forms in the setting of seventeenth-century Seekerism, Quakerism, and 'covenantal' theology, see the early chapters of Douglas Gwyn, *The Covenant Crucified: Quakers and the Rise of Capitalism* (Wallingford, Pennsylvania: Pendle Hill Publications, 1995 and London: Quaker Books, 2006); and *Seekers Found: Atonement in Early Quaker Experience* (Wallingford, Pennsylvania 1986, 2000).

5. For which see Gareth Stedman Jones, 'Rethinking Chartism', in *Languages of Class: Studies in English Working-Class History, 1832–1982* (Cambridge: Cambridge University Press, 1983); and the discussion of 'Theory' in Chapter 1 of Mark Bevir, *The Making of British Socialism*, pp.1–21.

6. Bevir, *The Making of British Socialism*, p.298. 'People actively made socialism as they struggled to make sense of their world and their aspirations.'

7. Bevir, *The Making...* pp.299–300 puts these in neat chronological order: 'It was only in the late nineteenth century that the collapse of classical political economy and evangelicalism created the space in which socialism then appeared. In a first phase, a few popular and Tory radicals moved toward Marxism. In a second phase, a few liberal radicals moved toward humanitarianism, engaged Marxist and anarchist ideas, and forged a distinctive Fabian socialism based on an ideal of fellowship and attempts at personal and communal transformation.' John Dunn, *The Politics of Socialism: An Essay in Political Theory* (Cambridge: Cambridge University Press, 1984), pp.42–3, also has a triad of socialisms, but in this case they are within 'European social democracy, a political tendency, or a style of socialist politics, which has taken at least three distinct forms'.

8. Bevir, *The Making of British Socialism*, p.313.

9. For this project see also Stephen Yeo, 'Towards co-operative politics: using early to generate late socialism', in the *Journal of Co-operative Studies*, vol. 42:3 (No.127), December 2009, pp. 22-35, an essay which owes everything to Gregory Claeys, as does my 'Afterword: looking forward, co-operative politics or can Owen still help?', in Noel Thompson and Chris Williams, *Robert Owen and his Legacy* (Cardiff: University of Wales Press, 2011), pp.239-258. See also Stephen Yeo, 'Living the Vision: Co-operative Principles in Contemporary Practice: An Address to the UK Society for Co-operative Studies, September 2006', in *Journal of Co-operative Studies*, vol. 40:1, April 2007, pp.52-57. And 'The new mutualism and Labour's Third Way', in Johnston Birchall (ed.), *The New Mutualism in Public Policy* (London: Routledge, 2001), pp.226-242; and *Co-operative and Mutual Enterprises in Britain: Ideas from a Useable Past for a Modern Future* (Centre for Civil Society, London School of Economics, Report no.4, 2002).

10. The titles of chapters in Peter Ackers and Alastair J. Reid (eds.), *Alternatives to State-Socialism in Britain: Other Worlds of Labour in the Twentieth Century* (Cham, Switzerland: Palgrave Macmillan, 2016). This collection of essays includes a retrieval of the early work of G.D.H. Cole as 'a socialist and pluralist' by David Goodway. See also S. Meredith and P. Catney, 'New Labour and associative democracy: old debates in new times?' in *British Politics* 2,3, (2007), and M. Bevir (ed.), *Modern Pluralism. Anglo-American Debates since 1880* (Cambridge: Cambridge University Press, 2012). In my *Victorian Agitator: George Jacob Holyoake : Co-operation as 'This New Order of Life'* , which is volume 1 of *A Useable Past* (Brighton: Edward Root Publishers, 2017), pp.105-157, I worked with the idea of the Co-operative Movement as an embryonic autonomous, ethical or moral 'tradition', using Alasdair MacIntyre's philosophical work on rival 'traditions' as a base. Bram Bamford (ed.), *The Tradition of Workers' Control: Selected Writings by Geoffrey Ostergaard* (London: Freedom Press, 1997) is a rich contribution to associational socialism as (residual? re-emergent?) tradition, carefully distinguished from 'Fabianism and the Managerial Revolution', 'Socialism by Pressure Group', etc. See pp. 86-95 for how 'the tradition survives'.

11. For which see Stephen Yeo, 'Social movements and political action', *Universities Quarterly*, 24(4) (Autumn 1970), pp.402-21, reprinted in *School and Society, A Sociological Reader* (Open University, 1971). Tom Bottomore entitled part 3 of his *Sociology as Social Criticism* (Oxford: Blackwell, 1975) 'Social movements and political action'.

12. Mike Hales, *Living Thinkwork: Where Do Labour Processes Come From?*

(London: CSE Books, 1980), p.112.

13. R.H.S. Crossman, *The Backbench Diaries of Richard Crossman* (London: Hamish Hamilton, 1981), pp.769-70.

14. Beatrice Webb, diary entry for 18 April 1940 in the Passfield Papers at the London School of Economics, Vol.54.

15. *Justice*, 9 March 1901.

16. Asa Briggs, 'Drawing a new map of learning', in David Daiches (ed.), *The Idea of a New University: An Experiment in Sussex* (London: Deutsch, 1970), pp. 60-80. For my take on what happened, see also my 'Asa Briggs, an appreciation', in *Labour History Review*, vol.83, no.1 (2018), pp.69-79.

17. Walter Benjamin, 'The author as producer' in *Understanding Brecht*, translated by Anna Bostock (London: Verso,1977), p.103.

18. István Mészáros, *The Necessity of Social Control* (London: Merlin Press, 1971), p.64. For a fine antidote to the structure of thought and feeling that I am recalling here, see David Bollier, *Think Like a Commoner: A Short Introduction to the Life of the Commons* (Gabriola Island, British Columbia: New Society Publishers, 2014) chapter 10, 'The Commons as a different way of seeing and believing', pp.147-168.

19. Eileen and Stephen Yeo, 'On the uses of "community": from Owenism to the present', in Stephen Yeo (ed.) *New Views of Co-operation* (London: Routledge, 1988), pp.229-258.

20. For which see FWWCP *Book List 1985-6*, available from Consortium, Janet Burley, 16 Cliffsend House, Cowley Estate, London, SW9. See also D. Morley and K. Worpole (eds.), *The Republic of Letters: Working Class Writing and Local Publishing* (London: Comedia, 1982); Stephen Yeo 'The politics of community publications', in Raphael Samuel (ed.), *People's History and Socialist Theory* (London: Routledge, 1980), pp. 42-48; and 'QueenSpark books, selections and comment', in *South East Arts Review* (Winter 1977), pp.21-35.

21. A Brighton Labour Process Group typescript paper for the Conference of Socialist Economists (CSE) conference-meeting of July 1979 was central for me: 'Collectivism, Statism and the Associated Mode of Production: Notes towards the Critique of the Political Economy of Socialism as it Actually Exists'.

22. 'The poverty of theory', in *The Poverty of Theory and Other Essays* (London: Merlin Press, 1978), p.363. E.P. Thompson, *Customs in Common: Studies in Traditional Popular Culture* (London: Merlin Press, 1991). The (small p) politics of Thompson's work, as well as its historical

genius, has been well continued in that of his students, particularly Peter Linebaugh, *The Magna Carta Manifesto: Liberties and Commons for All* (Berkeley: University of California Press, 2008).

23. Sheila Rowbotham, 'The women's movement and organising for socialism', in Sheila Rowbotham, Lynne Segal, Hilary Wainwright (eds.), *Beyond the Fragments: Feminism and the Making of Socialism* (London: Merlin Press, 1979).

24. Alun Burge, *William Hazell's Gleaming Vision: A Co-operative Life in South Wales, 1890–1914* ((Talybont: YLolfa, 2014), p. 196. 'Joyous, co-operative, hopeful travelling' echoes Ivan Illich's recommendation of 'conviviality' as prefigurative politics in his *Tools for Conviviality* (1973). I owe this insight to Mike Hales. In *Activists and the Long March Home: Class Geography, Conviviality, Melancholy Territory – Some Prospects for Libertarian Socialist Adventures* (Brighton: Barefoot Documents, 2017), Hales is inspired by Illich to ask: 'In a world of sophisticated ways of knowledging and elaborate forms of artifice – the kind of world a chemical engineer, for example (or a doctor, a transport planner, an architect, a computer systems developer, a food scientist, an app. designer) wakes to each day – how can these extended assemblies of artefacts be made available as means for sociability and compassion and facilitation and commonality? ... opened into a cornucopia of means of self-determination and self-management and mutuality and mutual regard, in brotherhood and sisterhood ... to guarantee the "kind" in humankind?'

25. *Co-operative News*, 9 December 1950, quoted in Alun Burge, *William Hazell...*, p.155.

26. E. Durkheim, *Socialism* (1896); A. Gouldner (ed.) (New York: Collier Books, 1962), pp.61-2. A.V. Dicey made a similar distinction, based on a similar distrust of workers' socialism, in his 1914 'Introduction' to his *Lectures on the Relations between Law and Public Opinion* (London: Macmillan, 1905), 1962 edition p. xl.

27. E. J. Hobsbawm, *Industry and Empire* (London: Weidenfeld, 1968), p. 208.

28. Walter Benjamin, 'Conversations with Brecht', in Ernst Bloch et al., *Aesthetics and Politics* (London: Verso, 1977), pp. 96-7.

29. Philip Corrigan, Harvie Ramsay, and Derek Sayer, 'The state as a relation of production', in P. Corrigan (ed.), *Capitalism, State Formation and Marxist Theory* (London: Quartet Books, 1980), pp. 1-25.

30. J.R. Seeley, *The Expansion of England* (Cambridge: Cambridge

University Press, 1883). These lectures sold 80,000 copies in two years. The quotation is from the 2nd edn, 1899, p. 30.

31. For vivid material on this, see Ian Bullock, 'Socialists and Democratic Form in Britain, 1880-1914', unpublished D.Phil. thesis, University of Sussex, 1981. The quotations that follow are from this thesis, rather than from the book into which it fed: Logie Barrow and Ian Bullock, *Democratic Ideas and the British Labour Movement, 1880-1914* (Cambridge: Cambridge University Press, 1996).

32. See Part 2 chapter 4 of Logie Barrow and Ian Bullock, *Democratic Ideas and the British Labour Movement, 1880-1914* (Cambridge: Cambridge University Press, 1996), 'Conflicts in the ILP', pp.75-87.

33. Ramsay MacDonald, *Socialism and Government*, vol. I (London: Independent Labour Party, 1909), pp. 11-12. See a perceptive review of the same work in *Labour Leader*, 26 November 1909: 'Volume 1' because this book was Part VIII of 'The Socialist Library' Series edited by MacDonald, a venture for which the National Administrative Committee of the ILP had agreed to take full financial responsibility Logie Barrow and Ian Bullock, *Democratic Ideas and the British Labour Movement, 1880-1914* (Cambridge, Cambridge University Press, 1996), p.163, n.3. See also MacDonald on 'Socialism' in Bernard Barker (ed.) *Ramsay MacDonald's Political Writings* (London: Allen Lane, 1972). In his *Socialism and Society* (London: Independent Labour Party, 1905), p.70, MacDonald wrote that 'the democratic State is an organisation of the people, democratic government is self-government, democratic law is an expression of the will of the people who have to obey the law'. Move forwards to Lenin fifteen years later and substitute 'the Soviet State' for 'the democratic State' and 'proletariat' for 'people'. For how 'the state' need not, and should not, be conceived as 'owning' and 'doing' things or (social) relations, see David Bollier, *Think Like a Commoner: A Short Introduction to the Life of the Commons* (Gabriola Island, British Columbia: New Society Publishers, 2014), p.93.

34. MacDonald, *Socialism and Society*, pp.70, 133.

35. See note 21 above, Brighton Labour Process Group, 'Collectivism, Statism …' (July 1979), p.2.

36. For philosophical statism and the freezing of the imagination, see Anthony Skillen, *Ruling Illusions: Philosophy and the Social Order* (New Jersey: Humanities Press 1978); and 'The statist conception of politics', in *Radical Philosophy*, 2 (1972), quoted in Philip Corrigan, 'State Formation and Moral Regulation in Nineteenth-century Britain: Sociological Investigations', unpublished D.Phil. thesis, University of

Durham, 1977, p. 381. See also N. Johnson, *In Search of the Constitution* (London: Routledge, 1977).

37. See Nicholas Deakin, *In Search of Civil Society* (Basingstoke and New York: Palgrave, 2001).
38. Senex, in *The Pioneer*, 22 March 1834, in Letter II (one of a series of such letters) 'To the productive classes'. For further material on the Owenite legacy, see Stephen Yeo, 'Towards Co-operative politics: using early to generate late socialism', in the *Journal of Co-operative Studies* (vol.42:3, no.127, December 2009), pp. 22-35.
39. S. and B. Webb, *The History of Trade Unionism* (London: Longman, 1894), pp. 475-6.
40. Beatrice Webb, *My Apprenticeship* (1926) (Cambridge: Cambridge University Press, 1979 edition), pp.59 and 161.
41. J.M. Keynes, 'Am I a Liberal?', in *The Nation and Athenaeum*, an essay published in two parts: I, 8 August 2015 pp.563-4; II, 15 August 2015 pp.587-8. I owe this reference to Hilary Wainwright from her work in progress on *The Politics of Knowledge*, forthcoming from Polity.
42. Beatrice Webb, *Diary* entry for 11 August 1940. I owe this reference to Hilary Wainwright.
43. Thomas Burt, quoted in Robert Currie, *Industrial Politics* (Oxford: Oxford University Press, 1979), p. 51.
44. For this perspective, see S. Yeo, 'State and anti-state: reflections on social forms and struggles from 1850', in Philip Corrigan (ed.), *Capitalism, State Formation and Marxist Theory* (London and New York: Quartet Books, 1980), pp. 111-41; and Currie, *Industrial Politics...*, on the 1906 Trades Disputes Act and the 1926 General Strike. The Webbs were in favour of the Taff Vale judgement, making Unions liable for the damages inflicted by 'industrial' action.
45. Stephen Yeo, 'On the uses of "apathy"', in the *European Journal of Sociology* XV (1974), pp. 279-311.
46. Paul Hirst (ed.), *The Pluralist Theory of the State* (London and New York:Routledge, 1989), 'Introduction', pp.16-22, on 'corporate personality and associationalism'.
47. *Labour Leader*, 1 February 1907.
48. P. Williams, *Hugh Gaitskell: A Political Biography* (London: Cape, 1979), p.391.
49. For the best study of the Trade Union-Labour Party relationship, see Lewis Minkin, *The Contentious Alliance, Trade Unions and the Labour*

Party (Edinburgh: Edinburgh University Press, 1991). And for a revealing 'moment' in the Co-operative Movement's history, see the *Co-operative Independent Commission Report* (Manchester: Co-operative Union, 1958). The papers of this Commission are now in the National Co-operative Archive. Its Chair was Hugh Gaitskell, and its Secretary Anthony Crosland; its view of the Co-op was as an (ailing) business needing modernisation in order to become more competitive, rather than as the cell of a new social order needing to inform Labour's entire project.

50. Hilary Wainwright, *The Politics of Knowledge*, forthcoming from Polity in 2018, is lucid on 'the prevailing knowledge of the political stratosphere, where governmental knowledge has been understood as "scientific" in the narrow sense of codified, centralised laws deployed by professionals expert in this knowledge and where other kinds of belief or knowhow do not count'.

51. A.J. Polan, *Lenin and the End of Politics* (Berkeley: University of California Press,1984), pp. 3, 78.

52. Caroline Humphrey, *Karl Marx Collective. Economy, Society and Religion in a Siberian Collective Farm* (Cambridge, Cambridge University Press. 1983), 'The collective farm and the state in Soviet theory', pp. 92–102. Svetlana Alexievich's many books based on sustained interviews, most notably *Second-Hand Time, The Last of the Soviets* (London: Fitzcarraldo Editions, 2013) provide rich material of this kind.

53. *The Observer*, 29 July 1979.

54. Asa Briggs, 'The world economy: interdependence and planning' in C.L. Mowat (ed.), *The Shifting Balance of World Forces 1898–1945, The New Cambridge Modern History* vol.XII (Cambridge: Cambridge University Press, 1968).

55. Brighton Labour Process Group, 'Collectivism, Statism …', p.2.

56. Raymond Williams, *Politics and Letters* (London: Verso,1979), p. 377.

57. Raymond Williams, *Culture and Society 1780–1950* (London: Chatto and Windus, 1958), the first book in a lifetime body of work on this and cognate themes. In this setting, see his *Culture* (London: Fontana New Sociology series, 1981); and *Keywords*, A *Vocabulary of Culture and Society* (London: Croom Helm 1976, extended in an Oxford University Press edition, Oxford, 1984).

58. Peter Nettl, 'The German Social Democratic Party as a political model', in *Past and Present* no. 30 (April 1969), pp.65–93.

59. Schumpeter called the socialism of the period 1790–1870 'associationist',

by which he meant that it was extra-scientific, having to do with blueprints, not with analysis. In a judgement which is stretched to include Thompson, Hodgskin, Gray, and Bray, Schumpeter regarded the work of the 'associationist socialists' as trivial, with the exception of Blanc, Owen, Fourier, and St-Simon: see J. A. Schumpeter, *History of Economic Analysis* (New York: Oxford University Press, 1954), pp. 452-62.

60. S. Webb, *Socialism True and False*, Fabian Tract no. 51 (1899), p. 10.
61. Quoted in R. Page Arnot, *William Morris: The Man and the Myth* (London: Lawrence and Wishart, 1964).
62. The citation is from the *Saturday Review*, 8 May 1880. The piece deals with the development of anarchist ideas within 'The International', where 'the doctrine of Collectivism forced its way to the front ... By Collectivism is meant that everything is done and managed by a society. Railways, mines, forests, and even the soil, are to be worked by associations ... What is remarkable in this impracticable conception is that it gets rid of the idea of the State. The associations include everyone, but there is nothing above the associations.'
63. *Co-operative News*, 20 October 1894. In John Dunn, *The Politics of Socialism: An Essay in Political Theory* (Cambridge: Cambridge University Press, 1984), p.47, 'collectivism' is used in the context of 'the internal political pressures towards collectivism which stem from the experience for the majority of its population of what it is like to live in a capitalist society'.
64. S. Collini, *Liberalism and Sociology* (Cambridge, 1979). And more recently by Mark Bevir in *The Making of British Socialism* (2011). Bevir rightly portrays Fabian socialism as much more mixed and overlapping with Ethical Socialism and liberal radicalism than I have allowed it to be here.
65. *The Wheatsheaf*, vol.II, no. 1 (May 1898), p.162.
66. Asa Briggs, 'Introduction' in Asa Briggs and John Saville (eds.), *Essays in Labour History 1886-1923* (London: Macmillan, 1971), pp.1-16, and his *William Morris: Selected Writings and Designs* (Harmondsworth: Penguin, 1962), p.17.
67. S. Webb to Edward Pease, October 1886, in Norman Mackenzie (ed.), *The Letters of Sydney and Beatrice Webb* (Cambridge: Cambridge University Press) vol. I, 1873-1892 (1978), p. 101.
68. Royden Harrison, *The Life and Times of Sidney and Beatrice Webb, 1858-1905, The Formative Years* (Basingstoke: Macmillan, Palgrave, 2000), and Royden Harrison, 'Sidney and Beatrice Webb', in Carl Levy (ed.), *Socialism and the Intelligentsia 1880-1914* (London: Routledge, 1987),

pp.59–60: 'between the Webbs' professional labour leader and Lenin's professional revolutionary there lay a world of difference, but there was also a notable area of common ground'.

69. Beatrice Webb, *Our Partnership* (London: Longmans,1948), diary entry for 25 February 1903, pp. 259–60.

70. T. Kirkup, *History of Socialism* (London and Edinburgh: A. and C. Black, 1st edition 1892; 5th edn, revised by Edward Pease, 1913, p. 379). Kirkup also wrote on related topics for the now-classic 1911 edition of the *Encyclopedia Britannica*.

71. Bernard Shaw, letter to W. P. Johnson, 24 April 1893, in Dan H. Laurence (ed.), *G.B. Shaw, Collected Letters, 1874–1897* (London: Viking Adult, 1965), p. 389.

72. S. and B. Webb, 'Social movements' in A.W Ward (ed.), *The Latest Age* (Cambridge: Cambridge University Press, 1910).

73. *The Letters of S. and B. Webb*, Norman Mackenzie (ed.), (Cambridge, Cambridge University Press with the LSE, 1978) vol. I, p. 196. Letter of Sydney to Beatrice Potter, 22 September 1890. See also Royden Harrison, 'Sidney and Beatrice Webb' in Carl Levy (ed.), *Socialism and the Intelligentsia 1880–1914* (Routledge, 1987), pp.35–89, and Royden Harrison, *The Life and Times of Sidney and Beatrice Webb, 1858–1905, The Formative Years* (Basingstoke: Macmillan, Palgrave,2000).

74. *Justice*, 9 March 1901.

75. Particularly as a parent body of the Fabian Society was the Fellowship of the New Life (1883–1898), whose prophet was Thomas Davidson, for whom see William Knight *Memorials of Thomas Davidson* (Boston: Ginn and Company, 1907). The Fellowship's members included Edward Carpenter, Henry Stephens Salt, and Havelock Ellis. Originally a 'Guild', its 'Object' was 'the cultivation of a perfect character in each and all'. They wanted to transform society by setting an example of clean simplified living for others to follow. Their 'Principle' was 'the subordination of material things to spiritual things'. But discipline was important. 'Fellowship' had one 'sole and essential condition … a single-minded, sincere and strenuous devotion to the object and principle'. Davidson explicitly contrasted 'co-operation' with 'socialism' in 'Cooperation' in the *Freethinkers Magazine*, Feb.1887, reprinted in Michael H. De Armey, *The St Louis Hegelians* (London: Continuum, 2001), pp.50–59. I owe this reference to Jonathan Ree. Bevir, *The Making of British Socialism*… emphasises the range of socialisms within the Fabian Society (p.150) and challenges the view

that Sidney Webb in particular is best understood as a champion of a New, Professional-Managerial class or cadre (p.193). 'He was an ethical and evolutionary positivist whose later socialism was still dominated by a historical sociology that articulated the functional differentiation and development of social institutions.' But elsewhere in *The Making...* he sees Sidney as a 'collectivist' who turned away from neoclassical economics to positivist sociology'. 'Webb defined permeation in terms of giving expert advice to the political elite' (p.19). And 'The Fabians' (p.213) 'rarely promoted greater popular participation in government', 'looked on political reform not as a way to solve social ills but as administrative measures to facilitate good government ... Generally they welcomed the rise of a professional civil service and policy experts.'

76. For which see Carl Levy, 'Introduction: historical and theoretical themes' and 'Conclusion: historiography and the new class' in Carl Levy (ed.), *Socialism and the Intelligentsia 1880–1914* (Routledge, 1987), pp. 1–34 and 271–290.

77. See Hilary Wainwright, *A New Politics From The Left* (Cambridge: Polity, 2018).

78. I am indebted to Mike Hales for the starkness of this observation.

79. Barbara and John Ehrenreich, 'The professional-managerial-class', in *Radical America* (2), March–April 1977, pp.7–31, reprinted with commentaries in Pat Walker, *Between Labour and Capital* (Hassocks: Harvester Press, 1979), and elaborated in Barbara Ehrenreich, *Fear of Falling: The Inner Life of the Middle Class* (New York: Pantheon, 1989).

80. Barbara and John Ehrenreich, *Death of a Yuppie Dream: The Rise and Fall of the Professional-Managerial Class* (New York: Rosa Luxemburg Stiftung Office, February 2013). I owe this reference to Mike Hales. The little-known Rosa Luxemburg Foundation is 'an internationally operating, progressive non-profit institution for civic education. In co-operation with many organizations around the globe, it works on democratic and social participation, empowerment of disadvantaged groups, alternatives for economic, and social development, and peaceful conflict resolution.'

81. Barbara and John Ehrenreich, 'The professional-managerial class...', p.1.

82. Stephen Yeo, 'Intellectuals versus cultural producers: mainly from Raymond Williams's fiction', in *The Journal of Historical Sociology* Vol.2 No.3 (September 1989), pp.265–286, particularly 'our common,

associative life', pp.282-4. This conflict/struggle informs much of Williams' later work. It is evident in his relationship with his interviewers in *Politics and Letters* (London: New Left Books, 1979) and in his *The Politics of Modernism: Against the New Conformists* (London: Verso, 1989); and in John McIlroy and Sallie Westwood (eds.), *Raymond Williams in Adult Education: Border Country* (Leicester: National Institute of Adult and Continuing Education, 1993).

83. For 'Class, politics and socialism', see pp. 153-174 of Raymond Williams, *Towards 2000* (London: Chatto and Windus, 1983). In this now neglected work, which concludes with a magnificent chapter called 'Resources for a journey of hope', Williams reconsiders the analyses and proposals in his better known *The Long Revolution* (London: Chatto and Windus, 1961), and responds to Rudolf Bahro's *The Alternative in Eastern Europe* (London: New Left Books/Verso, 1978). The ground for this kind of work was broken for Western radicals, particularly those working in adult education, by Ivan Illich, in *Deschooling Society* (New York: Harper and Row, 1971) and *Tools for Conviviality* (New York: Harper and Row 1973); and by Paolo Freire, *The Pedagogy of the Oppressed*, first published in Portugese in 1968, in English in 1970, and still in print in 2017 as a Penguin Classic.

84. See Mike Hales, *Humble Origins – All Roads Lead to Halifax* (Seven Dials, Brighton: Barefoot Documents, October 2017). In a section of this text called 'The story starts here – class geography, the landscape into which M was born', there is a vivid account of a transformative moment (from a class point of view) in Mike's life in the University of Sussex in 1972.

85. Mike Hales, *Living Thinkwork: Where Do Labour Processes Come From?* (London, CSE Books, 1980), p.112.

86. Mike Hales, *Activists and the Long March Home: Class Geography, Conviviality, Melancholy Territory. Some Prospects for Libertarian Socialist Adventures* (Seven Dials, Brighton: Barefoot Documents , October 2017) .

87. Mike Hales, *Living Thinkwork*, pp. 94-5, 147, 153, 173. He has continued to develop this work recently in a cluster of publications-on-demand available through his 'Barefoot Documents' imprint, including the work cited in notes 84 and 86 above. Mike publishes under a Creative Commons Share-Alike non-commercial 3.0 licence. The huge, more than contingent obstacles to be overcome in his class project, as lucidly described here, can be followed every day now in the press, for example Aditya Chakrabortty, 'If capitalism fails, 26 Greek workers can show us how to fill the void', in *The Guardian* 18 July 2017, p.29, where 'what

will happen next?' cannot be kept from the socialist reader's mind.

88. M. Hales, *Living Thinkwork: Where do Labour Processes Come From?* (London: CSE Books, 1980), p.110.

89. L.F. Urwick and E.F.L. Brech, *The Making of Scientific Management* (London: Management Publications Trust 1945, 1951-7, republished by the Thoemmes Press, 2002). In *Labour and Monopoly Capital: The Degradation of Work in the Twentieth Century* (New York: Monthly Review Press, 1974). Harry Braverman referred to Urwick as 'the rhapsodic historian of the scientific management movement'.

90. For the St Simonians in this context (the word *'socialisme'* being coined in *Le Globe* newspaper in the late 1820s to early 1830s) and for Goethe's vision of 'a historically new synthesis of private and public power, symbolized by the union of Mephistopheles, the private freebooter and predator, and Faust, the public planner who conceives and directs the work as a whole', see Marshall Berman, *All That is Solid Melts into Air* (London: Verso, 1983).

91. B. Kirkman Grey, *Philanthropy and the State, or Social Politics* (London: P.S. King, 1908), p. 13. For this crucial figure, see H. B. Bins, *A Modern Humanist: Miscellaneous Papers of B. Kirkman Grey* (1910). I owe the former reference to Asa Briggs, and the latter to Chris Waters, 'Socialism and the Politics of Popular Culture in Britain, 1889-1914', unpublished DPhil thesis, Harvard University, 1985, pp. 188-9.

92. G. J. Harney (a Chartist) in the *Red Republican*, 21 September 1850.

93. New York: Harcourt, Brace, Jovanovich, 1979.

94. Royden Harrison, *The Life and Times of Sidney and Beatrice Webb, 1858-1905, The Formative Years* (Basingstoke: Macmillan, Palgrave, 1999) particularly on 'The Man with No Inside', Sidney Webb 1859-90. Harrison's essay 'Sidney and Beatrice Webb' in Carl Levy (ed.) *Socialism and the Intelligentsia 1880-1914* (London: Routledge, 1987), pp.35-90, is a brilliant anticipation and overview of his entire work on the Webbs, including Sidney's devotion to Roman un- or anti-individual ends: 'a beacon light to all successive ages' (p.57).

95. E. T. Keeling (ed.), *Letters and Recollections* (London: George Allen and Unwin, 1918), pp. 57, 38-9, 32, 62, 59-60. In his introduction to this book, H. G. Wells wrote that Keeling was 'as complete and expressive a specimen of the educated youth of the first decade of the twentieth century ... as perhaps we are likely to get'.

96. S. and B. Webb, *Soviet Communism: A New Civilisation* (London: Longman, 2nd edn. 1937), pp. 1215- 6.

97. From 'Concerning the ego and the collective', an essay by Malevitch in the first number of the *Almanac* of UNOVIS, a Suprematist group in Vitebsk, for which see T.J. Clark, *Farewell to an Idea: Episodes from a History of Modernism* (New Haven: Yale University Press, 1999), p.226.
98. *Leeds Co-operative Record*, no. 196 (April 1894), p. 6. Balfour was to inherit his Prime Minister brother's Earldom in 1930.
99. Quoted in Jeremy Seabrook, *What Went Wrong?* (London: Gollancz, 1978), p.59; see also p.183.
100. Jose Harris, *William Beveridge: A Biography* (Oxford: Oxford University Press, 1977, revised and enlarged in 1998).
101. Bentley Gilbert, *The Evolution of National Insurance in Great Britain. The Origins of the Welfare State* (London: Michael Joseph, 1966, Gregg Revivals, 1993).
102. A good example of which is *Quaker Faith and Practice: The Book of Christian Discipline of the Yearly Meeting of the Religious Society of Friends (Quakers) in Britain* (London: The Yearly Meeting. 1994, 1998, etc.).
103. London: George Allen and Unwin, 1948, pp. 323-4. For a deeply felt, twenty-first century echo, or new/old beginning of such visioning, see David Bollier, *Think Like a Commoner: A Short Introduction to the Life of the Commons* (Gabriola Island, British Columbia: New Society Publishers, 2014): Introduction, 'Think like a Commoner', p.4, on 'countless real-life commons'. 'These commons integrate economic production, social co-operation, personal participation and ethical idealism into a single package.They represent a practical paradigm of self-help and collective gain. The commons is essentially a parallel economy and social order that quietly but confidently affirms that another world is possible. And more: we can build it ourselves, now.'
104. The quotation is from Alun Burge, *William Hazell's Gleaming Vision: A Co-operative Life in South Wales, 1890–1964* (Talybont: Y Lolfa Cyf, 2014), p.196.
105. Philip Corrigan, 'State Formation and Moral Regulation in 19th Century Britain: Sociological Investigations' (University of Durham: D.Phil, 1977), p.96. Philip Corrigan, an historical sociologist and socialist, co-authored with Derek Sayer, *The Great Arch: English State Formation as Cultural Revolution* (Oxford: Basil Blackwell, 1985). A 'great arch' was Marx's metaphor for capitalism's long revolution. Corrigan's book describes the eight-hundred-year transition to capitalism as cultural revolution, thereby conveying the idea of a socialist revolution more extended than Raymond Williams' version of the same in *The Long*

Revolution (1961). *The Great Arch* works with the idea that it is, in both cases, *construction* which is at issue, in any long transition. That is to say, the making of prefigurative forms of association – or cells – which carry a possible future in the present. Peter Gurney worked the same seam on behalf of Co-operative association as cultural revolution, in '"Labour's Great Arch", co-operation and cultural revolution in Britain, 1795-1926', in Ellen Furlough and Carl Strickwerda (eds.) *Consumers against Capitalism. Consumer Co-operation in Europe, North America and Japan 1840-1990* (Maryland: Rowman and Littlefield, 1999). For Andrea Weber, a theoretical biologist, on *biopoesis* in this setting, see David Bollier, *Think Like a Commoner: A Short Introduction to the Life of the Commons* (Gabriola Island, British Columbia: New Society Publishers, 2014), pp.147-9.

106. Philip Gross, 'Wetland, thinking...' in *A Bright Acoustic* (Hexham: Bloodaxe Books, 2017), p.68.

107. G.J. Holyoake, *The Co-operative Movement Today* (London: Methuen, 1903 edition), pp.187-8.

108. Mike Hales, *Activists and the Long March Home: Class Geography, Conviviality, Melancholy Territory. Some Prospects for Libertarian Socialist Adventures, 2017* (Seven Dials, Brighton: Barefoot Documents, October 2017).

109. I owe this story entirely to Aditya Chakrabortty, 'If capitalism fails, 26 Greek workers can show us how to fill the void', in *The Guardian*, 18 July 2017, p.29.

110. 'Retrieving pluralism', in William Outhwaite and Michael Mulkay, *Social Theory and Social Criticism: Essays for Tom Bottomore* (Oxford: Basil Blackwell, 1987, Gregg Revivals, 1992), pp. 154-174. See also Paul Hirst, *From Statism to Pluralism: Democracy, Civil Society and Global Politics* (London: Routledge, 1997).

111. Paul Hirst, *Associative Democracy: New Forms of Economic and Social Governance* (Cambridge: Polity, 1984); *The Pluralist Theory of the State: Selected Writings of G.D.H. Cole, J.N. Figgis, and H.J. Laski* (London: Routledge, 1989); Grahame Thompson, Paul Hirst, and Simon Bromley, *Globalization in Question: The International Economy and the Possibilities of Governance* (Cambridge: Polity, 1996); 'Renewing democracy through associations', in *Political Quarterly*, vol. 73, issue 4 (October 2002), pp.409-421. This essay was the stimulus for a fertile seminar in the Coin Street Neighbourhood Centre in October 2010.

112. For the same question, see Stephen Yeo, 'The new mutualism and

Labour's Third Way', in Johnston Birchall (ed.), *The New Mutualism in Public Policy* (London: Routledge, 2001), pp.226–242; and *Co-operative and Mutual Enterprises in Britain: Ideas from a Useable Past for a Modern Future* (London School of Economics: Centre for Civil Society Report no.4, 2002). And for a promising co-operative and mutual answer, see David Blunkett, *Politics and Progress: Renewing Democracy and a Civil Society* (London: Demos, 2002).

113. The quotations from *Associative Democracy* are from pp.173, 11, 189, 13, 17–8, 20.

114. Interview in *The World*, 3 July 1871. In section 5, 'Co-operative labour', of Marx's *The International Working Men's Association, 1866. Instructions for the Delegates of the Provisional General Council*, written at the end of August 1866, Marx wrote: 'We acknowledge the co-operative movement as one of the transforming forces of the present society based upon class antagonism. Its great merit is to practically show that the present pauperising and despotic system of the subordination of labour to capital can be superseded by the republican and beneficent system of the association of free and equal producers.' However, he went on to argue that 'the co-operative system will never transform capitalist society' by means of 'the dwarfish forms into which individual wage slaves can elaborate it (i.e the co-operative system) by their private efforts. To convert social production into one large and harmonious system of free and co-operative labour, general social changes are wanted, changes of the general conditions of society; never to be realised save by the transfer of the organised forces of society, viz., the state power, from capitalists and landlords to the producers themselves.'

115. *The Communist Manifesto*: 'All previous historical movements were movements of minorities, or in the interests of minorities. The proletarian movement is the self-conscious, independent movement of the immense majority in the interest of the immense majority. The proletariat, the lowest stratum of our present society, cannot stir, cannot raise itself up, without the whole superincumbent strata being sprung into the air.'

116. R. Bahro, *The Alternative in Eastern Europe* (London: Verso, 1978), pp. 287–8. The internal quotes from Goethe are from *Faust*.

117. Raymond Williams, *Politics and Letters* (London: Verso, 1979), pp. 434–7.

118. Raymond Williams, *The Country and the City* (London: Chatto, 1973), p. 306.

119. *The Communist Manifesto*, and *The German Ideology*, as read by Marshall

Berman, *All That is Solid Melts Into Air* (London: Verso, 1983), pp. 95-7.

120. Quoted in E.P. Thompson, *William Morris, Romantic to Revolutionary* (London: Merlin Press, 1977 edition), p.593.

121. A. E. Bestor, 'The evolution of the socialist vocabulary', in *Journal of the History of Ideas*, IX (3) (1948), pp. 259-302.

122. For Holyoake on the co-operative 'state within the state', and on 'the moral art of association', 'associative intelligence', 'a new art of association', 'the association of labour', etc., see Stephen Yeo, *Victorian Agitator, George Jacob Holyoake (1817-1906): Co-operation as 'This New Order of Life'* (Brighton: Edward Everett Root, Publishers, 2017), pp.33, 37, 52, 90, 157, 174, etc. And for co-operative socialism more generally in this context, see also Stephen Yeo, 'Towards co-operative politics: using early to generate late socialism', in the *Journal of Co-operative Studies*, vol.42:3 (No.127) December 2009, pp. 22-35.

123. K. Marx, *Capital*, III (Harmondsworth: Penguin edn.1981), pp. 571-2.

124. *The Producer*, 15 February,1917.

125. T.W. Mercer, *The Co-operative Movement in Politics* (Manchester: Co-operative Union, 1921). The phrase about introducing Co-operation into politics but not politics into Co-operation originates with William Maxwell, President of the Scottish CWS, speaking at the Co-operative Congress of 1897 in Perth; see *Co-operative News*, 12 June 1897 pp. 622-3. Within the Co-operative Movement there was much scepticism, even thought-through antagonism, towards the creation of a Co-operative Party in the, by then, orthodox sense of what a Political Party was. See Thomas F. Carbery, *Consumers in Politics: A History and General Review of the Co-operative Party* (Manchester: Manchester University Press, 1969).

126. T. F. Carbery, *Consumers in Politics* ..., p.13. The quotation is from a verbatim report of a debate on co-operative politics in the *Report of the Cooperative Congress of 1913*, pp.494-9. Part One, chapters 1 and 2 of Carbery..., 'Prelude to the Party' and 'The birth of the Party', pp. 3-23, are essential reading for the molten years of the formation of the Party, as is Sidney Pollard, 'The foundation of the Co-operative Party', in Asa Briggs and John Saville (eds.), *Essays in Labour History, 1886-1923* (London: Palgrave Macmillan, 1971), pp.188-210, and Bill Lancaster, *Radical Co-operation and Socialism: Leicester Working-class Politics, 1860-1906* (Leicester: Leicester University Press, 1987).

127. London: Swan Sonnenschein, 1898.

128. Howard, *A Peaceful Path...*(1898), pp. 96-8, 121.

129. For examples brought to life by graduate students and faculty at the University of Sussex and presented to J.F.C. Harrison, see Stephen Yeo (ed.), *New Views of Co-operation* (London: Routledge, 1988). See also my 'State and anti-state, reflections on social forms and struggles from 1850', in P. Corrigan (ed.), *Capitalism, State Formation and Marxist Theory* (London: Quartet, 1980) and 'Working-class association, private capital, welfare and the state in the late-nineteenth and twentieth centuries', in N. Parry, M. Rustin, and C. Satyamurti (eds.), *Social Work, Welfare and the State* (London: Edward Arnold, 1979).

130. Stephen Yeo, *Religion and Voluntary Organisations in Crisis* (London: Croom Helm, 1976) ; Eileen and Stephen Yeo (eds.), *Popular Culture and Class Conflict: Explorations in the History of Labour and Leisure* (Brighton: Harvester, 1981).

131. From a base in modern Manchester, Michael Symmons Roberts' book of poems, *Mancunia* (London: Cape Poetry, 2017) has some wonderful 'difficult-recovery' poems in it. For example, 'Superintendent of Public Spectacles' (p.15), and 'Terra Pericolosa' (p.35). From the former:

> Even he (who understands spectacle,
> who knows how it can seize the attention
> so an audience forgets its future)
>
> can imagine this consummate age,
> this commonwealth, all lost except a single square
> of woven glass-fibre from a transistor radio,
> washed up on a distant shore,
> with the ghost of a circuit mapped onto it.

132. Stephen Yeo, 'Some Problems in Realising a General Working-class Strategy in Twentieth-century Britain', paper to the British Sociological Association conference on Power and the State (1977), Sheffield. See David Bollier, *Think Like a Commoner: A Short Introduction to the Life of the Commons* (Gabriola Island, British Columbia: New Society Publishers, 2014), pp.147–9, on Andreas Weber and *biopoetics*.

133. K. Marx, *Capital,* vol. I, Penguin, edn. (1976), p. 198.

134. Timothy Garton Ash, *The Polish Revolution: Solidarity 1980–2* (London: Jonathan Cape, 1983), pp. 9, 231.

135. Stephen Yeo, 'William Morris and modern socialism', in *The Spokesman* no.20, December 1971/ January 1972, pp. 3–7. For how 'our culture and language do not equip us to see fthe humanistic and spiritual

roots of the commons', see David Bollier, *Think Like a Commoner: A Short Introduction to the Life of the Commons* (Gabriola Island, British Columbia: New Society Publishers, 2014), p.151

136. A book edited by David Daiches (London: Deutsch, 1964) in which Asa Briggs wrote his most radical and original essay, on the School-based, interdisciplinary curriculum with which the University of Sussex began: 'Drawing a new map of learning'.

137. For which see Stephen Yeo, 'Social movements and political action', *Universities Quarterly* 24(4) (Autumn 1970), pp.402-21, reprinted in *School and Society, A Sociological Reader* (Open University, 1971). Tom Bottomore entitled part 3 of his *Sociology as Social Criticism* (Oxford: Blackwell, 1975) 'Social movements and political action'.

138. For which see the Asa Briggs essay in note 16 above, and my 'Asa Briggs: an appreciation', in *The Historian: the Magazine of the Historical Association* (Issue 133, Spring 2017), pp.16-20.

139. Mike Hales expressed both its centrality and its difficulty in *Living Thinkwork: Where Do Labour Processes Come From?*: 'The problem of a politics of knowledge is to bring theoretical knowledge within the grasp of all significant social practices, and to create theoretical knowledge which can be mapped into immediate personal knowledge in ways sufficiently direct and visible to be brought under social control by democratic means. Knowledge is abstraction. But in producing socialist knowledge, the *how* of the abstraction must be part of what the knowledge knows. In working towards this kind of knowledge, the theory of literatures is at least as much use to us as the theory of sciences.' See also Hilary Wainwright, 'A New Politics of Knowledge', in *A New Politics From the Left* (Cambridge: Polity, 2018) pp. 1-37.

140. The title of an essay by Robin Murray (of the Greater London Council Economic Policy Group) in Ben Pimlott (ed.), *Fabian Essays in Socialist Thought* (Fabian Society, 1984).

141. QueenSpark was a co-founder and continuing member of the Federation of Worker Writers and Community Publishers (FWWCP), for which see Dave Morley and Ken Worpole (eds.) *The Republic of Letters: Working-class Writing and Local Publishing* (London: Comedia Publishing Group, 1982), re-published with a new section on 'Afterthoughts: the past, present, and future of worker writers and community publishers: historical currents' (Philadelphia and Syracuse, New City Community Press and Syracuse University Press, 2009), pp .179-271.

142. Sheila Rowbotham, Lynne Segal, and Hilary Wainwright, *Beyond the Fragments: Feminism and the Making of Socialism* (London: Merlin Press, 1979), republished by the same press in 2013 with three new essays by the same authors.

143. Robin Murray, *Danger and Opportunity: Crisis and the New Social Economy* (London: NESTA, Provocation 09, September 2009), pp.4–5); see also Robin Murray, Julie Caulier-Grice, and Geoff Mulgan, *Social Venturing* (London: The Young Foundation and NESTA, Social Innovator Series, July 2009) and *The Open Book of Social Innovation* (March 2010).

144. Greater London Council, *London Industrial Strategy* (1985), p. 213.

145. R. Murray, 'New Directions in Municipal Socialism', pp. 228–9. Among much else which shows renewed interest in voluntary association as a *sine qua non* of any majority socialism, see Ken Worpole, 'Volunteers for socialism', *New Society*, 29 January 1981; Jeff Bishop and Paul Hoggett, *Organising Around Enthusiasms* (Comedia, 1986), series on Organizations and Democracy, no. 2.

NOTES AND REFERENCES FOR PART II

146. Adopted at the general conference 5 July 1885; reprinted as Appendix 1 in E.P. Thompson, *William Morris, Romantic to Revolutionary* (London: Merlin Press, revised edition, 1977), pp.732–740. The Edinburgh socialists objected to the use of 'religion', preferring 'cause' – a word Morris also often used: see A.K. Donald to J.L. Mahon, 21 Jan. 1885, in Socialist League papers, Amsterdam. I owe this and the Eleanor Marx reference below to Edward Thompson, who also told me that Donald went on objecting to Morris's 'moral tone', became the opponent in the Bloomsbury 'Marxist' section whom Morris most distrusted, and turned eventually into a total cynic, leaving the cause in about 1895 to resume his own legal career. See Thompson, *William Morris, Romantic to Revolutionary* (London: Lawrence and Wishart, 1955 edition), p.698. All subsequent references to Thompson, *Morris* come from this original, 1955 text. For another Morris argument for 'Religion', see *Commonweal*, 28 Aug. 1886.

147. Raymond Williams, *Keywords* (London: Croom Helm, 1976).

148. Hilary Wainwright, p.1.

149. Eleanor Marx Aveling to Council, Socialist League 5 Oct. 1885 in SL papers, Amsterdam; E.B. Bax, *The Religion of Socialism* (London: Swan

Sonnenschein, 1885); Katherine St J. Conway and J.B. Glasier, *The Religion of Socialism; Two Aspects* (Manchester: Labour Press Pamphlet no. 18, 2nd edition, 1894); R. Blatchford, 'The New Religion', Pass On Pamphlets no. 9: Clarion Press, 1892); G. Lansbury, *My Life* (London: Constable, 1928), pp. 78-9.

150. For this body of work, see Part I of this book,'The Three Socialisms'.

151. John Rae, *Contemporary Socialism* (New York: Scribners,1st ed., 1884. London: Swan Sonnenschein, 1891), p. 84; William Morris and E.B. Bax, *Socialism: its Growth and Outcome* (London: Swan Sonnenschein, 1893), pp. 269-70.

152. Ben Turner, *About Myself 1863-1900* (London: Cayme Press, 1930), pp. 78-9.

153. Alex M. Thompson, *Here I Lie, The Memorial of an Old Journalist* (London: G. Routledge and Sons, 1937) with a Preface by Lord (H.H.) Snell.

154. The quotations are from *News from Nowhere*, published in instalments in *Commonweal* 1890, in book form in 1891; for a moment of millennial joy in the prospect of 'barbarism once more flooding the world', see a letter of May 1885 in Philip Henderson (ed), *The Letters of William Morris to his Family and Friends* (1st edition, University of Michigan:1950, New York and London: McGraw-Hill, 1960), p. 236.

155. Edward Carpenter, *My Days and Dreams* (London: G. Allen and Unwin, 1916); for the 'spirit wife' relationship between Katherine Conway and Dan Irving, the ex-merchant seaman, foreman shunter on the Midland Railway, see Laurence Thompson, *The Enthusiasts: A Biography of John and Katherine Bruce Glasier*, London: Gollancz, 1971), pp. 70-1. For Carpenter, see also work published after I had completed the first version of this essay: Sheila Rowbotham and Jeffrey Weeks, *Socialism and the New Life*, London 1977; Sheila Rowbotham, 'In search of Carpenter', *History Workshop* 3, Spring 1977; Sheila Rowbotham, *Edward Carpenter: A Life of Liberty and Love* (London: Verso, 2008).

156. H.W. Nevinson, *Changes and Chances* (London: Harcourt, 1923), p. 121.

157. Beatrice Webb, *My Apprenticeship* (1st ed., 1926. London: Longmans, 1945), pp. 154-5; P.T. Cominos, 'Late Victorian sexual respectability and the social system', *International Review of Social History*, VIII, 1963, pp. 249-50.

158. James, *Varieties ...* (London: Fontana, edition, 1960), pp. 382-4. The two lectures on Conversion are excellent background for the cases used below, see pp. 194-257; for Trevor see Stanley Pierson, 'John Trevor and the Labour Church Movement in England 1891-1900',

in *Church History*, Dec. 1960, pp. 463-76, and J. Trevor, *My Quest for God* (1st edition 1897, 2nd edition Horsted Keynes, 1908; for B. Webb's concern, see *Our Partnership* (London: Longmans, 1948), pp. 85-6, diary entry for 21 Sept. 1894. There is important new material on Trevor (1855-1930) recently deposited in the Modern Records Centre, Warwick University: MSS. 143, *Trevor Working Papers*, of late Rev. G.W. Brassington, deposited by Mrs. R. Brassington of Kikby-in-Furness. The papers include biographical information collected from the family, and two important letters of 1925.

159. R. Blatchford, *Merrie England* (London: Clarion, 1894), p. 96; for Blatchford's own conversion, see *Sunday Chronicle*, 3 Mar. 1899 and following issues.

160. *Clarion*, 23 Mar. 1895, p. 94.

161. *Justice*, 17 Nov. 1894, p. 2, quoted in Stanley Pierson, *Marxism and the Origins of British Socialism* (Cornell University Press, 1973), pp. 226-7; for more cases see *Clarion*, 16 June 1894, p. 6; and 29 Nov. 1907; *Labour Prophet*, May 1894, p.53, and June 1894, p. 77. I owe the *Clarion* reference to Logie Barrow, 'The Socialism of Robert Blatchford and the Clarion Newspaper 1889-1918', unpublished PhD thesis, London 1975.

162. Such as Mark Rutherford, *The Autobiography of Mark Rutherford, Dissenting Minister and edited by his friend Reuben Elhapoot* (London: Trabner, 1881). This was followed in 1885 by a second volume, *Deliverance*. See also Edmund Gosse, *Father and Son* (1907); George Moore, *Confessions* (1886); and Richard Jefferies, *The Story of My Heart* (1883).

163. H. H. Snell, *Men, Movements and Myself* (London: J.M. Dent, 1936), p. 55; see also p. 198 for his faith in a New Way of Life.

164. Margaret McMillan, *Life of Rachel McMillan* (London: J.M. Dent, 1927), pp. 27-8, 30, 39.

165. Samson Bryher, *An Account of the Labour and Socialist Movement in Bristol* (Bristol: Bristol Socialist Society, 1929), Part II, p. 29. She described this experience frequently in subsequent lectures; for another version see *Bradford Labour Journal*, 30 Sept. 1892, quoted in Pierson, *Marxism ...*, pp. 163-4.

166. Thompson, *Enthusiasts*, p. 66.

167. D.B. Foster, *Socialism and the Christ and the Truth. My Two Great Discoveries in a Long and Painful Search for the Truth* (Leeds, 1921), p. 27.

168. For example: Mrs Humphrey Ward, *Robert Elsmere* (1888), the best-selling best-seller in nineteenth-century fiction; Samuel Butler, *The*

Way of All Flesh (1903); Mark Rutherford, *The Revolution in Tanners Lane* (1887).

169. G.D.H. Cole (ed.) *William Morris Selected Writings* (London: Nonesuch Press 1934), pp. 372-4.
170. Royden Harrison, 'The Young Webb: 1859-1892', duplicated paper for Society for the Study of Labour History, Anglo-American Colloquium (1968).
171. For the Reading SDF branch in this context, see Stephen Yeo, *Religion and Voluntary Organisations in Crisis* (London: Croom Helm, 1976), pp. 253-89.
172. See, for example, Harry Quelch's editorial attack on 'Morality Mongers' in *Justice,* 7 April 1888, p. 2.
173. 'Socialism' by The General, *The War Cry,* 27 Feb. 1888; General Booth, *In Darkest England and the Way Out,* London: Salvation Army, 1890), Preface, October 1890.
174. Pierson, *Marxism...,* pp. 147-8.
175. H.W. Hobart edited 'Labour Notes' for *Justice* for a time, was in the St Pancras and then the Islington SDF, a candidate for the LCC in 1889, a teetotaller, and wrote a pamphlet for the SDF on temperance. I owe this information to Victor Rabinovitch. For Sparling see *The Labour Annual,* 1895, p. 187.
176. Belfort Bax, in *Justice,* 21 June 1884; and the essays by Grant Allen and Frank Smith in A. Reid (ed.) *The New Party* (London: 1894).
177. Percy Redfern, *Journey to Understanding* (London: Allen and Unwin, 1946), pp.100-03; H.M. Reade, *Christ or Socialism* (undated but 1909). John Trevor is another case. For a time he could hold individualism and collectivism, action and contemplation, sexual emancipation and politics together. Then the pressures, external and internal, became too intense. See Warwick, MSS. 143, *Trevor Working Papers,* notes on *Labour Prophet,* June 1896, p.93, Feb. 1898, p.28; and on Trevor's *The One Life,* 1909. By 1909 Trevor was writing (p.20): 'The Redemption of Love from the curse of Tradition in the name of Natural Religion is the work to which I must devote the rest of my life'. George Sturt is another case. He was a Socialist League supporter, and contributor to *Commonweal* in the late 1880s, but then began to oppose individual to social change and become sceptical about, for example, *Towards Democracy's* fusions. See *The Journals of George Sturt 1890-1927,* a selection edited and introduced by E.D. Mackerness in two volumes (Cambridge University Press, 1967, entries for 4 and 6 November. Geoffrey Grigson's 1941 edition of

the *Journals* quotes Sturt as arriving at the position where ' The Golden Age is a state of inward being'.

178. For Fred Brocklehurst see *The Labour Annual*, 1895, p. 163. He attempted to imitate the Salvation Army's Self-Denial Week in the ILP, see *Clarion* 23 June 1894, p. 2, and 7 July 1894, p. 6. For a sermon of his at Bolton see *Labour Leader*, 17 Oct. 1896, p. 365: 'His afternoon address took the form of queries which every member of the ILP and Labour Church ought to put to himself. Was the world any better for his profession as a socialist and was he himself any more elevated, enlightened and self-sacrificing than before? Had they endeavoured to live socialism as the true propagandism? Were their own lives and those of their families, their neighbours and friends, and the lives of the poor and suffering around them brighter and happier because of their devotion and work? He thought that "We shall not have much influence upon the world until we hold our political and social faiths with all the ardour of religious conviction", and that "It is of much more importance to teach and live socialism than it is to elect socialist representatives ... A million theoretical socialists are of less real and ultimate value than one earnest soul whose socialism is the expression of his heart's religion and life', see *Clarion*, 23 June 1894 and 23 Mar. 1895. Before dismissing such evangelicism as not-quite-socialism, it is salutary to remember that it was part of the revolutionary convictions of Tom Maguire, among others, too; see Pierson, *Marxism* ... , pp. 147-8; for Maguire see *The Labour Annual*, 1896, p. 211, and E.P. Thompson, 'Homage to Tom Maguire', in Asa Briggs and John Saville (eds), *Essays in Labour History* (London: Macmillan, 1960, pp. 276-316); for a 'sermon' by Tom Mann, see *Workman's Times*, 14 May 1892, p. 5.

179. For Hardie's early convictions see Fred Reid, 'Keir Hardie's Conversion to Socialism', in A. Briggs and J. Saville (eds), *Essays in Labour History 1886-1923* (London: Macmillan, 1971), pp. 17-46.

180. John Trevor, *Unspoken Address to the 1896 International* (London: Labour Prophet Tracts, no. 4, 1896). 'Our business was to make socialists: to go on making 'em until we had roped in all the human race', Alf Mattison, a Leeds socialist organiser remembering old times in *Leeds Weekly Citizen*, 4 Oct. 1929, quoted in Thompson, *Morris* (1955), p.496. For a good exposition of the 'making socialists' option, see R. Blatchford, *Merrie England* (1894) 1908 edition, p.243. And William Morris, 'Introduction' to Frank Fairman, *The Principles of Socialism Made Plain* (London: William Reeves, 1888).

181. *Royal Commission on Labour, Minutes of Evidence,* Group A, 11 Feb. 1892,

question no.13172; W. Stewart, *J. Keir Hardie* (London: ILP Publications, 1921), pp.212-4.
182. Tom Mann, 'Preachers and the Churches', in Andrew Reid (ed.) *Vox Clamantium: the Gospel of the People* (London: 1894), p.303. For a slightly later source for Mann's views, see 'A Talk with Tom Mann' in *The Labour Prophet*, June 1897. For his later gloss on these years, see Tom Mann, *Memoirs* (London: Labour Publishing Company, 1923), p.49. For Mann on the religion of socialism in the ILP, see *Dewsbury Reporter*, 8 June 1895, speech at Orsett.
183. John Burns, *The Man with the Red Flag: being the speech delivered at the Old Bailey by John Burns Social Democratic candidate for Nottingham 1885 .. .in the trial of the 4 Social Democrats for seditious conspiracy 5 April–10 April 1886* (London: Twentieth Century Press Limited, undated); for involuntary asceticism in the later 1880s, see G.N. Barnes, *From Workshop to War Cabinet* (London: Jenkins, 1924), pp.35-6 .Twelve editions of this autobiography of a West London engineer and trade-union official were published between 1924 and 1973. In his retirement Barnes served as Chairman of the Co-operative Printing Society. There are many details of financial adversity in G. Haw, *The Life of Will Crooks, MP – From Workhouse to Westminster* (1st ed. 1907), popular ed. (London: Cassell 1917), the biography of a London cooper sacked for agitation, with many details of financial adversity, and an Introduction by G.K. Chesterton; see pp. 44-56, 81-4. Likewise the engineers J. L. Mahon and Lorenzo Quelch were two other examples of agitators who were sacked, although Mahon later returned to the trade and dropped out of the movement.
184. For Caroline Martyn see Lena Wallis, *Life and Letters of Caroline Martyn* (London and Glasgow: Labour Leader Publishing Department 1898); for two stories by Margaret McMillan about martyrdom and sacrifice, see *Clarion*, 15 Feb. 1896, p. 56, 8 Sept. 1894, p. 5. The classic description of the mid-century bourgeois lifestyle as perceived by late-Victorian rebels is in Beatrice Webb, *My Apprenticeship* (London: Longmans,1926) chapters I and II.
185. 'Art and The People', in May Morris, *William Morris, Artist, Writer, Socialist* (London,1936) II, pp. 404-5, quoted in Thompson, *Morris*, 1955 edition. p. 353.
186. *Workman's Times*, 25 Mar. 1893, p. 2, quoted in Pierson, *Marxism ...*, p.228, n.22.
187. For complaints, and answers to them, see *Clarion*, 3 Nov. 1894, p. 8; 2 Nov. 1895, p. 348; 9 Nov. 1895, p. 256; 16 Nov. 1895, p. 365; 23 Nov. 1895,

p. 372. This controversy showed a depth of feeling against fee'd lecturers as 'place hunters' and 'men on the make'. For later complaints, see East Ham ILP Minutes, 14 Oct. 1909 (I owe this reference to T.G. Ashplant); Thompson, *Enthusiasts*, p. 183 (1912); G.H. Haw, *The Life Story of Will Crooks, MP*, London 1907, protests too much about Crooks's income as an MP, as if it was a live issue which had to be answered. The economics of the socialist movement as a developing career from the mid-1890s onwards needs separate treatment in another essay – for leads and denials, see S.G. Hobson, *Pilgrim to the Left* (London: Longmans Green and Company 1938), pp. 42–3; Thompson, *Enthusiasts*, pp. 71, 96; Pierson, *Marxism...* p. 199; Joseph Clayton, *The Rise and Decline of Socialism in Great Britain* (London: Faber and Gwyer, 1926), pp. 85–93; Judith Fincher, 'The *Clarion* Movement', unpublished M.A. thesis Manchester, 1971, p. 21; H.M. Reade, *Christ or Socialism: A Human Autobiography* (Glasgow, 1923), pp. 12–13.

188. *Trade Unionist*, 27 Feb. 1892, quoted in Fincher, 'The *Clarion* Movement', p. 32n. 35; *Clarion*, 1 Dec. 1894.

189. W. Stewart, *J. Keir Hardie ...*, p. 213; for similar examples of doubts about class interest as the motivating power for socialism, see Pierson, *Marxism ...*, p. 95 (Bax), p. 100 (Carpenter), pp. 169–70 (H. Burrows, H.W. Lee, H.W. Hobart); Thompson, *Enthusiasts*, pp. 70-2 (Conway); Fincher, '*Clarion* ...', p. 211 (Blatchford); *Dewsbury Reporter*, 8 June 1895 (Mann).

190. *Clarion*, 18 April 1896, p. 124, 25 April 1896, p. 133; and a pamphlet *Altruism, Christ's Glorious Gospel of Love versus Man's Dismal Science of Greed*, London 1898; for Blatchford on class, see also *Clarion*, 9 Feb. 1895, p. 44.

191. Redfern, *Journey to Understanding...* p. 19.

192. *Justice*, 1 July 1893, p. 5, letter from W. Ford.

193. *Justice*, 29 March 1893, p.5. I owe this reference to Victor Rabinovitch. For catechising of intending members before they could join a branch (in this case Reading), see Lorenzo Quelch, 'The Pioneers' in *The Reading Citizen*, Feb. 1931; for a 'socialist catechism class' in the ILP in Middlesborough, see *Clarion*, 29 Sept. 1894, p.2.

194. E.P. Thompson, 'An Open Letter to Leszek Kolakowski', in *Socialist Register* (London: Merlin, 1973), p. 51.

195. For Blatchford's early anti-clerical pamphleteering, see *Three Open Letters to the Bishop of Manchester on Socialism* (London: Clarion pamphlet no 3, 1894); for accusations from the *Methodist Times* about Blatchford's

alleged sell-out, see *Clarion*, 30 March 1895, p.101; 20 April 1895, p.125. For fascinated antagonism from the church side, see an unusually long article in the *Wesleyan Methodist Magazine* 1893 volume, pp. 738–47 on 'The Labour Church'. In the *British Weekly: a Journal of Social and Christian Progress*, there was a long debate on socialism in 1894, starting with articles by Rev. Marcus Dods (4 Jan. 1894) and Keir Hardie (18 Jan. 1894). The debate included an attack on 'millenial aspirations and on the religion of socialism' by H.H. Champion (8 Feb. 1894).

196. Stanley Pierson, *Marxism and* ... (1973); Mark Bevir, *The Making of British Socialism* ...(2011), Part Three: *The Ethical Socialists*, pp.215-297.

197. William James, *The Varieties of Religious Experience* (1st edition 1902; London: Fontana, 1960, p.96: 'the word "religious" cannot stand for any single principle or essence, but is rather a collective name'.

198. For theodicy see Max Weber, *The Sociology of Religion*, Methuen ed., London 1965, pp. 138–50. 'Theology, Salvation and Rebirth'; H.H. Gerth and C. Wright Mills, *From Max Weber: Essays in Sociology*, London 1948, pp. 122, 275, 358-9.

199. 'The devotion of all true Socialists today will be based on science and involve no cultus. The Socialist whose social creed is his own religion, requires no travesty of Christian rites to aid him in keeping his ideal before him ...', *Justice*, June 1884, p.2.

200. The section was called 'The Problem of Individual Life', *Progress and Poverty* (London: William Reeves edition, undated) pp. 429-36.

201. *Clarion*, 14 Jan. 1893, p. 4.

202. See W. Stewart, *J. Keir Hardie* ...(1921), p. 4; William Morris, 'Art and the Beauty of the Earth', Lecture 13 Oct. 1881 in Burslem Town Hall, in *Collected Works* (London: Longmans Green, 1910-15), vol.XXII, pp. 171-2.

203. Morris, *News from Nowhere* in G.D.H. Cole (ed.), *William Morris, Selected Writings* (London: Nonesuch, 1934) p. 131.

204. Philip Henderson (ed.), *The Letters of William Morris* (London: Longmans 1950), p. 181; also Bryher, Bristol ..., I. p.21.

205. A review of *Fabian Essays* (1889) in *Commonweal*, 25 Jan. 1890, quoted in Thompson, *Morris* (1955 edition), p. 637.

206. Henderson, *Morris...*, *Letters*, p. 176, a letter to C.E. Maurice, 1 July 1883.

207. For example *Clarion*, 22 Apr. 1893, p. 4, a talk to the Salford ILP branch by Alderman Tatterall on 'The cause and cure of Poverty and Crime'.

208. Redfern, *Journey to Understanding*..., p. 32; see also H.H. Snell, *Men,*

Movements and Myself... 1936; P. Snowden, *An Autobiography* (London: Nicholson and Watson, 1934) vol. I, p. 67, describing a meeting at Keighley in 1895: 'that meeting will for ever stand out in my memory. It was an inspiration. It was like a revival gathering. Socialism to those men and women was a new vision, a new hope of relief from the grinding toil and hard struggle which had been their lot.'

209. Tom Mann, *Memoirs*..., p. 75; for how Henry George's *Progress and Poverty* could have a similar effect, see also Goddard H. Orpen, in E. De Lavaleye, *The Socialism of Today* (London: Field and Tuer, 1886) p. 291, 'his [Henry George's] calm assumption of infallibility, his brilliant bursts of eloquence, his keen sympathy for the poor, his religious fervour and the very audacity of his proposal are exceedingly attractive to many minds'.

210. W.S. Sanders, *Early Socialist Days* (London: Hogarth Press edition, 1927), pp. 12-13; for the problem stated from a more elevated social angle, see H.S. Salt, *Seventy Years Among Savages* (London: G.Allen and Unwin, 1921), p. 242.

211. See, for example, three collections of essays by E.B. Bax, *The Religion of Socialism*, London 1887, *The Ethics of Socialism*, London 1889, *Outlooks from the New Standpoint*, London 1891. Each of these was published by Swan Sonnenschein and went quickly through several editions. For Bax's view in 1901 of these works, see E.B. Bax, *Reminiscences and Reflections of a Mid and Late Victorian* (London: G.Allen and Unwin, 1918), p. 158. For the quality of the socialism that they expressed see, for example, *The Religion of Socialism*, pp. ix-xi, 48-9, 51-3, 78, 80-2, 161-3. The foreshortening was not confined to socialists. Lloyd George, aged 26, caught the tone in February 1890 at the S. Wales Liberal Federation: 'there is a momentous time coming, the Dark Continent of wrong is being explored and there is a missionary spirit abroad for its reclamation to the Realm of Right. A Holy war has been proclaimed against man's inhumanity to man and the people of Europe are thronging to the crusade', Frank Owen, *Tempestuous Journey, Lloyd George His Life and Times* (London: Hutchinson, 1954), p. 54. So did Joseph Arch in 1893, by then supposedly a very different man from his earlier messianism of the 1870s. Yet in that year he wrote: 'Nemesis is at the door of those who in their selfish ease and soft-living never regarded the cry of the poor. Ruin is upon them and they will fall unmissed and unregretted to give place to a newer brighter state of things ... Sharp diseases require sharp remedies' ('Lords and labourers' in *The New Review*, 45, 1893, pp. 129-38).

212. *Commonweal*, 31 Mar. 1888, and *The Labour Annual*, 1895, pp. 131-3.
213. See *Fabian Essays in Socialism* (1889, London: Allen and Unwin, 6th edition with a new Introduction by Asa Briggs, 1962), pp. 56, 92-3, 132, 134, 155-61, 235-6, 239. For efforts to interpret Fabianism as always having been gradualist and uncatastrophic, see G.B. Shaw, 'Preface to 1908 edition', in *Fabian Essay...* , p. 283; E. Pease, *History of the Fabian Society* (1st edition, 1916, London: Cass reprints, 1963), p.235; G.B. Shaw, *The Early History of the Fabian Society*, London 1892, Fabian Tract No. 41. For Shaw's admission of earlier views and mockery of them, see 'The Idea of Citizenship' (1909), in W. S. Smith (ed.), *Shaw on Religion* (New York:1967, pp. 20-8).
214. Quoted in H.V. Fineberg, 'Attitudes towards the Working Class and Democracy in the Case of Bernard Shaw, 1883-1914', unpublished MA thesis, University of Sussex, p. 57.
215. S. Webb, *Socialism in England* (London: Swann Sonnenschein, 1893), pp. xx-xxi; see also *Clarion*, 11 Nov. 1893, p. 8, article by Simeon Twigg; Keir Hardie, 'The Independent Labour Party', in *The Nineteenth Century*, XXXVII, pp. 1-14; see also his speech at the 1896 ILP Conference in *Report of the 4th Annual Conference of the ILP 1896*, p. 5; Thompson, *Morris...* 1955 edition, p. 425n.1; H. Bland, 'The Outlook', in *Fabian Essays...*, pp. 237-55; Pease, *History of the Fabian Society*, p. 117; Webb, *Our Partnership* (London: Longmans, 1948), pp. 115, 121, 127.
216. *Workman's Times*, 20 Feb. 1892, p. 4.
217. Keir Hardie, 'The Independent Labour Party', in *The Nineteenth Century*, XXXVII, 1895, pp. 1-14.
218. *Clarion*, 5 Mar. 1892, p. 2 and 12 Mar. 1892, p. 7.
219. *Justice*, 28 June 1890.
220. Thus Hyndman could write in 'The English Workers as they are', in *Contemporary Review*, LII, July, 1887, pp. 122-36: 'the working people, as a body, are in spite of all drawbacks more open to the reception of high conceptions of duty and far reaching ideals of what might be than the upper or middle class'. Hyndman's changes of tone are good signposts to the chronology of wider changes of attitudes. He would not have written this two-three years before, or six-seven years later. Before long he came to realise that he had been wrong, in his terms, to announce in 1887 that 'the period of social apathy is clearly at an end'. In 1901 Hyndman was 'quite astounded at the ignorance and apathy of my fellow countrymen', in a letter explaining his withdrawal from politics for a spell. Glasier's romanticism had also turned sour

by 1909: 'Katherine and I talk rather moodily about the movement. Both of us begin to doubt if it is socialist in spirit at all. All our high idealist teaching seems, as in the case of churches, not to have borne fruit. Egotism, mere self-assertion, disloyalty rampant. Its main motive is individualist – the hope of getting. Are we feeding wolves? I wonder ... I wonder ...', Thompson, *Enthusiasts*, p. 157. In just the same way Carpenter would not have written 'the battles of the Heroes of the future will be individualistic, but against the apathetic routine and inertia of the human masses' at the time of his initial decision to throw in his lot with the working class. The phrase is in his 'Transitions to Freedom' in E. Carpenter (ed.), *Forecasts of the Coming Century* (London and Manchester: Labour Press and the Clarion Office, 1897), p.192.

221. G. Haw, *The Life Story of Will Crooks MP...* (1907), pp. 63-4.
222. John Heather, 'The Ancient Faith in Providence', in Andrew Reid (ed.), *Vox Clamantium: The Gospel of the People by Writers, Preachers and Workers Brought Together* (London: A.D. Innes, 1894, pp. 264-5). The theology of the Labour Church was from the beginning a matter of dispute, with Trevor and Foster putting a harder line than those who saw the movement as a mere adornment to 'real politics'; see, for example *Clarion*, 18 Aug. 1894, p. 5; 1 Sept. 1894, p. 4; 20 Oct. 1894, p.3; 10 Nov. 1894, p. 7 and 17 Nov. 1894, p. 3; or Foster, *Socialism and the Christ and the Truth*, pp. 32-3, 49-50. For the best late-nineteenth-century follower of F.D. Maurice, see Stephen Yeo, 'Thomas Hancock' in Maurice Reckitt (ed.) *For Christ and the People* (London: SCM, 1968), pp. 1-60. In an address on 'The Relation of the Labour Movement to Free Religion' given to the New Fellowship, 29 Nov. 1895, Trevor said, 'Thus the Labour Church is doing work similar to the prophets of old, with this difference; they addressed themselves to those who thought they did God's service and did it not; we address ourselves to those who do God's service and know it not'; see *Seed Time*, 1896, p. 7, noted in Warwick MSS. 143, *Trevor Working Papers*.
223. J. Morrison Davidson, 'The Religion of Collectivism' in *Let There be Light* (London, 1895), pp. 16-19.
224. The title of a lecture given by Henry Hyndman in 1894.
225. For example, *Further Reminiscences* (London: Macmillan, 1912), pp. 5, 236, 438-9.
226. Information about the 46 is in some cases full and in some sparse (I have distinguished women by adding first names): R. Blatchford; F. Brocklehurst; H. Burrows; J.B. Glasier; Katherine St J. Conway; K. Hardie; W. Morris; F. Smith; Margaret McMillan; B. Bax; H.W. Hobart;

D. Irving; T. Maguire; Caroline Martyn; A.M. Thompson; H.S. Salt; E.R. Hartley; Hannah Mitchell; D.B. Foster; E.F. Fay; J. Leatham; Edith Nesbit; R. Balmforth; W. Diack; J. Clayton; J.W. Wallace; G. Meek; H.M. Hyndman; G. Lansbury; J. Trevor; P. Redfern; H.M. Read; E. Carpenter; T. Mann; H.H. Snell; Annie Besant; T.J. Cobden Sanderson; F. Henderson; Enid Stacy; H.W. Nevinson; W.S. Sanders; C. Allen Clarke; J. Hunter Watts; Eleanor Marx; L.T. Hall; G. Sturt.

227. For local equivalents of these women, see biographies of Helena Born and Miriam Daniell, and mention of Miss Gertrude Dix and Miss C.E. May in Bryher, *Bristol...*, II, pp. 6–8, 22. Eleanor Marx too was much in demand among ILP and SDF branches after 1889.

228. For the Manchester branch, see Pierson, *Marxism ...*, p. 88 n. 57; and J.B.S., 'Revolutionary Reminiscences' in *Co-operative News*, 5 Aug. 1905, noted in Thompson, *Morris*, 1955 edition, p. 652 n. 1.

229. For the problem and ways around it, see James Leatham, 'Sixty Years of World-Mending' in *The Gateway*, no. 341, p. 13; no. 347, p. 10; and W.M. Haddow, *My Seventy Years* (Glasgow: R. Gibson, 1943), p. 37; W.S. Sanders, *Early Socialist Days...* 1927, pp. 26–7; Bryher, *Bristol...*, I, p. 20.

230. Foster, *Socialism and the Christ and the Truth...* pp. 33, 48.

231. E.J. Hobsbawm, *Primitive Rebels* (Manchester: Manchester University Press, 1959), pp. 142–55, and chap. VIII.

232. For the fullest treatment of these phenomena, see Rev. D.F. Summers, 'The Labour Church and Allied Movements of the late-Nineteenth and early-Twentieth Centuries', unpublished PhD thesis, University of Edinburgh (1958).

233. *Clarion*, 12 May 1894, p. 6.

234. *Clarion*, 15 June 1895, p. 191; 7 Sept. 1895, p. 286.

235. Haddow, *My Seventy Years*, pp. 31–2.

236. *Clarion*, 27 Jan, 1894, p. 6; 18 Nov. 1893, p. 2; *Workman's Times*, 12 Aug. 1893, p. 3.

237. *The Labour Annual*, 1897, p. 166.

238. *The Workers' Cry*, 15 Aug. 1891.

239. Lord Snell, *Men, Movements and Myself...* (1938), p. 148.

240. *Clarion*, 14 Dec. 1895, p. 398; or, for Oldham, 18 May 1895, p. 158.

241. *The Labour Annual*, 1898, p. 75; for other evidence on this point, see Summers, 'The Labour Church...', pp. 98, 100, 121, 149, 268, 284, 687.

242. *The Spectator*, 21 April 1894, pp. 535-5.
243. Leatham, 'World Mending', in *Gateway*, vol. 29-30, no. 341, p. 12; *Workman's Times*, 20 Feb. 1892, p. 6.
244. In Gilbert Beith (ed.), *Edward Carpenter; An Appreciation* (London: Routledge, 1931), pp. 20-1.
245. Bryher, *Bristol...*, p. 26.
246. Lena Wallis, *Life and Letters of Caroline Martyn*, London/ Glasgow (1898), pp. 44, 68.
247. As in E.J. Hobsbawm's *Primitive Rebels...*; H. Pelling, *Origins of the Labour Party 1880-1900* (Oxford: Oxford University Press,1965), pp. 132-44.
248. *From Workshop to War Cabinet* (1924)..., p. 42.
249. For one who watched this happening, see A. D. Agostino, 'Intelligentsia socialism and the "Workers' Revolution"', in *International Review of Social History*, xiv 1969, pp. 54-89, on J.W. Machajski.
250. *Workman's Times*, 20 Feb. 1892, p. 6.
251. *Clarion*, 8 April 1893, p. 4; 21 Dec. 1895, p. 404; 11 Mar. 1893, p. 4; 11 Aug. 1894, p. 6; 13 May 1893, p. 4; for the specifically Labour Church cultus, see Summers, 'The Labour Church...', pp. 89, 97, 102, etc.
252. William Morris, 'Order and anarchy', in *Justice*, 9 Feb. 1884, p. 2.
253. *The Labour Annual*, 1895, p. 4.
254. *The Labour Prophet*, June 1895, p. 89, John Trevor, 'Starting a Labour Church'.
255. Bryher, *Bristol...*, I, p. 24; II, pp. 11, 21, 22, 25.
256. F.W. Jowett, 'What Made Me a Socialist', no date, quoted in Thompson, *Morris* ... 1955 edition, p. 774; see also *Clarion*, 2 Mar. 1895, p. 10 (Marylebone branch); H.H. Snell, *Men, Movements and Myself...* (1938), p. 108.
257. Joseph Clayton, *The Rise and Decline of Socialism in Great Britain 1884-1924...* (1936), p. 108.
258. Leatham, 'World-Mending', in *Gateway*, vol. 28 no. 334, pp. 12-13; and no. 331, p. 15; Bryher, *Bristol...*, I, p. 23; Hannah Mitchell, *The Hard Way Up* (London: Faber, 1968) p.108; *Workman's Times*, 5 Mar. 1892, p. 2.
259. *The Labour Prophet*, June 1895, p.6; *Clarion*, 2 Dec. 1893, p.4 (South Salford ILP); 12 Jan. 1895, p.14.
260. *My Days and Dreams...*, pp. 128-9.
261. Hannah Mitchell, *The Hard Way Up*, p. 74; for a theological expression

of this longing for unity – including that between body and soul – see Foster, *Socialism and the Christ and the Truth*, pp. 62-3.
262. Pierson, *Marxism...*, p. 212 for the case of Joe Terrett.
263. *Clarion*, 22 Sept. 1894, p. 6, 21 Sept. 1895, p. 300; 5 Oct. 1895, p. 318; 23 Nov. 1895, p.374; 30 Nov. 1895 p. 382; 7 Mar. 1896, p. 76. For the numerical estimate, and the Unity movement generally, see Fincher, '*Clarion...*', pp. 197 and following.
264. *Clarion*, 22 Dec. 1894, p. 4; for Tom Mann, 26 Jan. 1895, p. 30.
265. Leatham, 'World-Mending', in *Gateway*, vol. 29-30 no. 336, p. 14.
266. W.S. Sanders, *Early Socialist Days*, London 1927, p. 25.
267. I owe this point to Victor Rabinovitch; see N. Milton, *John Maclean* (London: Pluto Press edition, 1973), p. 37; H. Burrows in *Justice*, 30 July 1887, p. 1; *The Socialist Democrat*, IV, Dec. 1900, p. 363.
268. H. W. Nevinson, *Changes and Chances,...* (1923), p. 109.
269. Bryher, *Bristol...*, II, pp. 5, 69. See also *Justice*, 24 Oct. 1885, where Benjamin Crick writes from Poplar: 'Having during my short term of membership been the means of recruiting some 10 or 12 new members, I should be very sorry to see them turn back from the cause which they in common with other members have so much at heart.' He advocates a hall for the winter meetings and the setting up of a musical or literary club; 'even a "knife and fork tea" monthly for members and their sweethearts and wives, and then afterwards an entertainment at a low figure. Such a thing I think would bring us a large number of new members besides keeping the old ones together.' (I owe this reference to Anna Davin.)
270. *Clarion*, 10 Feb. 1894, p. 6; 27 April 1895, p. 130 (Liverpool); 23 Mar. 1895, p. 94 (Bolton); 5 Jan. 1895, p. 3 (Heeley).
271. Only later did it become 'That the Labour Church exists to give expression to the religion of the Labour Movement'.
272. J. Trevor, 'From the Hills: from ethics to religion', in *Labour Prophet*, Mar. 1893, p. 44.
273. J. Trevor, 'The Labour Church', in *The Labour Annual*, 1896, pp. 41-3.
274. *Clarion*, 18 Aug. 1894, p. 5; 1 Sept. 1894, p. 4; 20 Oct. 1894, p. 8; 10 Nov. 1894, p. 8; 17 Nov. 1894, p. 3; Pierson, *Marxism...*, pp. 239-42.
275. Foster, *Socialism and the Christ and the Truth...*, pp. 32-3, 49-50.
276. Pierson, *Marxism...*, pp. 130-3, the cases of Shaw, Clarke, Besant.
277. *Clarion*, 18 Feb. 1893, p. 8.

278. Clarion, 6 Jan. 1894, p. 3 (West Bowling ILP); 27 Jan. 1894, p. 6 (Battersea SDF); 10 Feb, 1894, p. 5 (Birmingham Cinderella); *Justice*, 19 Feb 1887, p. 1 (Clerkenwell SDF): Fincher, *Clarion*..., p. 143 and following.

279. *Clarion*, 14 Dec. 1895, p. 398; 21 Dec. 1895, p. 406; 11 Jan. 1896, p. 14 (Marylebone SDF).

280. W.M. Haddow, *My Seventy Years* (1943)..., p. 37.

281. Lena Wallis, *Caroline Martyn*, pp. 54–5.

282. Leatham, 'World-Mending', *Gateway*, vol. 29–30 no. 347, p. 10.

283. Tom Mann, 'Is it money we want or men?' in *Clarion*, 29 Sept. 1894.

284. *Workshop to War Cabinet*... pp. 42–3.

285. Haddow, *My Seventy Years*.., pp. 37–40.

286. This letter is reproduced in full in Dona Torr, *Tom Mann and his Times*, volume I, 1846–1890 (London: Lawrence and Wishart, 1956), pp. 255–7.

287. *Clarion*, 18 Nov. 1893, p. 4; 2 Dec. 1893, p. 6; 10 Mar. 1894, p. 5.

288. *Clarion*, 27 Oct. 1894, p. 6.

289. *Clarion*, 4 May 1895, p. 142 (Bradford); 11 May 1895, p. 150 (Bradford); 7 Mar. 1896, p. 76 (Barrow); 4 Jan. 1896, p. 6 (Greenwich).

290. For G. S. Railton's resistance to such displacement, see B. Watson, *Soldier Saint: George Scott Railton, William Booth's First Lieutenant* (London: Hodder and Stoughton, 1970). And for churches and chapels and a range of other voluntary associations surrounded by the same choices and constraints in a single town (Reading, Berkshire) during the same period, see Stephen Yeo, *Religion and Voluntary Organisations in Crisis* (London: Croom Helm, 1976).

291. *The Labour Leader*, 31 Oct. 1896, p. 380; 7 Nov. 1896, p. 387.

292. *Report of the 4th Annual Conference of the ILP, 1896*, p. 15.

293. *Labour Prophet*, Feb. 1898; G. Lansbury, *My Life* (London: Constable, 1928) p. 2.

294. G. Meek, *Bath Chair-Man by Himself*, London: Constable, 1910) pp. 264, 290–4.

295. *Ethical World*, 8 Oct. 1898, quoted in Pierson, *Marxism*..., p. 251; according to Marie Trevor, John Trevor became involved with the South Place Ethical Society when living in Hampstead from 1909 onwards; see Warwick MSS. 143, *Trevor Working Papers*.

296. Redfern, *Journey to Understanding*... pp. 100–3.

297. Leatham, 'World-Mending', *Gateway*, vol. 28 no. 329, p. 16, and no. 334, p. 13.

298. Margaret McMillan, *The Life of Rachel McMillan* (London: J.M. Dent, 1927), p. 121.
299. H. G. Wells, *Experiment in Autobiography. Discoveries of a Very Ordinary Brain* (1st edn. 1934. London: Victor Gollancz, 1966, vol. I), pp. 245-54.
300. *The Labour Prophet*, May 1895 pp. 65-7.
301. Reprinted in Warren S. Smith (ed.), *The Religious Speeches of George Bernard Shaw* (Pennsylvania State University: 1963, pp. 20-8.
302. 'At the point of decay', in E.P. Thompson (ed.), *Out of Apathy* (London: New Left Books, Stevens, 1960), pp.3-15.
303. See John Saville, 'Trade Unions and Free Labour', in Asa Briggs and John Saville (eds), *Essays in Labour History* (London: Macmillan, 1960), pp. 317-50.
304. The Jim Connell quotation from *The Socialist*, Oct. 1904, I owe to Ray Challinor; see also *The Labour Annual*, 1895, p. 42.
305. For blaming of 'How the Working Man Thinks' for this, see Shaw Desmond, *Labour: the Giant with the Feet of Clay* (London, New York: Scribners, 1921), pp. 32-3.
306. *Workman's Times*, 23 Jan 1891, p.8
307. *The Labour Annual*, 1900, p. 152.
308. Haddow, *My Seventy Years*... pp. 34-5; W.S. Sanders, *Early Socialist Days*... London 1927, p. 67.
309. I have examined it in 'News from Nowhere: an Appreciation' in *News from Nowhere*, issue 2, Brighton undated, pp. 6-11.
310. G.D.H. Cole, *William Morris Selected Writings* (London: Nonesuch Press, 1948). p.671.

NOTES AND REFERENCES FOR PART III

311. J.B. Priestley, *Postscripts* (London: Heinemann, 1940), p.2.
312. Public Records Office, CAB 24/105. Report on Revolutionary Organisations in the UK, Home Office, 6 May 1920.
313. H.M. Hyndman, *The Historical Basis of Socialism in England* (London: Kegan Paul, 1883), p.194n, p.433.
314. *Justice*, 3 Sept. 1910, quoted in C. Tsuzuki, *H.M. Hyndman and British Socialism* (Oxford: OUP, 1961), p. 211.
315. ILP Conference Report (1893), p.3.

316. *Clarion*, 21 Jan. 1893, *Clarion*, 14 and 28 Oct. 1899. I owe the 1899 references to Logie Barrow.

317. *Merrie England* (London: The Clarion Press, 1894), p. 123.

318. Ivor Morgan brought to light another egregious example in a letter to *The Observer*, 11 March 2018. Keir Hardie described the Lithuanian Poles employed by the Glengarnock Iron Company in Ayrshire as 'beastly, filthy foreigners'. 'He portrayed them as undercutting the wages of Scottish miners by surviving on garlic fried in oil they stole from street lamps. Moreover, these outsiders brought "Black Death" to "decent men".'

319. For an outline history here, see Hugh Cunningham 'The language of patriotism, 1750-1914', *History Workshop*, No.12 (Autumn, 191).

320. For rich details, dates, and references to recent work on Englishness, see Robert Colls, *Identity of England* (Oxford: OUP, 2002) and *George Orwell: English Rebel* (Oxford: OUP, 2013).

321. William Morris to Robert Thompson, 1 Jan. 1885, quoted in Paul Meier, *William Morris, the Marxist Dreamer*, trans. F. Grubb (Sussex: Harvester, 1978) II, 557-8.

322. See ILP Conference Report (1893), p.5.

323. *Clarion*, 18 Nov. 1899, and Logie Barrow ts. On schemes for Trades Federation in the late 1890s, p. 102.

324. Perry Anderson, *Arguments Within English Marxism* (London: Verso, 1980), p. 149, and 'Origins of the present crisis', in *New Left Review* 23 (1964), 43. One way into the Anderson-Nairn *versus* E.P. Thompson argument of the early 1960s is the text and footnotes of the latter's 1965 essay 'The peculiarities of the English' in *The Poverty of Theory* (London: Merlin, 1978), pp.35-91, pp. 399-400. The relevant issues of *New Left Review* are nos. 23 through 35.

325. In K. Marx and F. Engels, *On Britain* (Moscow: FLPH, 1962). The piece was written on 12 Sept. 1892.

326. P. Corrigan and D. Sayer, *The Great Arch: English State Formation as Cultural Revolution* (Oxford: Blackwell, 1985); and for a critique, and references to other uses of Marx's metaphor, Michael Barratt-Brown, 'Away with all great arches: Anderson's History of British Capitalism', in *New Left Review* 1/167, Jan-Feb 1988.

327. 'Modern Socialism' was a phrase much used by Lenin and other Second International Socialists. For a local example see R.C.K Ensor (ed.), *Modern Socialism* (London: Harpers, 1907).

328. The Nation/State distinction in these succinct terms was made by William Morris in his *True and False Society* (1887).
329. Doris Lessing, *The Memoirs of a Survivor* (London: Picador, 1976), pp. 135-6, see also p8. The William Morris quotes on State and Nation are from his *True and False Society* (1887).
330. M. Clanchy, *From Memory to Written Record, England 1066-1307* (London: Arnold, 1979), p.6; Nevil Johnson, *In Search of the Constitution* (Oxford: Pergamon, 1977), p. 81: Perry Anderson, *Lineages of the Absolutist State* (London: Verso, 1974), p. 113.
331. F. Braudel, *Afterthoughts on Material Civilization and Capitalism* (Baltimore: Johns Hopkins, 1976), pp.99-100.
332. Clanchy, *From Memory* ...p.30.
333. P. Corrigan and D. Sayer, *The Great Arch: English State Formation as Cultural Revolution* (Oxford: Blackwell, 1985); E.P. Thompson, "The peculiarities of the English', *Socialist Register* (1965), also in *The Poverty of Theory* (London: Merlin, 1978).
334. Quentin Skinner, *The Foundations of Modern Political Thought* (Cambridge: CUP, 1978), II 353.
335. 'This is an old European country' is underlined as part of the argument of 'The peculiarities of the English' (1965), p. 349; the quote about professionals comes from Geoffrey Holmes, *Augustan England: Professions, State and Society, 1680-1730* (London: Allen and Unwin, 1982), p.239. He is analysing what he calls 'new men of English government', p.250.
336. J.H. Plumb, *The Growth of Political Stability in England 1675-1725* (London: Macmillan, 1967) is a key work here, as is P. Corrigan and Sayer's referred to in n.23 above.
337. The Morris quote comes from 'Art and Socialism', Collected Works XXII, 208. For Adam Smith see Donald Winch, *Adam Smith's Politics: An Essay in Historiographical Revision* (Cambridge: CUP 1978).
338. Barrington Moore, *Social Origins of Dictatorship and Democracy* (Boston: Beacon Press, 1966), p.32.
339. This gloss on Wallerstein comes from D. Levine, *Family Formation in an Age of Nascent Capitalism* (York: Academic Press, 1977), p.10.
340. The essay is in Carlo Cipolla (ed.), *The Fontana Economic History of Europe* (London: Fontana, 1973), III, 301-57.
341. Robin Murray, in a typescript memo for the Labour Process Group in Brighton. This group was affiliated to the Conference of Socialist

Economists and produced important unpublished work.

342. K. Marx, *Instructions for the Delegates to the Geneva Congress* (1866).

343. Edmund Burke, *Reflections on the Revolution in France* (1790).

344. On the walls of Rochdale Town Hall (1870s) Cromwell appears naturally in the sequence of Monarchs; in Whitaker's Almanack the King was held to be ruling even where he could not reign during the Interregnum: see Christopher Hill, *Some Intellectual Consequences of the English Revolution* (London: Weidenfeld, 1980); for the statue, and much else about English national history, see J.W. Burrow's *Liberal Descent: Victorian Historians and the English Past* (Cambridge: CUP, 1981).

345. Herbert Butterfield, *The Englishman and His History* (Cambridge: CUP, 1944), p.2, p.79.

346. For sharp analysis of this, see Raymond Williams, *Towards 2000* (London: Chatto, 1983), pp. 102–27.

347. 2nd Edition (1899), p.30, quoted in Burrow, *A Liberal Descent*, p. 295.

348. Editorial for 21. Nov. 1979.

349. *Lineages*, pp.114–15.

350. Raymond Williams, 'Democracy and Parliament', *Marxism Today* (June 1982), p.15.

351. R.H.S. Crossman's long introduction to Walter Bagehot, *The English Constitution* (first published in 1867) (London: Watts New Thinkers Library,1963) provides an exceptionally clear analysis of this by an experienced Labour politician, MP, and Minister.

352. W.C. Costin and J.S. Watson, *The Law and Workings of the Constitution: Documents 1660–1914*, I (London: Black, 1952), p.376; Johnson, *In Search...*, pp.84, 90.

353. The Report was published by the Fabian Society in Nov. 1906. I owe the reference to Ian Bullock's 'Socialist and Democratic Form in Britain, 1880–1914', unpublished D.Phil. thesis (University of Sussex, 1981).

354. Raymond Williams, *Keywords* (London: Croom Helm, 1976) on 'Representative', and his 'Democracy and Parliament', p.16.

355. Raymond Williams, *Towards 2000*, and 'Democracy and Parliament'.

356. The phrases are Lord Hailsham's and Raymond Williams' (*The Long Revolution*) respectively.

357. *Labour Leader*, 23 March 1901.

358. Nevil Johnson, *In Search of the Constitution*, p. 53.

359. K. Marx, *Capital*, volume 1, Chapter 3 part 2, in a section on 'The Means

of Circulation'.

360. K. Marx, *Capital*, I (Moscow edit.), p.744.
361. See Nevil Johnson, *In Search Of*..., and Perry Anderson, *Lineages*.... The latter regards Henry VIII's need to pay for his attack on France in 1543 as a turning point here.
362. Perry Anderson, *Lineages*.
363. J.H. Plumb, *The Growth of Political Stability in England 1675-1725* (London: Macmillan, 1967).
364. E.J. Hobsbawm, 'The general crisis of the seventeenth century', in T. Aston (ed.), *Crisis in Europe, 1560-1660* (1965), pp.47-9.
365. Marx, 'German Ideology' in *Collected Works*, V, p.89: 'Civil society embraces the whole material intercourse of individuals within a definite stage of the development of productive forces. It embraces the whole commercial and industrial life of a given stage and, insofar, transcends the state and nation, though, on the other hand again, it must assert itself in its external relations as nationality and internally must organise itself as stage. The term "civil society" emerged in the eighteenth century when property relations had already extricated themselves from the ancient and medieval community. Civil society as such only develops with the bourgeoisie.'
366. Marx, 'Critique of Hegel's Philosophy of Right', *Collected Works*, III, 32.
367. Marx, 'Critical Marginal Notes on the Article "The King of Prussia and Social Reform. By a Prussian"', *Collected Works*, III, 198.
368. The quotations are all from Chapter 10 of *Capital*, I.
369. Gareth Stedman Jones, 'Engels and the genesis of Marxism', *New Left Review* 106 (Nov./Dec. 1977); see also his 'Engels and the history of Marxism', E.J. Hogsbawm (ed.), the *History of Marxism*, I (Sussex: Harvester, 1982).
370. William Thompson, *Labour Rewarded* (1827), p.23.
371. 'Dialogue between an Artificer in a dockyard and those who required his Vote in the next election for Kent', in *Lloyds Evening Post*, 18-21 July 1760, quoted in C.R. Dobson, *Masters and Journeymen: a Prehistory of Industrial Relations 1717-1800* (London: Croom Helm, 1980), pp.98-9.
372. Lawrence Stone, 'The new eighteenth century', *New York Review of Books*, 29 March 1984.
373. Dobson, *Masters and Journeymen*, p.98; information from *Lloyds* 4-6 Jan., 26-9 May 1758.
374. E.P. Thompson, *The Making of the English Working Class* (London:

Gollancz, 1963), p.86, and chapter IV 'The free-born Englishman' as a whole.

375. For the Chartist Convention see Malcolm Chase, *Chartism, a New History* (Manchester: Manchester University Press, 2007) chapters 3 and 4. And Keith Judge, 'Early Chartist organisation and the Convention of 1839', in *International Review of Social History* 20.3 (1975), pp.370-97; and D.J.Rowe, 'The Chartist Convention and the Regions', in *Economic History Review*, vol.22 no.1 (April 1969), pp.58-74.

376. W.H. Greenleaf, 'Toulmin Smith and the British political tradition', *Public Administration*, 53 (1975), 25-44, 36-9.

377. The quotations in this paragraph are from Engel's writings of the early 1840s, cited in the Stedman Jones article 1977, see n. 59.

378. *Capital*, I, 413.

379. 'Education' or 'educated', in the sense of what Marx calls Hegel's 'very heretical views, on the division of labour'. In his *Philosophy of Right* he says: 'By educated men we may *prima facie* understand those who ... can do what others do'; see Marx, *Capital*, I, 485 n. 51. As large-scale industry develops, the proportion of such people, for capital (but potentially also for labour) presumably increases greatly.'The mass of misery, oppression, slavery, degradation and exploitation grows; but with this there also grows the revolt of the working class, a class constantly increasing in numbers, and trained, limited and organized by the very mechanism of the Capitalist process of production'; see *Capital*, I chapter 24.

380. *Capital* I (Penguin edition), pp.449-50.

381. The 1864 reference is to the *Inaugural Address of the International Working Men's Association*; the 'social barrier' quote and the Magna Carta quote come from *Capital*, I,16.

382. *Instructions for Delegates to the Geneva Congress* (1866).

383. *Inaugural Address* (Penguin edit. Political Writings 3, 1974), pp.79-80.

384. *Capital*, I, 449.

385. *Capital*, III, ch.27.

386. *Capital*, III, ch.23.

387. *The Civil War in France* (Penguin edit. Political Writings 3, 1974), p.212.

388. H.A.Turner, *Trade Union Growth, Structure and Policy: A Comparative Study of the Cotton Unions in England* (London: G. Allen and Unwin, 1962).

389. J.M. Baernreither, *English Associations of Working Men* (London:

Sonnenschein, 1889), 1893 edit. p.6, p.21, p.146.

390. Baernreither, pp.xiii, 146.

391. *The Englishman*, 7 Dec. 1910, quoted in T.G. Ashplant, 'The C.I.U. and the I.L.P.: Working Class Organisation, Politics and Culture, c. 1880-1914' unpublished D.Phil thesis (University of Sussex 1983), p. 524.

392. A.D. Murray (ed.), *The Autobiography of John Ludlow* (London: Cass, 1981) but written in the 1890s, p.188.

393. See my 'State and anti-State: reflections on social forms and struggles from 1850', in Philip Corrigan (ed.) *Capitalism, State Formation amd Marxist Theory* (London: Quartet Books, 1989), pp.111-143.

394. *Report of the Nineteenth Annual Co-operative Congress*, held in Carlisle (1887) pp.6-7.

395. *The Producer*, 15 Feb. 1917.

396. Quoted in Neil Killingback, 'The Politics of Small Business in Britain during the 1930s', unpublished D.Phil thesis (University of Sussex), 1980, p. 294. The full quotation is in *The Law Times*, 175, 3 June 1933, p.428.

397. Stephen Yeo, 'Working-class association, private capital, welfare and the state', in M. Rustin and N. Parry (eds), *Social Work and the State* (London: Arnold, 1979) pp.48-71.

398. For which see John Saville, 'Trade unions and free labour: the background to the Taff Vale decision', in Asa Briggs and John Saville (eds), *Essays in Labour History* 1886-1923 (London: Macmillan, 1960, revised edition 1967) pp.317-250. John Saville was a fine historian and analyst of class struggle and associational form. See also his 'Sleeping partnership and limited liability, 1850-1856', in the *Economic History Review* vol.8, issue 3, pp.418-442.

399. Edgar Snow, *Red Star Over China* (London: Gollancz, 1937), p.153. The other two books were the Communist Manifesto and 'the first Marxist book ever published in Chinese, *Class Struggle* by Kautsky'. Kirkup is mis-spelt as Kirkupp in the quote from Mao used by Snow. Incidentally, Kirkup's work was noticed in the *Co-operative News* as well as in the rest of the socialist press. His works were *An Inquiry into Socialism* (London: Longmans, 1887, 1888, and 1907 editions); *The History of Socialism* (London: A & C Black, 1892, 1900, 1906, 1909, 1913 editions); plus an entry on Socialism in the *Encyclopaedia Britannica*. It is the different editions of *The History* that I have used here.

400. The phrase is in Jack Grey's review, 'The road that matters' in *New*

Society, 25 Jan. 1979. He counterposes communalist socialism with etatist socialism, and refers to 'Kirkup's *History of Socialism* in which the description of Robert Owen's socialist community is point by point the precedent of the Chinese commune'.

401. The quotes are from *The History* (1892 edit.), Preface p.vi, pp.7-8, p.5, pp.231-2, p.218.
402. *The History* (1913 edit.) p.405, p.412.
403. The quotes are from *The History* (1892 edit.), p.263, p.218, p.273, p.217, p.216.
404. The *History* (1909 edit.), p.402.
405. *The History* (1892 edit.) pp.272-3, p.222, pp.222-3, p.4.
406. *The History* (1909 edit.), p.406, pp.400-01.
407. Socialists as interested in Morris's more obviously political work as in his multifarious Arts and Crafts practices and productions now have E.P. Thompson's deeply felt 'Postscript:1976' to mine. This is pp.763-816 of the revised edition of E.P. Thompson, *William Morris, Romantic to Revolutionary* (London: Merlin Press, 1976). See also for Thompson, and for Morris (particularly on 'The Policy of Abstention' and for English inflections of socialism, Perry Anderson, *Arguments within English Marxism* (London: Verso, 1980).
408. Paul Meier, *William Morris: the Marxist Dreamer* (1972), II, 416.
409. 'The Policy of Abstention' (1887), May Morris, *William Morris, Artist, Writer, Socialist* (Oxford: Blackwell, 1936), II, 434-53.
410. I re-told it in an obscure Brighton publication edited and issued by David Morgan during the 1970s. I focused on this single chapter, 'How the change came', of *News...*: Stephen Yeo,'News from Nowhere – an appreciation', in *News from Nowhere* (Brighton, 20 Bedford Square, n.d.) Issue 2, pp. 6-11.
411. 'The Policy of Abstention' (1887).
412. Meier, *Morris*, II, 311-16 and all of ch.V. 'The Withering Away of the State' collects the main references in Morris to direct democracy. The quotes in the sentence here are from 'What Socialists Want' (1888) and a letter to Dr John Glasse, 23 May 1887.
413. 'What Socialists Want' (1888), quoted in Meier, pp.311-13.
414. 'Monopoly', in *Collected Works*, XXIII, 253.
415. Letter to Rev.G. Bainton, 6 May 1888, P. Henderson (ed.), *The Letters of William Morris to his Family and Friends* (London: Longmans, 1950), p.290.

416. E.P. Thompson, *The Communism of William Morris. A Lecture* (A pamphlet; London: Merlin, 1965.)
417. 'The Policy of Abstention' (1887). Letter to Joseph Lane, 20 March 1887, in British Library, Add.Ms 45, p.345, quoted in Florence Boos (ed.), 'William Morris's Socialist Diary', in *History Workshop*, 13 (Spring,1982) p.7.
418. Morris, 'True and False Society' (1887).
419. 'Dawn of a New Epoch' (1885) quoted in Meier, II, p.308.
420. 'Artist and artisan', in *Commonweal* Sept. 10, 1887. All of chapter 8 of Meir, II, 'To everyone according to his needs', is excellent on the question of work and privilege, and needs as opposed to input, as criteria for reward.
421. William Morris and E.B. Bax, *Socialism, Its Growth and Outcome* (London: Sonnenschein, 1896 edition), p.282
422. Morris, 'How Shall We Live Then', quoted in Meir, II, p.315. In the work of Morris's friend John Carruthers, *Communal Commercial Economy* (1883) pp.323-5, there is a clear attempt at detailing 'communalism', 'without pretending to offer a cut-and-dried scheme of communal government, we may here shortly discuss the form that would be most readily evolved from the existing system'.
423. 'The Policy of Abstention'.
424. 'True and False Society' (1887).
425. 'Statement of Principles of the Hammersmith Socialist Society', 10 January 1891, British Museum Add.Mss 45894, quoted in Meir, II, p.301.
426. 'Art under Plutocracy' (1883).
427. See Raymond Williams, 'Afterword' to *Modern Tragedy* (London: Verso, 1979 edition) and his attempt to write through this loss, towards coming out on the other side, in chapter 5 of *Towards 2,000* (1983): 'Resources for a Journey of Hope'.
428. Quoted in R. Page Arnot, *William Morris, the Man and the Myth* (London: Lawrence and Wishart, 1964).
429. Kirkup, 1913 edition, Preface, p.ix.
430. Clearly there, for instance, in Kirkup 1909 edition pp.400-02.
431. Kirkup, 1913 edition, p.379, see also pp.395-6.
432. *Keeling, Letters and Recollections. With an Introduction by H.G. Wells*, edited by E.T. (London: G.Allen and Unwin, 1918) p.62, and 59-60.

433. 'If I were in power, and were driven by urgent military needs or political pressure to do something drastic, I should decree Universal Submission to the national need – not young men for the trenches only, but everyone for what he was fitted, and not persons only but property and possessions – everything to be placed at the disposal of the Government', quoted in J.M. Winter, *Socialism and the Challenge of War* (London: Routledge, 1974), p.210.

434. *Justice*, 9 March 1901. See also E.J. Hobsbawm, 'The Fabians Reconsidered' in *Labouring Men* (London: Weidenfeld, 1964) pp.250-71.

435. Well studied in Philip Corrigan, 'State Formation and Moral Regulation in 19th century Britain: Sociological Investigations', unpublished D.Phil. thesis, (University of Durham, 1977).

436. For this group in its context, see B.Semmel, *Imperialism and Social Reform: English Social-Imperial Thought 1895-1914* (New York: Doubleday, 1960), chapter 3. Also H.C.G. Mathews,*The Liberal Imperialists: The Ideas and Politics of a Post-Gladstonian Elite* (Oxford: Blackwell, 1971); and A.M. McBriar, *Fabian Socialism and English Politics 1884-1918* (Cambridge: Cambridge University Press, 1966).

437. See the Preface to the 1920 edition of S. and B. Webb, *Industrial Democracy* (London: Longmans, 1920), p.xxxi.

438. S. and B. Webb, *The Consumers' Co-operative Movement* (London: Longmans, 1921) p.161. For the changes in the Webbs' views on co-operation as production versus co-operation as consumption, see D.C. Jones, 'The Economics of British Producer Co-operatives', unpublished D.Phil. thesis (Cornell University, 1974).

439. Keir Hardie, *The ILP: All About It* (1908), p.4.

440. *Labour Leader*, 31 May 1912. I owe this reference to Ian Bullock.

441. *Annual Conference of Trades Councils, Report* (1946). I owe this reference to Michael Bor's work on Trades Councils.

442. Quoted in Kevin Theakston,'The 1964-70 Labour Government and Whitehall Reform', University of Leeds, Polis Working Paper no.2, Feb. 2004, wwwpolis.leeds.ac.uk.

443. E.P. Thompson, 'At the point of decay', in E.P. Thompson (ed.), *Out of Apathy* (London: Stevens and Sons, 1960), pp.3-15.

444. 'At the point of decay', pp.11-12, and 5.

445. A Co-operative Independent Commission, led by the Leader of the Labour Party, Hugh Gaitskell, and with C.A.R. Crosland as its active Secretary, was set up in 1955. Its papers are now in the National Co-

operative Archive in Holyoake House Manchester and, with its *Report*, they deserve as much detailed study as the *Report* and papers of the more recent Independent Commission, also catalysed by the Leader of the Labour Party (and Prime Minister) Tony Blair in 2000–1.

446. As I was revising this essay, Hilary Wainwright's *A New Politics from the Left* (Cambridge: Polity, 2018) came out and addressed this question more sharply than I now can.

Index

Allende, Salvador, 38
Anagnostou, Makis, 75
Anderson, Perry, 208
Arnold, Matthew, 140, 194
Arts Research Support Fund, 184
Associate, The, 85
Association of All Classes and All Nations, 76
associationism
   associative democracy, 76-79
   effects, 81-95
   introduction and definition, 70-71
   use of term, 85-86, 245-246
   voluntary action, 71-74
   workers control of work, 39, 74-76
associations, 48-51, 162-169, 257-258, 272-273
Auden, W.H., 74, 92
Aveling, Eleanor Marx, 109, 127

Baernreither, J.M., 232-234
Bahro, Rudolf, 34, 82
Balfour, G.W., 69
Barnes, G.N., 154, 169
Bax, Belfort
   Fabianism, 21, 57
   politics, 123, 164
   socialism, 109, 112, 132, 134, 136, 265
Baxter, John, 224
Belisha, Hore, 240-242
Bellamy, Edward, 260
Beloff, Max, 53
Benewick, Bob, 103
Benjamin, Walter, 27, 189
Benson, T.D., 35
Berman, Marshall, 84
Bernstein, Edouard, 194
Besant, Annie, 109, 119
Beveridge, William, 41, 71-72
Bevir, Mark, 16-17, 110, 132
Billcliffe, B., 173
Blatchford, Robert

   Cinderella Clubs, 167
   conversion to socialism, 145
   Merrie England, 117-118, 130, 138
   nationalism, 192-193, 194
   religion, 132, 133
   socialism, 107, 109, 111, 150, 156, 162, 182-183
   speaker, 168
Booth, William, 123-124, 153, 265
Bottomore, Tom, 14, 15, 19, 76, 96, 103
Bradford Central Independent Labour Club, 173
Brecht, Bertolt, 34, 92-93, 214
Briggs, Asa, 5, 26, 54, 97
Brighton Labour Process Group, 3, 14-15, 28-29
Bristol Socialist Rambling and Propaganda Society, 165
Britain (see also Englishness), 190-191
Brocklehurst, Fred, 125, 148
Burke, Edmund, 205-206
Burns, John, 56, 128, 146, 169, 172
Burnside, John, 70, 73, 75
Burrows, Herbert, 118
Burt, D.O., 126
Burt, Thomas, 41

Campaign for Nuclear Disarmament, 24, 108, 209
capitalist system, 2, 216-217, 252, 256, 258
Carpenter, Edward
   England's Ideal, 120-121
   My Day and Dreams, 119
   socialism, 122, 132, 162, 182
   speaker, 151, 156
   Towards Democracy, 114-115, 124
Chamberlain, Neville, 242
Champion, H.H., 142
charity work, 167
Chartism, 225-226
Chile Socialist Party, 38

Cinderella Club, 166, 167
citizens, 48-51
civil society, 39, 43, 219
Claeys, Gregory, 16
Clarion, 113, 132, 149, 150, 162, 163, 165, 168, 182, 192
class (see also working class)
  activism, 144
  definitions, 25, 33, 42, 79-81
  middle class, 128, 214, 217
  organising class, 35
  professional and managerial, 22, 23, 57-66, 236
  struggle, 16, 41-42, 218, 230, 243
Cobden, R.J., 125
Cole, G.D.H., 18, 41
Cole, Margaret, 262
collectivism, 51-69
Collini, Stefan, 53, 103
communism, 68-69, 111, 183, 250, 255
Communist Manifesto, 79-81, 84
Communist parties, 24, 203, 204
Conference of Socialist Economists, 3, 28, 99, 100-101
Connell, Jim, 131, 181
Conservative Party, 24, 69, 76, 101, 140, 240, 242
Conway, Katherine St. John
  conversion to socialism, 120-121, 122, 127, 129-130
  relationships, 114
  socialism, 109, 143, 148, 157, 162
co-operation
  associationism, 85-90, 234-235
  connections with Labour Party, 44, 171, 212, 238-239, 242, 273
  democracy, 234-235
  development, 231-232
  ILP co-operative, 173
  Marx, 80, 229-230
  politics, 88
  productive, 89, 223, 237-238, 267
  state within a state, 32
  taxation, 240-241, 273
  wholefood and Fair Trade, 99-100
  working class, 89
co-operative commonwealth, 31, 32
Co-operative News, 32, 85

Co-operative Union/Co-operatives UK, 31, 89, 90, 91, 100, 232
Co-operative Wholesale Society, 31, 52-53, 89, 186, 237-239, 242
Corrigan, Philip, 73, 198-199
Cramp, C.T., 151
Crane, Walter, 106
Crooks, Will, 140-141
Crosland, Anthony, 20-21, 44, 273
Crossman, Richard, 21
Curran, Pete, 173
Czechoslovakia, 65

Davin, Anna, 184
democracy
  associative, 76-79
  co-operative, 234-235
  industrial, 67-69, 91, 163, 182, 267
  parliamentary, 207-214, 219-220, 225-226, 250, 263
  primitive, 163
  social, 35-37
Democratic Federation, 112
Derfel, R.J, 125
Directorate of Army Education, 190
Disraeli, Benjamin, 23
Djilas, Milovan, 64
Duc, Andre le, 184
Dunn, John, 16, 30-31
Durbin, Evan, 21
Durkheim, Emile, 32-33

education
  labour movement, 19-20, 232, 241
  universities, 19-21, 24-26, 57, 96-97, 99
Edwards, Joseph, 162
Ehrenreich, Barbara and John, 57-58
elections, 170-171, 182, 222-223
Ellis, T., 140
employment
  labour control, 39, 74-76
  public-sector and state, 33, 46, 266
Engels, Friedrich
  Communist Manifesto, 79-81, 84
  England, 195, 215, 221, 226-227
  patterns in labour, 29
  Salvation Army, 113

Index

English state, 205-214, 217-244, 248-249, 252-254
Englishness, 189-202, 265-266
Ensor, James, 12
Enzensberger, Hans Magnus, 13

Fabian Society, 112, 139, 210, 249, 262-264
Fabians, 21, 32, 51-56, 65, 265
factory legislation, 228
Fair Trade, 100
Fay, Edward Francis, 168
Federation of Worker Writers and Community Publishers, 28
feminism, 27, 99, 108, 143, 233
Figgis, J.N., 77
Foot, Michael, 270
Football Association, 90
Foster, D.B., 119, 121, 123, 145
Fowles, John, 214
franchise, 36, 43-45
friendly societies, 72, 91, 232, 242, 273
funerals, 157-158

Gaitskell, Hugh, 20-21, 43, 273
garden cities, 89-90
George II, 35, 209, 269
George, Henry, 134, 146
Germany, Social Democratic Party, 49
Gilray, John, 119
Gissing, George, 115
Glasier, John Bruce, 109, 125, 148, 149, 156, 163, 171
Gore, Hugh Holmes, 177-179
Gramsci, Antonio, 27, 31, 243
Gray, Kirkman, 64
Greater London Council, 59, 99-103
Greece, 74-76
Gross, Philip, 73

Hales, Mike, 33, 42, 59-62, 66, 74
Hall, Leonard, 145
Halliday Sparling, H., 124
Hammond, J.L. & B., 243
Hancock, Thomas, 141
happiness, 137
Hardie, Keir
  ambulance work, 167
  ILP and Labour Party, 43, 163, 212, 244, 268
  religion, 131, 132, 133, 148
  Royal Commission on Labour, 126
  socialism, 125, 131, 133, 135, 140
  speaker, 168, 194
Hardy, Thomas, 224
Harrison, W.H., 30, 269
Hartley, E.R., 182
Hazell, William, 31-32, 72-73
Henderson, Fred, 141
Heseltine, Michael, 209
Hines, William, 161
Hirst, Paul, 70, 76-78, 96, 97
Hobart, H.W., 118, 124
Hobhouse, L.T., 56, 243
Hobsbawm, E.J., 18
Hobson, J.A., 243
Hobson, S.G., 174
Holyoake, George Jacob, 1-2, 51, 52, 73, 75, 85, 237
Home Office Reports on Revolutionary Organisations, 191
Hornsey Labour Party, 22-24, 28
Howard, Ebenezer, 52, 89-90
Hughes, Kathryn, 188-189
Hungary, 65
Hunter Watts, J., 161
Hyndman, Henry, 36, 140, 142, 157, 191-192, 193, 194

Independent Labour Party
  activists, 109, 121
  business activities, 169, 172-173,
  democracy, 163, 212
  formation, 112
  influence, 174-185, 269
  statism, 35, 268
industrial democracy, 67-68, 91, 163, 182, 267
Industrial Revolution, 51, 201, 233, 262
intellectuals, 40-41, 43-44, 54-56, 58
International Socialism, 24
Irving, Dan, 114
Italy, 203-204

James, William, 117
Jenkins, Roy, 20-21

Johnson, Nevil, 35, 207, 209, 214
Jones, Ben, 89
Jones, Merfyn, 184
Jowett, Fred, 160, 269
Joynes, J.L., 131
Jung, C.G., 30

Keeling, Frederick 'Ben', 67
Keynes, J.M., 40
Killingback, Neil, 184
Kirkup, Thomas, 55, 244-249, 250, 261, 262-263
Klein, Naomi, 76
knowledge control, 62-66, 97
Kolonitsky, Boris, 19
Konrád, George, 66
Koumatsioulis, Dimitris, 75

labour
　control of employment, 39, 74-76
　effects of associationism, 81-83, 94-95
　Royal Commission on Labour, 238, 240
Labour Annual, 162
Labour Army, 147, 149
Labour Church
　activities, 148, 150, 157-161
　members, 117, 125, 149, 150
　principles, 124, 162
　religion of socialism, 107, 109, 147, 166
Labour Leader, 30, 35, 174, 269
labour movement (see also socialism)
　charity work, 167
　control of, 40-41, 43-44, 54-56
　education, 19-20, 232, 241
　events, 147-150
　fundraising, 167-169, 170-173
　leadership, 163-164
　social activities, 165-169, 170-171, 234
　unity of organisations, 162-169
Labour Party
　activism, 22-24
　association, 87-88, 93-94, 167
　connections with co-operatives and trade unions, 44, 171, 212, 238-239, 242
　control of, 40-41, 43-44, 213, 269, 270, 273

Hornsey, 22-24, 28
intellectuals, 40-41, 43-44, 54-56
New Labour, 18, 77
Labour Prophet, 107, 177
language, relative autonomy, 16
Lansbury, George, 109-110, 174-175
Lawrence, D.H., 42
Leatham, James, 175
Leeds Labour Exchange, 264-265
Left, the, 57, 59, 77, 212
Lenin, Vladimir, 45, 49, 54
Lessing, Doris, 197
Lever, W.H., 242
Levy, Carl, 67, 103
Liberals, 139, 214, 243, 244 Lloyd, Henry Demarest, 89
Ludlow, J.M., 233, 235

MacDonald, Ramsay, 36-37, 161, 163, 269, 270, 273
Maguire, Paddy, 103
Maguire, Tom, 124, 129
Manchester, 173, 221-222
Mann, Tom, 126-127, 130, 131, 132, 172-173, 238
Mao Zedong, 92, 245
March-Phillipps, Evelyn, 164
Marshall, H.E., 205
Martyn, Caroline, 129, 143, 147, 149, 152-153, 168
Marx, Karl
　Capital, 3, 28, 46, 94, 215, 220, 227-228, 230
　capitalism, 216
　class, 243
　collective, 45
　Communist Manifesto, 79-81, 84
　co-operatives, 229-231
　need for change, 28
　trade unions, 203, 231
Marxism, 14, 26-29, 259
Maurice, F.D., 133
Maxwell, Sir Robert, 24
McMillan, Margaret, 130-131, 143, 176
McMillan, Rachel, 119-120
Mercer, T.W., 88
middle class, 128, 214, 217
Millgate Monthly, 85

Mitchell, Hannah, 145, 162
Mitchell, J.T.W., 52-53, 237-238
monopoly, 81-82
Moore, George, 115
Morris, William
   change in society, 85, 95, 98, 129, 144, 182-183
   England, 187, 189, 193, 208
   labour and art, 52, 152
   News from Nowhere, 47, 82, 95, 111, 135-136, 156-157, 158, 183, 251, 255, 258, 260
   religion, 131
   socialism, 112, 118, 122, 132, 135-136, 164, 249-262
   Socialist League, 107-108
   speaker, 152
   World Market, 47-48, 267
Morrison, Herbert, 211
Mulkay, Michael, 103
Murray, Robin, 3, 14-15, 59, 99-103, 204

National Deposit Friendly Society, 72
National Socialist Party, 192
nationalisation, 32, 223, 273
nationalism (see also Englishness), 193
Neale, Edward Vansittart, 85
Nevinson, H.W., 116, 164-165
New Left Review, 83, 108
News from Nowhere, 47, 82, 95, 111, 135-136, 150, 156-157, 158, 183, 251, 255, 258, 260
nuclear disarmament, 24, 73-74, 108, 209

Orwell, George, 191, 193, 205
Oswald, Alice, 51
Outhwaite, William, 103
Owen, Robert, 229

Paine, Tom, 26, 205
Palmer, John, 24
parliamentary democracy, 207-214, 219-220, 225-226, 250, 263
Payne, Will, 181
Pease, Edward, 55, 262
Pierson, Stanley, 110, 144
Plebs League, 241
Plumb, J.H., 218-219

Poland, 95
political activism, 22-24, 43-45
Pond, Alan, 184
Ponting, Clive, 34
poverty, 20, 136-138
Power, Eileen, 21
Priestley, J.B., 190, 193
Princeton University, 184
Producer, The, 87, 186, 238
production
   co-operative, 89, 223, 237-238, 267
   socialism, 60-61, 89, 233-234, 237-238, 250-251, 254-255, 267
   statism, 46-48, 49
professional and managerial class, 22, 23, 57-66, 236

QueenSpark, 28, 99
Quelch, H., 142

Rakowski, M.F., 30
Rassaby, Elaine, 184
Redfern, Percy, 119, 125, 175
Reid, Andrew, 139
religion of socialism, 107-111, 131-138
Revolutionary Socialist Students Federation, 96
Rogers, F., 142
Rowbotham, Sheila, 13, 29, 100, 204
Royal Commission on Labour, 238, 240
Ruskin, John, 83, 90, 95, 259
Ruskin College, 32
Russia, 68-69, 246

Salvation Army, 113, 123-124, 167, 174, 265
Samuel, George A.H., 35
Schumpeter, J.A., 50
Scotland, 112
Seabrook, Jeremy, 70
Seeley, J.R., 34, 207
self-help, 20
Semmel, Bernard, 267
Sharples, H., 135
Shaw, George Bernard, 56, 66, 139, 179, 181-182
Shaw, Jennie, 103
Shore, Peter, 47

singing, 159-161
Smiles, Samuel, 82
Smith, Adam, 200
Smith, Frank, 139, 148, 167
Smith, John, 117
Snell, H.H., 113, 119, 175
Snowden, Philip, 163
Social Democratic Federation, 21, 36, 109, 113, 123, 163, 172
Social Democratic Party, 22, 49, 210
socialism (see also labour movement)
   1880s and 1890s, 111-142, 147-157, 155-184, 260-262
   1970s and 1980s, 26-29, 46, 47
   alternatives to state socialism, 18
   aristocratic creed, 35
   associationism and collectivism, 15, 51-69, 70-95, 247-248
   connections between bodies, 142-169, 212
   conversion to socialism, 111-146
   co-operation, 234-235
   democracy, 138-142
   funerals and weddings, 157-158
   influence, 174-184
   intellectuals, 40-41, 43-44, 54-56
   majority self-direction, 20
   militancy, 254
   religion, 107-111, 131-138
   social history of, 16-19
   statism, 15, 30-51, 196, 200, 236, 252-254
   unity of organisations, 162-169, 257-258, 272-273
   work, 60-61, 74-76
   working class, 1
socialisms
   conflicting socialisms, 14-17
   term, 14, 15, 16
   three socialisms, 14-17, 29
Socialist League, 108, 109, 193
Socialist Society, 120
Socialist Workers Party, 24
speakers
   events, 144, 148-153
   lectures, 90, 118, 156-157, 158, 162, 179, 183, 218-219
   socialism, 24, 69, 112, 130, 168

Stacy, Enid, 143, 149, 168
State, the, 196-202, 205-214, 220-221, 252
statism
   associations, 48-51
   control, 65
   introduction and definitions, 30-32
   production, 46-48, 49
   role of the state, 33-45, 155, 266, 268-272
   state socialism, 32-35
   welfare, 175-177
Stead, W.T., 119
Stedman Jones, Gareth, 221
Stevenson, Robert Louis, 188
Stiftung, Rosa Luxemburg, 58
Stubbs, William, 206
suffrage, 36, 43-45
Sunlight Soap, 242
Supple, B.E., 201-202
Sussex University, 19-20, 26, 57, 96-97, 99
Szelényi, Ivan, 66

Taff Vale judgement, 242
Tawney, R.H., 166
Thatcher, Margaret, 33, 103, 197
Third World Information Network, 99
Thompson, Alex, 113
Thompson, E.P.
   associationism, 73-74
   England, 215, 225, 243, 272
   religion, 123
   socialism, 18, 29, 180, 189, 195, 259, 261
Thompson, William, 256
Tillett, Ben, 132, 192, 194
Toole, Joseph, 123
Toulmin Smith, Joshua, 226
trade unions
   anti-union legislation, 38, 240, 241, 242
   connections with Labour Party, 44
   development, 231
   England, 192, 229
   Italy conference, 203-204
Trades Union Congress, 91, 232
Transport and General Workers Union, 24

Trevor, John
  autobiography, 119, 146
  Labour Church, 109, 117, 157
  socialist religion, 126, 133, 141, 174
Trotsky, Leon, 46
Turner, Ben, 142, 162

Ure, Andrew, 266
Urwick, L.F., 63

voluntary action, 39, 43, 71-74, 212, 247, 273

Wainwright, Hilary, 108
Wallerstein, Immanuel, 201
Walzer, Michael, 220
Webb, Beatrice
  associated bargaining, 85
  co-operation, 237
  family, 266
  industrial democracy, 67-68, 91, 182
  producers and consumers, 24
  public opinion, 55
  socialism, 20-21, 77, 116-117, 267
  Soviet Communism, 68-69
  working class, 39-41, 56
Webb, Sidney
  associated bargaining, 85
  collectivism, 51-52, 54, 56, 66, 122, 265
  industrial democracy, 67-68, 91, 182
  producers and consumers, 24
  socialism, 21, 113, 139, 262, 267
  Soviet Communism, 68-69
  state, 271
  working class, 39-41, 56
Weber, Max, 15, 25, 134
welfare activities, 175-177
Wells, H. G., 21, 56, 178
West, Alick, 13, 97
Wheatsheaf, 53
Wilde, Oscar, 66, 115
Williams, Raymond, 1, 29, 35, 48, 58, 83, 108
Williams, Shirley, 210
Williams, William Carlos, 193-194
Wilson, Harold, 23, 37, 56, 270
women, 27, 43, 99, 108, 143, 233
Workers Educational Association, 241

working class
  capability, 39-43, 90-91, 231, 240-244, 246, 253, 258-260
  government, 263-264
  organisations, 89, 99, 228-229, 232-242, 243
  press and thinking, 176, 191
  recreation, education and leisure, 155-156, 232, 241
  socialism, 91, 155-156
Working Men's Club and Institute Union, 90, 232, 234-235, 241-242

Yeo, Stephen
  family, childhood and education, 24-25
  Italy conference, 203-204
  Labour Party activism, 22-24
  religion and socialism, 108
  Sussex University, 19-20, 26, 57, 96-97, 99